GREEN

In Melissa Fite Johnson's b
and a heart are both things that can ᵥᵤ
looks at the way grief has its own language and nᵤᵥ.
mouth is a thing that can both create and erase. In these
poems, the past has crystallized into desire lessons, the fear
that accompanies those first encounters, and the inherited
legacies that shape how we see ourselves. This book knows
time slips away quickly but holds us in unflinching memory
before releasing us to the wide and green world.

> —**Traci Brimhall, author of**
> *Come the Slumberless to the Land of Nod*

In her latest poetry collection, Melissa Fite Johnson
somehow manages to lace grief with hope, and questioning
with reckoning. Love is at the heart of this collection, but
not simple love: love that questions, love that demands,
love that is irreverent and taxing, love in its fragility and
strength. The poems dig through the rubble of youth and
uncover hard truths, and the poems show how when we are
young, we may think something horrible will swallow the
rest of our lives, and then it doesn't, and how this is terrible
and beautiful all at once. This poet writes of the connection
we have as humans to each other, even when the string that
ties us is so thin it can barely be found; yet she finds it, and
she plucks.

> —**Shuly Xóchitl Cawood, author of**
> *Trouble Can Be So Beautiful at the Beginning*

The poems in *Green*, both searing and soft-hearted, span from early childhood to old age, and demonstrate with consistent poignancy that girlhood and womanhood are not separate phases of life but as interconnected as fibers in a leaf. Through the unique lens of the color green and all its complicated connotations—newness, nature, jealousy, and more—Johnson unflinchingly examines the many shades of human relationships, asking "What if?" before "time rusts the gate closed." These touching, impeccably crafted poems dare to heal the emotional wounds that come from living and loving in a gendered world.

—**Marianne Kunkel, author of** *Hillary, Made Up*

The poems of Melissa Fite Johnson's *Green* excavate the bittersweet tenderness invoked by the collection's title. To be green is to be naive, heading into a sea of defining experiences, a vantage Johnson wonderfully explores in poems that chart the pains of girlhood: the casual critiques that stick, the difficulty of relationships with boys, family, friends. She also writes movingly of her disabled father. Grappling with the grief and guilt evoked by his death, Johnson admits, "If a poem resurrects, how many times have I tried?" While some losses cannot be reversed, it is in this act of writing that Johnson offers readers another vision of green: to grow through challenge, to will oneself to flourish despite pain, is to be fully alive, a trajectory *Green* reminds is possible for us all.

—**Ruth Williams, author of** *Flatlands*

GREEN

Melissa Fite Johnson

Riot in Your Throat
publishing fierce, feminist poetry

Johnson, Melissa Fite.
1st edition.
ISBN: 978-1-7361386-0-1

Cover Design: Jai Johnson
Cover Photography: Meryl Carver-Allmond
Book Design: Shanna Compton
Author Photo: Meryl Carver-Allmond

Riot in Your Throat
Arlington, VA
www.riotinyourthroat.com

For Marc—

I tried to tell my sixteen-year-old self about you.

CONTENTS

I.

II.

When I was learning to creep, my mother set me down on the beach to see what I thought of it. I crawled straight for the coming wave and was just through the wall of green when she caught my heels.

—Sylvia Plath

I'm free but I'm focused
I'm green but I'm wise

—Alanis Morissette

I.

I'M ONLY HAPPY WHEN IT RAINS

after the Garbage song

My song came on and I jerked the volume up,
stomped on the gas, sang along: *My only comfort
is the night gone black.* Since his laryngectomy,
my father couldn't talk. He studied me
from the passenger seat. I had to chauffeur him around
after his strokes. I wished the Toyota were a rocket
shooting me out of this town. *Pour your misery
down on me.* The song ended. I'd cried
through the last chorus: *I'm riding high upon
a deep depression. I'm only happy when it rains.*
He gestured to his paralyzed side—his right hand
a claw resting in his lap, his right leg limp
against the car door. He pointed to his chest,
mouthed, *Me, too.* He struggled to sit up. *Me, too.*

THE IMMEDIACY

Once my father wanted yogurt
but couldn't remember the word.
Once he tried to carry his own cereal,
brace the bowl's lip against his cane handle,
and my mother came home to flakes
crusted to the kitchen floor. When he
mouthed *Elden* again and again, I guessed
my brother had a new girlfriend, Ellen, but
it was the name of his dead uncle.
So what? I asked, then left the room.

The day my father died,
I smelled the cologne-tinged
rubber handle of his cane, held it tight
in my hand, pretended it was his hand.

GONE

Our last easy conversation   I was six.
I don't remember it.

      I remember   stage-whispering

     he was walking too slowly,
    people were staring,

as he dragged   his right half
                    behind him.

    I waved for him to hurry.

He woke in a hospital bed,   unable to form my name

with his hand or mouth, sounded syllables
the way a child

     inches a finger under words
     in a picture book.   His eyes met mine.

He tried the first breath   of my name,
                    clenched his left fist,

    shook his head. His eyes

met my mother's,
my brother's.

Their names died on his lips.

His strokes another death, the father I knew, lifting me

onto his shoulders, drawing

caricatures of cats,   typing as I narrated   stories

from my perch on his lap,

my head against his broad chest.

IF A POEM

If a poem resurrects, how many times have I tried?
I place him on his scooter, turtle speed to rabbit.
I place him on the thing meant to liberate but
infantilizes, swerve him again through the neighborhood
where he breaks down. I place him in the story
my parents don't tell me, but I hear my mother's part,
every conversation between them one-sided,
my father's nod, his lip-synching the script in his head,
his misspelled left-handed scraps of words. The boys
sharing the basketball as they pass. They roll the ball
into the grass, pretend to help. Snatch my father's keys
and throw, run away laughing. How long
was he stranded? Who found his keys? My mother
doesn't say. He died in 1998. No cell phone.
How this century would've helped him.
If he could have waited. If a poem were a bridge.

I place him at home. I place my mother and myself
at her friend's for a mother-daughter tea party.
Spoons murmur against our dolls' closed mouths.
Our mothers smile, summoning some future memory
of themselves as doting grandmothers. The phone insists
all afternoon, our only interruption. *Pranks*,
my mother's friend reports, returning to the table,
flourishing her napkin once more into her lap.

Heavy breathing. Finally, she sneers *pervert*,
threatens the police. The calls stop. My mother and I
the last to leave. I place us back home, my father
on the floor. The cordless phone beside him.

If a poem makes amends—
the boys ask for my father's license, find his name
in the phone book. My mother answers
her friend's phone. I am with my father when he dies.

CORNER BOOTH AT CAFÉ DEL RIO, TWO
WEEKS AFTER MY FATHER'S DEATH

Through the window an old couple
power-walks the air-conditioned mall.
My father built strength this way
after his strokes—planted
the rubber soles of his cane
with his left hand, scraped his
right sneaker against the linoleum.

The waitress brings chips, salsa,
root beers with crushed ice.
Someone asks how I'm doing, real
concern, and I lurch. Force
my voice light. *I'm lucky.*
I got sixteen years with him.
He was a great man. My friend
smiles. *My dad still is*, she says.

She slurps, pushes her empty
glass to the edge of the table.
The others look from me to her.
I excuse myself. I stay
in the bathroom a long while,
waiting for a pattern in the floor tiles.

FROM MY PARKED CAR, I STARE AT THE SNOW

At five, I ran away. August. I packed
nothing but wore my winter coat.
I'd be gone long enough to need it.

I imagined myself in a snowstorm,
my mother biting her lip in worry at home
while I discovered an uninhabited log cabin.

The gun rack by the front door
would teach me to hunt; the fishing pole
in the mudroom would teach me to fish.

My mother found me still in the backyard,
seized my shoulders and shook.
I startled at her wet eyes and cheeks.

Tonight, flakes design patterns
on glass. I'm the mittened figure inside
a snow globe. How to describe the sound:

No running engine. No radio. Ice soft
on the windshield, a small spoon
scratching against my mother's sugar bowl.

MY MOTHER SAID

No one will marry you if.

If I couldn't   bake a pie,
crust and all.

    If I couldn't corset   my body.

A father sat silent on the couch.   A father disagreed
    or didn't.

Girls in leotards knelt at the barre.
Girls drank water

     to keep from eating lunch.

No one noticed my brother
   coming home drunk.

No one will marry you if,   my mother said.

But they will   if you learn.
They will   if I teach you.

WATCHING *CASABLANCA* AT OMA AND OPA'S HOUSE

At five o'clock, my grandfather proposed dinner,
my grandmother a swim. He said, *My stomach!*
She said, *Old man*, stomped into the bedroom.
Fighting, they switched to Dutch, *Godverdomme*,
then back to English, a radio flickering between stations.
Oma reappeared in a blue bathing suit and cap,
slivered through the deck's door, raised her arms
glorious as a peacock thrilling its feathers,
cleaved the water. Opa sputtered, then barked at me,
asked if I'd ever seen *Casablanca*. I shook my head.
He said he thought we'd watch it before dinner.
And we did, volume up to drown Oma's splashes.

LAUNDRY DAY

My mother rolled socks slowly—
bend the ankle, squeeze the cuff, open

the mouth until it swallows itself—
arranged them in neat rows

for my colorblind father,
blue in back, black in front, each Sunday

for twenty-five years, a one-woman
assembly line. Her purpose

at the start of marriage:
render this professional writer

the part when he crossed
his legs at a book signing, or stood

to lead a meeting, a band of wool
flashing. In the end, she gave

this man with a cane dignity
as he lugged half his body behind him.

FREEWHEELIN' BOB DYLAN AND THE
NAMELESS GIRL

I used to rifle through my mom's records,
basement floor, until I found this one. This was love,

Dylan in the thin jacket trying not to look cold,
the girl bundled in a trench, pressed against him.

In his memoir: *erotic, fair-skinned, golden-haired;*
the air suddenly filled with banana leaves.

The girl in the photo, seventeen, would be
Dylan's girlfriend for three years. She smiles

but shivers. Dylan doesn't smile or hold her hand.
He considers only the snow-covered street.

She died at sixty-seven, lung cancer, married
to Enzo Bartoccioli forty-four years. I search online,

Bartoccioli and Suze Rotolo, try to find their photos—
clearly *this* was love—but she's trapped in the sixties

at seventeen. She saunters on Dylan's arm,
lights his cigarette, sprawls across their bed.

In her memoir: *Dylan was an elephant in the room*
of my life; I was a string on his guitar.

VISITING MY SIXTEEN-YEAR-OLD SELF

I want to smooth your hair
the way a big sister would
as you lie on your bed, raw.
You wasted the last weeks
of your father's life still
and uncomfortable beneath a boy,
his hand down your pants,
his small pink tongue erasing
and erasing your breasts.

I stand, time-traveling ghost
in the corner, watch you
dress for school. Your mother
at the funeral, the black skirt
she laid out still on your bed,
you tread the halls, tiny
in baggy jeans and your brother's
hoodie, your eyes smeared black.

I follow you, class to class,
a few steps behind, never quite able
to catch up, to touch the backpack
strapped to your shoulders,
a defective parachute.
I sit beside you on the bus ride home.

You'll become an English teacher
like he was. You'll write. You'll give
your wedding bouquet to his grave.
I tell you the ways it gets better,
but you look through me,
out the window at nothing.

I BEGIN TO FORGIVE MYSELF

After I broke my leg at seventeen,
too late, I understood on a small scale
what it was like for my father
in his last years, as he stared the barrel
of our staircase, cane in hand,
as he balanced on his bath board
waving the shower wand in his weak left grip.
I wished myself next to him
on our couch. Prop my left leg on the ottoman
beside his right. Laugh with him,
shrug hopelessly, *Aren't we a pair?*
To go downstairs, I sank to the top step,
pitched my crutches through
the narrow aisle, crab-walked
on three limbs. Before bathing, I slipped off
the brace, my second skin.
My mother washed my hair in the sink—
each cup a waterfall down the drain.

II.

IT'S NOT MY MOTHER'S FAULT

she cast insecurities
onto me, her only copy—

brightly, *You and I both
need to lose 20 pounds.*

Too tall, both of us;
women should be folded

wings. Never go bowling
and admit your shoe size.

When did I stop slipping
from the bathroom

before the steam cleared?
When did I first feel glad

to see myself, a Polaroid
born from shower mist?

Now I tuck my hair behind
my ear, gently, finally gently.

I hold my mother's hands
so she can't shield her belly

with her crossed arms, an action
a little like giving herself a hug.

BOOKENDS

Innocence, not innocence
lost, a friend and I

lying in the bleachers, facing
the wall, not the court,

our legs elevated a tier,
jackets for pillows.

He hadn't kissed anyone,
neither had I,

and we were so old,
fourteen, so he asked

if we should try. That's what
the kiss felt like, trying,

pressing our tongues together
like bookends without books.

No dating, no breakup,
no second kiss.

When I see him now
I'm happy, we catch up

at the farmers market, his wife,
my husband, the past, the present.

I thought to write
the next kiss, the next,

a hand on my neck, a body
blocking the doorway,

but let this poem be
only sweet beginning, only sweet end.

FIFTEEN

Learning my friend had sex
was like pinning on the donkey's tail:
the blindfold came off, and
suddenly tails could grow from snouts
or be stomped by hooves, and
she could stretch naked alongside a man.

▼

Holden Caulfield: proof Austin
from English 10 loved me instead of
all those lip-glossed freshmen he took out.
Jane Gallagher, patron saint of good girls.

▼

On a trip with my friend and her parents,
I sat in back, sang with them when
I knew the words, license plate game,
anything to quit thinking
I am the only virgin in this car.

▼

The most romantic moment of my life:
Austin snapped the eraser from his pencil
when I asked to borrow one for a test.

▼

The mirror told me what was wrong.
Love me, I said
with my eyes, never my mouth.

▼

Our youth pastor outlined twelve steps
of sex. Step 1, eye to body:
you see someone. Step 2, eye to eye:
someone sees you. Step 3,
voice to voice: conversation. My friend
whispered, *We're sluts. We've done
the first three with hundreds of guys.*

▼

When Austin kissed me, I worried
my breath, my braces. I didn't worry
my breasts, my zipper, whether
this was something I'd chosen.

THE PENIS ENTERS THE ROOM

For years I framed the story as a joke,
the guy who unzipped his jeans to jerk off
while we kissed. Basement couch,
ignoring *Almost Famous* on the VCR.
I opened my eyes when I felt his fist
tapping the inside seam of my jeans.

When the penis enters the room,
your friends don't ask if you'd minded.
And you don't ask them. Most of them
have a story like this one. When the penis
enters the room, you'll donate to Goodwill
the new blouse you'd bought for this date.
You'll pretend you hadn't liked it much.
You'll pretend you hadn't liked him.

When the penis enters the room,
your mother is upstairs reading
Princess Di's biography and your father's
been dead three years.

When the penis enters the room,
it's a year after your last boyfriend raped you.

When the penis enters the room, you're stunned
into silence. He says *Is this OK?* and you don't answer.

NINETEEN

My boyfriend told me which *Maxim*
spreads he jerked off to. I dawdled
at work alphabetizing CDs,

impersonating our coworker
the male model, teaching the staff
how to jazz square in the parking lot.

I could've stayed forever
at that record store, vouching for
Exile in Guyville and scanning

barcode barcode barcode, the beeps
blocking out whatever he'd said
that day. Once, he urged me into

a body toning class, where I met
a girl missing a hand—she duct taped
her almost fist to a free weight

when it was time to work our biceps.
I wondered if she had a boyfriend
and what he must say to her.

PANTOUM FOR KIM KARDASHIAN

You cannot display your wealth, then be surprised that some people want to share it. –Karl Lagerfeld, blaming Kim Kardashian for her own 2016 robbery

Easy target. Look what she wore:
$4 million ring flaunted online,
diamonds in her cleavage.
She asked for it. She deserved it.

$4 million ring flaunted online
and no guard outside her hotel door.
She asked for it. She deserved it.
What did she expect?

No guard outside her hotel door
when the men came in ski masks.
What did she expect?
They pressed a gun against her temple,

the men in ski masks. They
tied her hands and feet, never
releasing the gun from her temple,
dragged her to the bathroom.

Her hands and feet tied, she pleaded,
told them her children were babies.
Before locking her in the bathroom,
they taped her mouth shut.

Her children were babies.
Easy target. Look what she wore
in her sex tape. *You cannot display your*
diamonds, cleavage, *wealth, then be surprised.*

SUBMERGED

When I wore stockings and boots, buttoned my body
to the neck,   men still stared.   38D? 36DD?
I sketched the funhouse mirror. Non-pregnant belly
swollen   to seven months. Hips   cracked open,
pushed   farther apart.   Breast reduction, took back
          what men first notice.

                    I set myself before a mirror
                    but wouldn't let me see myself,

tried to blink   invisible,   rested my elbows
            on the surface of a cool lake.   Underneath,
a lock of hair   from my first cut   caught in an envelope.
          My mother's writing. A letter
my father sent me,   our house   to our house.
Flute head   separated   from its body of keys.

APOLOGY TO TAYLOR SWIFT

These kinds of wounds they last and they last
                    –Taylor Swift, "Bad Blood"

I'm sorry I hailed *1989* a masterpiece
only after Ryan Adams covered the album,
each song stripped of pop and joy,
each song now a dirge.
Condescension masked as compliment.

My ex once made me a mix CD:
"Music You May Have Missed."
His own song, track 13.
Condescension masked as gift.

I'm sorry I bought Ryan Adams' story,
remaking your album healed him
after his divorce. No—a predatory move
from the married man who once
disrobed to meet a 15-year-old online.

Ryan Adams told his wife (Mandy Moore!)
she wasn't a real musician.

My ex never read one of my poems
but arranged me on his bed
for a private concert
each time he wrote a new song.

I'm sorry I posted the article
"What Ryan Adams' *1989*
Can Teach Taylor Swift."
He clamped his hand over your guitar,
undressed your melodies, forced
your words into his mouth.

BLANK

A guy I used to date runs by
in street clothes, panic
on his face, clips the corner

and he's gone. We haven't
spoken since he returned
my Christmas card in the mail.

My life a loaf of bread. Halve it—
that's when I slept in his room. A port,
I thought, but just more storm.

Easy to blame a version of him
for hurting a version of me.
He could be anyone now.

Fill in the blank: He's running after

_____.

I can't. I can't begin to guess.

AA ABECEDARIAN

An addict and I walk into the
basement meeting holding hands.
Court-appointed. We
drink coffee, Styrofoam cups,
edge closer to the circle,
finally sit. I believe a
good man is buried inside
him. When he becomes the bottle,
I shut my eyes, try to
justify his hands on my throat.
Kill the drunk not-him.
Love the sober true-him.

Most people share only their
names. A few tell stories. I—
observer, lurker, fraud—
pass. What would I say,
quiet girl who's never been high?

Rain outside. He and I
stand under the awning, waiting.
Thank you for coming, he says,
understanding what I don't: no
veil between not-him and true-him.
We're so good at fooling,

X marks any spot we want.
You're welcome, I say. The camera
zooms out. We become small, smaller still.

THE WOMAN AND THE WOLF

He strangled little sounds from me
in his doorway. Later
he called the word *strangle*
dramatic. *You could breathe fine.*

Hand over my mouth, he shushed
into my ear. Later he said,
You can't rape your girlfriend.
I lay awake while he slept.

Easter morning I cried
in church, quietly
so my mother couldn't hear.
Another bowed chin in a pew.

Sometimes I imagine wolves
as wounded birds. From a distance,
they're not so different, the howling
head, a wing puncturing the sky.

III.

THE FRAGILE DOMESTIC

title after Amy Meissner's mixed-media piece

We played house in her basement.

As mother, Ellie crouched

behind the plastic oven. As father,

I moved to kiss her forehead.

She frowned. *You're doing it wrong.*

▼

My mother cut the little girl
from the magazine, placed the picture

in her hope chest years before
she met my father. I was a kid

when she showed me
the girl, blonde, blue-eyed, like me,

like looking in a mirror.

▼

At my friend's shower,
she was the last one pregnant
except me. I listened
to their stories over cake and punch.

▼

I only looked   like that girl   for a while   until
        one day

                        I didn't.

                          ▼

That year, Ellie's father

visited the grocery store

where her mother worked.

She steered him

to the storage room,

where he shot her

dead, then himself.

▼

My mother woke early to grade
elementary cursive. Her hand tidied
wild loops, taming a word, then
another, then a sentence. She clenched
each child's invisible fist.

▼

One decided against the tub,
smoothing a tarp instead
over her marriage bed,
saying she needed
to feel grounded.

One rubbed her belly
as she spoke—the six-year-old
beside her, a phantom limb.

▼

The picture treasured   in the chest   she forced me

      [to speak]   an octave higher
scolded me   for slipping

      into my own   voice. I stopped

      talking
      much.

I felt her   ventriloquist hand

      on the small of my back.

▼

We switched. As father,

Ellie hoisted a plate over her head,

slammed it to the floor.

As mother, I poured air

from plastic eggs into a red

mixing bowl.

BACKYARD

This scooped-out hole   was once the Bradford pear
canopying a friend and me last May   when
she lifted her shirt   to let me feel the life inside.
Through the dark soil   the tree's roots
still stretch   like lines   etching a cracked egg.

She became a mother. I didn't.   She secures
the stroller's strap,   follows her son
to the park. She meets other mothers
in the shade.   The older children pile acorns
in their laps, burdens disguised as gifts.

                              They spill to the ground.
At home my husband and I read, opposite ends
of the couch,   my feet tucked under his side.
     Our tea steeps   in the kitchen.
In the neighbors' yard, branches quilt patterns into sky.

BROODY

Our biggest hen lingers in vain
on a mound of eggs. Panting
in her sweatbox, her comb

tinged purple from dehydration,
she refuses to leave.

We have no rooster.
Those eggs might as well be
ping-pong balls. To break her

of her broodiness, my husband slides
an ice pack beneath her

damp haunches; I baptize
her head in a bowl of water.
We lock her outside the coop.

She paces the length of the cage,
desperate to return to her nest.

WHEN, WHEN

This morning, in front of the termite guy, I sobbed
because I couldn't force open the gate.
My arms weakened with effort; late for work, again.

You're so together, a friend texted recently. I haven't
heard her voice in a year. Last we talked, her list,
soccer and violin, softball in the summer,

her wistful *You must have so much time*. What do I do
with the minutes? I walk a dog, feed chickens,
plan lessons, grade. I do not call my friend,

whose floor I once slept on, heartbroken. If we
unburied the time capsule, one of us would hug first.
I imagine her on the front steps of our high school.

I imagine myself facing her, raising my hand
in a salute or to shield the sun. We passed notes
in chemistry. I can't name noble gases but I remember

Kevin applied lip balm each time he kissed her.
On Facebook, she calls someone else best friend.
How did we get to forty? She didn't marry Kevin.

Her kids keep having birthdays. Dust under
the TV stand, clear shoreline where the broom
doesn't reach. When, when, time rusts the gate closed.

ODE TO WEEDING

My universe shrinks
to the size of my backyard patio.
I jab the double-headed spear
deep into the dirt between two bricks,
grab as close as I can to the root
with my rubber glove, yank.
In the bucket, the satisfying plop of leaf
and spindly nerve. For three hours
I don't argue with my mother
in my head or wonder if my boss
has emailed me back. I don't
scroll sunstroke symptoms,
though I will later. I dig, sweat,
stretch, guzzle deep the garden hose.

THE LITTLEST CHICKEN

Alone again. The others left the coop
for a dirt bath. Across the yard,
their stop-motion bodies
squat and twist, kick up swirls.

The littlest chicken dreams. In the sun
her black feathers shimmer turquoise.
She flaps her wings for nothing,
struts in no particular direction.

I refill food and water, collect eggs.
The others ignore my approach,
camouflage their bodies in dust.
The littlest chicken, always

in profile, stares at me with one
unblinking eye, rotates to offer
the other. Against a patch
of prickly grass, her comb is a flame.

LOST

Kenneka Jenkins' body found in a hotel freezer,
September 9, 2017, Chicago

I am no one's mother
but something kicks from inside.
In the hotel, someone's daughter

pushes off one wall, careens into another,
her body a pinball. Watching the news, I cry,
though I am no one's mother.

She trips over a banister,
white metal, stumbles narrow hallways inside
the hotel. She was someone's daughter.

She rights herself, then wanders
into the kitchen to die.
I am no one's mother,

but I want to pause the footage, discover
a new ending. I want her to walk outside
the hotel—someone's *daughter*—

the whirring tape filming just another
night. She must have kicked from inside.
That poor mother—
in the hotel freezer, her daughter.

BELLS

One good egg is all it takes.
She longed to hold a baby to her breast,
let the child breathe milk. The nest
is a hen's truth. You can't make
a broody hen forsake her nest.
No matter how many eggs you replace
with small silver bells, she'll stay
forever waiting for the bells to hatch.

DONATING MY EGGS

In the fertility clinic   waiting room,

     I'm the youngest by ten years,   except
     for a toddler
my cousin   smiles at   wistfully.

     He wears cowboy boots and has a matching hat

his mother won't let him

        put on indoors. He says

        he's not   a real

        cowboy without it.

Before my ultrasound,
the boy's mother says,

     All it takes is one good egg.

       My cousin, forty-one and
       beautiful,

     so skinny I can't imagine her

with a curved silhouette   by Christmas,

      doesn't answer.
            Later,
            on the car ride home, she says,

If he were my son,   he could wear   that hat   to funerals.

IV.

SITTING NEXT TO MYSELF AS AN
OLD WOMAN

Both on vacation in San Diego, we prefer the lily pond
to the zoo. I know she's me, scribbling poems
on a legal pad. I'm less vain in the future—
toenails unpainted, the color of seashells scrubbed clean.
My black sandals' bulk conforms to the curve
of my arch. I sit on a folded blue tote, my legs
cooled by damp grass. She notes, and I note:
a man sings his bicycle up three steps, a woman
prays over her open map. I stop writing
only when my future self unfurls each yellow sheet.
On the top page, *legerdemain* and *punctilious*,
words I haven't learned yet. Before I walk away,
I take off my sunglasses. I look right through myself.

DUPLEX FOR MY FUTURE SELF

after Jericho Brown

My husband, making coffee in the kitchen
or dead. Tell me, future self, so I can be ready.

> If he's dead, I need to be ready, so tell me.
> In thirty years, will this house still be ours?

In forty years, will this house still be ours?
On the porch, I dare a glance behind me.

> On the porch, I glance behind me again—
> to my husband or my reflection?

My husband stars in my reflections:
the man on stage who shook his long hair back.

> The man on stage shakes his long hair back—
> my husband, an answer I don't yet know.

My husband, the answer I don't yet know:
Is he alive inside, making coffee?

ECHOES

The sullen student   muttering for me not to touch
his shoulder. The ex-boyfriend
                                        snapping for a towel.
My mother   bribing me with polish   not to bite
          my fingernails.
                                        The dead
fifth-grade classmate   caroling Christmas
outside my first home. The woman   buying eggs

                    ahead of me
in the grocery line.   Just the wreck risen to the surface.

ELEGY

Last year's days cling to my coat,
my boots, my hair. The past
glitters the street with debris.
Two students died last year, winter

and winter, ten months apart.
Car crashes, fast. Both brushed
sleep from their eyes
the morning of, parted drapes.

Their lives flashed like headlights.
The past is a pair of leather gloves.
My head in my hands,
the past cold against my cheeks.

MEETING

I read my first Eavan Boland poem today,
the day she died. A Master's in poetry, and still.

So many cracks in the syllabus. A bookcase
dedicated to poetry, but still. No way to meet

each brilliant voice. Some of the best musicians
I've heard were in living rooms, bands traveling

in vans from town to small town. How did I
happen upon them and not one of the world's

greatest poets? We live our lives. We take walks,
we take classes, we French kiss people we'll marry

and people we won't. There's no map except
the kind in *Family Circus*, dotted lines flinging us

far from home in loops, then home again.
We meet who we meet when we meet them,

and I like to think we meet them when we need to.
Today I met Eavan Boland, and today

she closed her eyes. Her meetings will not end
with death, and if only. If only I could be so lucky.

ABECEDARIAN FOR MY NEIGHBOR, WHOSE NAME I STILL DON'T KNOW

A garden born beyond my window. Not my
backyard, my neighbor's. Before
coronavirus, before isolation, she and I
didn't acknowledge each other.
Every night my dogs burst
from my back door, and she sat outside with a
glass of wine listening to—*something*. I'd
hush to spy but could never tell.
I imagined long-distance love, her voice
joined with his. Maybe Rosetta Stone, too low to
know what language. No wave, no hello.

Little pots line the wooden deck,
matching sprigs of green. A tarp covers
nothing, for now. She tells me, *You're the*
only person I've seen in days.

Planting's like praying, both
quests for communion. We
receive stale wafers on our
shining tongues, gather
tomatoes fallen off the vine too soon. I'm an
unbeliever who only pulls weeds, puts
voids in the ground instead of life. But
witness this small miracle: she was

X in her yard, I was
Y in mine. We're still rooted in these
zones, but now our voices soar over the fence.

WINTER

The trees undressed now,
I glimpse into my neighbor's kitchen,
single father eating breakfast

alone. Jelly from his doughnut
dabs his undershirt.
His son grabs something

from the fridge, stuffs it into
his backpack, hurries out.
My husband, dressed already,

joins me at our kitchen sink,
kisses the top of my head.
Last night's argument settled,

and not, our hug good-bye tentative.
Twist the dish wand inside
the coffee mug. Tug the string

that darkens the room.
When our garage doors lift,
our neighbor startles at my hello.

KARAOKE NIGHT, JB'S BAR AND GRILL

Everything heightened the night we met—
he didn't sing, he shouted; didn't dance, convulsed.
If I include Verve Pipe, could you guess the year?
When I was young, I knew everything.
Instead of listening, I decoded. His voice
the voice that rouses me now. He gripped
the microphone's head, that tiny disco ball.
In a few years, he'd stop smoking, but that night
a flame in his hand. My mouth moved with his.
After, the high-top table. Two empty bottles.
Only photo in his wallet, his grandfather,
whose vintage button-down he was wearing,
vertical patterns like rows of stamps.
I love Dawson's Creek, I warned. Better for him
to know me. His Creed joke—some said
he resembled Scott Stapp. Dark hair like a hood,
but otherwise I didn't see it. He tipped his head back,
arms wide open: *How about now?* Had I ever
laughed so hard? (No.) My water a small river
making its way to him. He helped me mop the spill.

ETHAN HAWKE AND I HAVE ONE OF THOSE DINNERS

inspired by the question of who I'd have dinner with,
living or dead. He picks me up at seven. I want
to ask—delicately, the way I slice into
my first bite of steak—if he misses being beautiful,
or if it's better being interesting. I could gaze at him
in *Reality Bites* on loop, his stringy hair,
his vulnerable throat-clearing, but he's certainly
better as the alcoholic priest in *First Reformed*.
Throw my vanity away. From a certain angle,
turning to check his blind spot on our drive home,
leaning in to kiss Winona Ryder before end credits,
Ethan Hawke is forever 23. At home, after
my husband waves to Ethan Hawke's taillights
and asks what he's like, I pull photo albums from
the top shelf and show the dogs my 23-year-old face
and hair—they look from picture to me in disbelief.

THE NIGHT BEFORE OUR DOG'S DEATH

my husband found a poem
about a dog slogging through
a snowy street behind his owner,
read it aloud, slid me the book.

I found a poem comparing
each of our remaining days
to a wooden block the child stacks.
My husband found a child reaching

for the wrong grown-up's hand.
I found an ambulance wailing
into the drive. He found a river.
I found a tricycle overturned

in the yard. He found a poem
about a dog sleeping in tree shadow.
I found his hand, our dog's fur,
my voice hollow in the near dark.

BEING HUMAN

Six, imagining my parents
in their coffins—my mother

in her teacher's corduroy
and wooden Christmas pin. My father
in a button-down shirt, notebook

peeking from the pocket,
as if he'd be charged with writing

a witty column about his own funeral.
I didn't know how people dressed
for death. I could see my brother

dead, too—stonewashed jeans,
ratty flannel, smirk. I knew

he would die if he didn't buckle up,
so every time we rode in the car,
to Florida or the grocery store,

I tattled. He glared, yanking
the strap across his chest.

My second year of teaching,
a student in his casket: blue suit
and tie, shadow scrubbed

clean from his face. No purple
bandana crowning his head.

I don't picture my father as he is,
ashes. I don't picture my student's tie.
Place them in my passenger seat,

the empty desk in the last row.
Close the lid on a stranger.

MY MOTHER MOVES TWO HOURS AWAY TO HER NEW LOVE'S HOME

I sit on her floor. She folds button-downs
on the bed, tries to smooth the creases out.
I place each shirt in a box. Then the phonograph
scratch of packing tape, the squeak of Sharpie

testifying to what's inside. We don't talk much.
She pauses once, looking down at the open arms
of a yellow blouse. *If I had grandchildren,
I wouldn't be able to leave.*

She crosses the arms of the blouse,
lifts the chest, hands it to me—
an offering. I lay the shirt into its box
slowly, like lowering a baby into his cradle.

VISITATION

If I squint hard against the sun,
I can materialize a crooked door
cut into the sky. For an hour
or two, I depart this place
and enter the blue-tinged light
of an old television. Beside
my father on his couch
for *Wheel of Fortune*, we try
to guess the phrases first.
During commercials, I show him
photos of my husband, laugh
when he scrunches his face
in mock disapproval.
I touch his Adam's apple—
new, plugging the hole cancer made—
and hear his gravelly voice
for the first time. Eventually,
I smooth my skirt, kiss his cheek,
slide open the screen door,
barefoot in the green.

THANKS

Thank you to Courtney LeBlanc for believing in this book and giving it the best possible home with Riot in Your Throat. I have loved working with you.

Thank you to Jai Johnson and Meryl Carver-Allmond, dear friends, for the beautiful cover. It is perfect.

Thank you to Maggie Smith for your generous feedback on *A Crooked Door Cut into the Sky*, the chapbook that led to this collection, and to Lisa Mangini at Paper Nautilus Press for selecting it for the Vella Chapbook Prize.

Thank you to Erin Adair-Hodges for helping me see what this book was meant to be. It would not exist without you. Thanks, too, to so many other poet friends for your feedback and support, especially Traci Brimhall, Marianne Kunkel, Ruth Williams, Shuly Xóchitl Cawood, Laura Lee Washburn, Allison Blevins, Roland Sodowsky, Chris Anderson, Katelyn Roth, Cameron Morse, Hyejung Kook, Jenny Molberg, Hadara Bar-Nadav, and Bridget Lowe.

Thank you to my family and friends for your love and encouragement, especially Emmy Fite and Carey Burke, David Fite, Glenda Madl, Donna Johnson, Jana Leigh, Juliet Traub, Angella Curran, Erin McChristy, Megan Knell, and Caleb Hoyer. As always, thank you to my late father, Jerry Fite.

Finally, thank you to Marc Johnson, who has never missed a poetry reading. Thank you for sharing all this with me.

ACKNOWLEDGMENTS

Many thanks to the editors of the journals and anthologies in which these poems first appeared, sometimes in earlier versions or with different titles:

3 Elements Review: "Watching *Casablanca* at Oma and Opa's House" (Best of the Net nominee)

Autumn Sky Poetry Daily: "Karaoke Night, JB's Bar and Grill"

Broadsided Press: "Backyard" and "The Fragile Domestic" (Best of the Net nominee)

Chiron Review: "Laundry Day"

Coal City Review: "Freewheelin' Bob Dylan and the Nameless Girl"

Flint Hills Review: "Ode to Weeding"

I-70 Review: "Sitting Next to Myself as an Old Woman" and "Visitation"

Noble / Gas Qtrly: "I Begin to Forgive Myself" and "I'm Only Happy When It Rains"

Pleiades: "AA Abecedarian"

Poetry Breakfast: "Winter"

Rat's Ass Review: "Blank" and "Fifteen"

Rattle: "The Woman and the Wolf"

Red Paint Hill Journal: "Bells"

Rise Up Review: "Gone"

Rogue Agent: "It's Not My Mother's Fault"

Sidereal: "From My Parked Car, I Stare at the Snow"

SWWIM: "Abecedarian for My Neighbor, Whose Name I Still Don't Know" (*Orison Anthology* nominee)

Valparaiso Poetry Review: "Being Human"

West Trestle Review: "Duplex for My Future Self"

Whale Road Review: "Donating My Eggs"

The Woman Inc.: "Submerged"

"Apology to Taylor Swift" was featured on the Instagram account Taylor Swift as Books.

"Broody" and "Visitation" also appear in the anthology *Ghost Sign* (Spartan Press, 2016).

The following poems are also in *A Crooked Door Cut into the Sky*, one of Paper Nautilus' 2017 Vella Chapbook Contest's winning manuscripts: "Backyard," "Being Human," "Bells," "Corner Booth at Café Del Rio, Two Weeks After My Father's Death," "Donating My Eggs," "Gone," "I Begin to Forgive Myself," "I'm Only Happy When It Rains," "The Immediacy," "The Littlest Chicken," "My Mother Moves Two Hours Away to Her New Love's Home," "The Night Before Our Dog's Death," "Ode to Weeding," "Visitation," and "Visiting My Sixteen-Year-Old Self."

Paper Nautilus Press nominated "I'm Only Happy When It Rains" and "My Mother Movies Two Hours Away to Her New Love's Home" for the Pushcart Prize.

New Rivers Press selected "Freewheelin' Bob Dylan and the Nameless Girl" as one of a hundred poems for their anthology *Visiting Bob*.

ABOUT THE AUTHOR

Melissa Fite Johnson's first collection, *While the Kettle's On* (Little Balkans Press, 2015), won the Nelson Poetry Book Award and is a Kansas Notable Book. She is also the author of *A Crooked Door Cut into the Sky*, winner of the 2017 Vella Chapbook Award (Paper Nautilus Press, 2018). Her poems have appeared in *Pleiades*, *SWWIM*, *Whale Road Review*, *Broadsided Press*, and elsewhere. Melissa teaches high school English in Lawrence, Kansas, where she and her husband live with their three dogs.

ABOUT THE PRESS

Riot in Your Throat is an independent press
that publishes fierce, feminist poetry.

Support independent authors, artists, and presses.

Visit us online:
www.riotinyourthroat.com

CPSIA information can be obtained
at www.ICGtesting.com
Printed in the USA
LVHW082021120421
684248LV00021B/997

9 781736 138601

The autonomous life?

Manchester University Press

CONTEMPORARY ANARCHIST STUDIES

A series edited by
Laurence Davis, *University College Cork, Ireland*
Uri Gordon, *Loughborough University, UK*
Nathan Jun, *Midwestern State University, USA*
Alex Prichard, *Exeter University, UK*

Contemporary Anarchist Studies promotes the study of anarchism as
a framework for understanding and acting on the most pressing
problems of our times. The series publishes cutting-edge, socially engaged
scholarship from around the world – bridging theory and practice,
academic rigor and the insights of contemporary activism.

The topical scope of the series encompasses anarchist history and
theory broadly construed; individual anarchist thinkers; anarchist informed
analysis of current issues and institutions; and anarchist or
anarchist-inspired movements and practices. Contributions informed
by anti-capitalist, feminist, ecological, indigenous and non-Western or
Global South anarchist perspectives are particularly welcome. So, too,
are manuscripts that promise to illuminate the relationships between the
personal and the political aspects of transformative social change, local
and global problems, and anarchism and other movements and ideologies.
Above all, we wish to publish books that will help activist scholars and
scholar activists think about how to challenge and build real alternatives
to existing structures of oppression and injustice.

The autonomous life?

Paradoxes of hierarchy and
authority in the squatters
movement in Amsterdam

Nazima Kadir

Manchester University Press

Published by Manchester University Press
Altrincham Street, Manchester M1 7JA
www.manchesteruniversitypress.co.uk

British Library Cataloguing-in-Publication Data
A catalogue record for this book is available from the British Library
An electronic version of this book is also available under a Creative Commons
(CC-BY-NC-SA) license.

Library of Congress Cataloging-in-Publication Data applied for

ISBN 978 1784 99410 5 hardback
ISBN 978 1784 99411 2 paperback
ISBN 978 1784 99756 4 open access

First published 2016

The publisher has no responsibility for the persistence or accuracy of URLs for
any external or third-party internet websites referred to in this book, and does
not guarantee that any content on such websites is, or will remain,
accurate or appropriate.

Typeset by Out of House Publishing
Printed in Great Britain
by Bell & Bain Ltd, Glasgow

CONTENTS

FIGURES

PREFACE

A few months before I left Amsterdam, I attended one of my last squatting actions. A former squatter housemate had organized the squatting of luxury condominiums. They had once been affordable social housing apartments, available for permanent rental to anyone whose number had come up after years on the waiting list. The squatters movement considered the practice of renovating and selling social housing apartments a betrayal to the Socialist ideals that led to the building of such housing a few decades earlier.

My friend was squatting these apartments because most had not sold, after nearly a year on the market following the global credit crisis. Mortgages were hard to come by and the apartments had become unexpectedly unaffordable. It was a confrontational action since squatters typically occupied abandoned spaces rather than luxury apartments. My friend felt unsure of how the police and the neighbors would react, so he organized hundreds of people to attend. The more support, the less likelihood of violence.

He planned well. By the time I arrived, the squatters had broken open the apartment doors and moved in, and the police had inspected the spaces and left. Hundreds of black clad punks in attendance milled around chatting in the newly squatted apartments, on the street, and on the sidewalks. It was a festive atmosphere.

However, a white Dutch couple in their late fifties who had purchased one of the condominiums was unhappy. They were now sandwiched in between squatters in the apartments above, below, and in the buildings on either side. I watched the husband lean out his window, stare craggily at the sea of white punks who had taken over the street, and say, repeatedly: "Fucking Muslims. Fucking Muslims."

This book is full of strange and contradictory stories like this one. I focus on micro-social interactions that reflect larger tensions around power, authority, belonging, and identity in the squatters movement specifically, and in urban life generally. These stories emerged from observations, interactions, and interviews during three-and-a-half years of anthropological research in a squatters community in Amsterdam. During this time, I resided in four squats where I was a member of living groups. I regularly attended squatting actions, political actions, worked as a cook in a squatted restaurant, worked on anti-gentrification campaigns and house defenses, and generally hung out in the citywide squatters' scene. I was evicted twice and jailed once.

Figure i Squatting Action Amsterdam, 2008

In addition to narrating stories, I systematically examine what people say versus what they do, and what these contradictions mean. Why did the older Dutch man curse Muslims when no Muslims were visually present nor responsible for the squatting? What does this incident reveal about an environment where it is acceptable to articulate xenophobic statements when feeling angry, powerless, and "surrounded?"

Since this book is about the squatters movement in Amsterdam, I focus on taboo dynamics that have yet to be examined in social movement literature. How do people silently practice hierarchy and authority in an anarchist community that rejects hierarchy and authority? How does that paradox structure every aspect of social life in this movement?

My tone and perspective differ radically from social movement literature, which often represents activists romantically. In contrast, my observations of this subculture are influenced by women/gender studies, queer theory, and subaltern studies. Hence, I view people in this movement as ... people, rather than heroes. Activists tend to consider their spaces and practices as, "heterotopias," that is, existing outside of hegemonic norms. I have found otherwise. I have witnessed activists unwittingly reproducing and being embedded in the very social and cultural norms that they verbally reject. Such contradictory practices are universal rather than hypocritical because people – all of us – are flawed and complicated. This is also what makes life interesting.

ACKNOWLEDGMENTS

First off, I give my heartfelt appreciation to my doctoral dissertation supervisor, Thomas Blom Hansen. This book is the result of his unconditional intellectual and emotional guidance, and unrelentingly high standards. I wish to thank the faculty and staff of the Anthropology Department at Yale. The National Science Foundation Doctoral Dissertation Improvement Grant and a plethora of Yale fellowships generously funded fieldwork and writing.

In Amsterdam, I wish to thank Martin Herzberg and Julia Roesselers for their research assistance and to Lynn Owens, Abbe Blum, and Ron Eyerman for feedback on early drafts of chapters. The Amsterdam Institute of Social Science Research (AISSR) and the International Institute for Social History (IISH) both provided affiliations, workspaces, and eventually, employment. Heartfelt thanks to Jose Komen of the AISSR and Marcel van der Linden and Karin Hofmeister of the IISH for access to these resources. I have been honored to collaborate with Maiko Tanaka, Binna Choi, and Maria Pask in the production of the sitcom, "Our Autonomous Life," inspired by this book.

In London, I have been privileged to receive invaluable editorial assistance from Heiba Lamara, who examined the manuscript with a fine toothcomb for linguistic and intellectual clarity. Special thanks to Sara Farris and Mihnea Chijdea for proposal feedback.

I want to thank the Dutch welfare state, which provided unemployment benefits, subsidized health insurance, and affordable housing. These benefits were essential to complete my PhD with peace of mind. I feel privileged that by remaining in welfare state Europe to write, I avoided financial duress in the United States.

I would like to express thanks to the squatters with whom I lived and worked. Unfortunately, due to anthropological standards of anonymity, I am forbidden from naming anyone. Moreover, many of my fellow squatters continue to be politically active, and to identify them puts them at risk. Thanks to all twenty of my housemates and the residents of a specific squatted neighborhood for making space for me in your lives. I treasure the bonds that I share with all of you despite the evictions and the heartaches. Looking back, we were a family, experiencing the joys and the struggles of family life. I also want to extend special thanks to the collective of a particular squatted social center as well as to the activists with whom I worked on the defense campaigns of the houses where I resided. I would also like to thank the brave members of the black bloc, who powerfully avenged my evictions. Last, I am grateful to certain squatters who read chapters and provided engaged and critical feedback.

Finally, I dedicate this book to my partner. He has listened to and debated with passion and precision every narrative and theoretical concept in this book. He has been a well of emotional and intellectual support. My love: as an activist, friend, and husband, you inspire me every single day. I am privileged to share my life with you.

Introduction: the autonomous life?

Every Saturday night for thirty years, the renowned Vrankrijk, a squatters' social center, has hosted a dance party which attracts a mix of squatters, punks, artists, radical left activists, hippies, university students, and tourists seeking to taste the underground scene in Amsterdam. Located on a beautiful street in the inner city, the building is enormous, standing four-stories tall, its facade covered by colorful murals in stark contrast to the eighteenth-century dollhouse architectural landscape of the neighborhood. Tour guides often stand in front of the Vrankrijk, explaining the importance of the squatters movement in the 1980s and how the building represents its achievements in maintaining affordable housing and encouraging cultural innovation in the city. The mainstream media and the municipal politicians call it a squatters' bulwark.

For squatters, the building has an entirely divergent set of meanings. Having been legalized nearly twenty years earlier, the building is no longer a squat or in any way at the political core of the movement, but a reliable place to party and consume cheap drinks. As is the norm for radical left European social centers, a rotating collective, mainly comprised of baby punks, enthusiastically manages the bar. As volunteers, they organize the bar shifts, the cleaning, the bouncers, the finances, and the themes of the Saturday dance nights – ranging from benefits for Polish queer organizations, Latin American solidarity info-evenings, to 1980s pop parties. Former squatters, referred to sarcastically as pensioners by activists, reside in living groups upstairs.

In September 2008, tremendous violence dismantled the tradition of the Saturday night dance party at the Vrankrijk. Around 8 p.m., two veteran squatters, Yoghurt and Joseph, both involved in the movement for over fifteen years, arrived drunk and high from a prodigious cocktail of drugs, with a hefty dog. The bouncer, a twenty-two-year-old punk who knew these men, refused them entrance with the dog. Ignoring his request, they barged in anyway. The bouncer and other bar workers, including a staff member nicknamed "Macho," ordered the men to leave. Finally, threatening them with a bat, the two men exited the bar. They then returned shortly afterwards and

Figure 0.1 The Vrankrijk legalized squat, 2006

the situation escalated, to the point where the bar staff locked the door to keep the men out while they pummeled the door and demanded entrance. Multiple versions of what happened next exist, but with the mix of alcohol, drugs, a barking dog, a bat, wooden sticks, and the involvement of someone nicknamed "Macho," the possibility of conflict resolution seemed slim at best. The situation ended with Yoghurt falling backwards (or being pushed), cracking his head, and permanently injuring his inner ear.

Discussions of the "Vrankrijk incident" in the squatters' scene were pervasive in the months following the event. What exactly happened? Was it a crime or self-defense? Who were the victims and who were the perpetrators? If a crime had been committed, how should the perpetrators be punished? Months passed without decisions but in numerous conversations, people complained and proclaimed furiously.

"Someone needs to take responsibility," I heard Chris, a Belgian squatter say loudly with conviction late at night at a squatted bar. "This is unacceptable behavior," declared Marie, over breakfast in the squat where I resided at the time. Meanwhile, for months, the collective who managed the Vrankrijk had been meeting nightly, wrangling over appropriate solutions for hours. Although regretting the violence and the permanent injury, most supported the staff, believing that Yoghurt had provoked the incident which spiraled out of control. They found it unfair to expel those involved from the squatters' community when they had merely done their best in an impossible situation.

Eventually, a citywide squatters' meeting was called to settle the issue. The majority in attendance – who had passionate opinions about the matter in bars and at breakfast tables – remained silent, while a handful of the attendees, mainly squatter bosses, argued about what to do. Was it fair to ban the perpetrators from the movement? Should they collect money towards the costs of Yoghurt's rehabilitation? Would Yoghurt report the perpetrators to the police? The meeting failed to produce a plan of action. A month later, the police resolved the movement's dilemma when they arrested and imprisoned the so-called perpetrators and the mayor announced that the city had removed the Vrankrijk's liquor license and had closed the space to the public.

This conclusion embarrassed the squatters movement, which prides itself as an anarchist, "Do-It-Yourself" (DIY), emancipated alternative to the capitalist, authoritarian, hierarchical Mainstream.[1] The incident demonstrated that in terms of internal conflict, the squatters movement could not "Do-It-Themselves." Instead, after months of waiting, the squatters' articulated enemy, the state – in the form of the mayor and the police – rectified the issue on their behalf. To add injury to insult, the mayor, acting in his role as the benevolent father figure of the city, grounded his naughty, punk, squatter children, taking away their liquor license and chiding them for their inability to manage their "playground," valued at millions in the 2008 real estate market.

The incident encapsulates many of the contradictory internal dynamics of the movement which form the basis of examination in this book. Like many social movements the squatters movement has two faces: "the front stage," which interacts with the Mainstream, consisting of the state, politicians, the media, and an imagined "public"; and the other, more complicated and perplexing "backstage," which directs itself towards the internal community, or "the scene."

Presented with a clear enemy, a determinate external Other such as the state, squatters can easily unite to work together using a well-rehearsed repertoire of tactics to reach their goals. But an internal problem, such as the incident at the Vrankrijk, involving members of this community who make their own claims for inclusion, support and justice, upsets an underlying logic. It proves impossible for squatters to perform "backstage" as the articulate, assertive "front stage" activist who unwaveringly proclaims and acts on one's ideals. The example points to a persistent contradiction between the two faces of squatting, and an unresolved problem in the heart of the squatters movement for the past forty years.

This book is an ethnographic study of the internal dynamics of a subcultural community that defines itself as a social movement. While the majority of scholarly studies on this movement focus on its official face, on its front stage, I am concerned with a series of ideological and practical paradoxes at work within the micro-social dynamics of the backstage, an area that has so far been neglected in social movement studies.

The central question, which I explore from a variety of angles, is how hierarchy and authority function in a social movement subculture that disavows such concepts. The squatters movement, which defines itself primarily as anti-hierarchical and anti-authoritarian, is profoundly structured by the unresolved and perpetual contradiction between both public disavowal and simultaneous maintenance of hierarchy and authority within the movement.

This study analyzes how this contradiction is then reproduced in different micro-social interactions, examining the methods by which people negotiate minute details of their daily lives as squatter activists in the face of a funhouse mirror of ideological expectations reflecting values from within the squatter community, that, in turn, often refract mainstream, middle-class norms.

In the examination of this question, I repeatedly revisit questions of performance and habitus. I use the term performance for self-conscious behavior exhibited by activists with a range of audiences in mind, which include a number of characteristics. First, I argue, they should display a specific socialization into a movement subculture through the practice of squatting and by learning skills that gain prestige in this community, which I term squatter capital. Moreover, I demarcate that an essential element of this socialization is to render invisible the long and arduous process of skill acquisition, thus demonstrating a process of mastery and rejection. Finally, I contend that activists should present a hostility and rudeness that is in itself a rejection of imagined middle-class insincere politeness.

While performance reflects a self-conscious display of internal movement socialization, I use habitus to refer to the types of unselfconscious quotidian behaviors and style preferences that reflect an activist's upbringing, and thus, his/her class, culture, and education. While performance is movement specific and theoretically accessible to all within the community to reproduce, habitus reflects class, culture and education and hence hierarchy and differential status, which I assert, are taboo to acknowledge transparently in a subculture that claims emancipation from differential status hierarchies.

Although these socializations exist independently of each other, I focus on the relationship between habitus and performance. For example, I illustrate when habitus contributes to the seamless performance of the ideal squatter self in the case of authority figures and their ability to mobilize their often educated, upper-middle-class habitus to effortlessly perform conviction. Or, on the other hand, I highlight when habitus undermines the convincing performance of the autonomous, defiant activist, such as in the case of people addicted to alcohol or drugs, who lack capacity to manage both movement and mainstream tasks, or simply originate from working-class backgrounds.

Both performance and habitus require recognition, and therefore, an audience. In addition to analyzing both successful and failed performances and the various types of habitus possessed by people in this community, I also consider how others recognize these performances mainly at the level of discourse. Moreover, I argue that when people in this community both gossip and classify each other negatively this reflects a squatter's status and capital in the movement in unexpected ways. Since members of this subculture are fiercely individualistic and view themselves as unclassifiable non-conformists, I contend that the best way to understand norms and values is through the negative classification of others that dominate subcultural discourse. In analyzing these interactions and methods of organization, I place as much value on the meaning of the silences and on the unstated assumptions as on the articulations.

Squatters are constantly negotiating elements of performance and habitus before a range of audiences. Some audience members, such as the state and the media, are temporary, tuning in for only selected, dramatic episodes. Some, such as one's housemates and the gaze of others who participate in the squatter "scene," are ever-present. Squatters juggle multiple ideals, many of which are premised on mastery and rejection and which are never explicitly defined. This lifestyle is especially labyrinthine, I assert lastly, when one examines the paradox surrounding the ideal of the "autonomous self." This study demonstrates that it connotes someone who is independent, non-conformist, emotionally self-contained, entitled, and anti-capitalist.

Reflecting on all of these factors and considering that this community of people – of different skills, habitus, and backgrounds – live and work intensively together on the legal margins of a tiny, wealthy, northern European, highly bureaucratized, multicultural city dominated by religious and ethnic tensions, the autonomous life is more often complex and fraught than liberatory and utopic.

Historical context of the squatters movement in Amsterdam

In this section, I will first review the main sources from which I have constructed this narrative, then present a critical historiography, followed by an overview of the main points of this history. I conclude by discussing the impact of this history on the current movement and summarizing structural changes in the political landscape during my fieldwork.

Description of sources

The three most comprehensive histories on the squatters movement in Amsterdam are *De stad in eigen hand* (The city in our own hands) (1992) by Virginie Mamadouh, *Cracking Under Pressure* (2009) by Lynn Owens, and *Een voet tussen de deur* (A foot between the door) (2000) by Eric Duivenvoorden. The academic monographs by Mamadouh and Owens are both based on their archival research for their doctoral dissertations and situate themselves in social movement studies. Duivenvoorden presents a narrative to a popular audience without an explicit argument. He was also instrumental in the making of a well-known and influential full-length documentary, *De stad was van ons* (The city was ours) (Seelan 1996), which relates a history of the squatters movement in Amsterdam.

These three books and the film have a Russian doll effect on the historical record. Mamadouh's book was published first, and Duivenvoorden then bases his work partially on her research in which he duplicates what she argues are the main points of historical development. Duivenvoorden works on the documentary by conducting the main interviews and providing the historical expertise that form the bedrock of the film. Duivenvoorden's film and book then provide the data for Lynn Owen's monograph.

Mamadouh's monograph, *De stad in eigen hand* (1992), is a foundational text. Mamadouh contends that the influence and impact of urban social movements is difficult to measure in terms of class conflict. Instead, these movements were directed towards enacting a vision of the city that challenged the types of municipal policies and the social norms of urban lifestyles at the time. Mamadouh investigates how urban social movements interpreted the city ideologically, their attempts to modify the built environment, and how their methods and tactics compared with each other.

In *Cracking Under Pressure* (2009), Lynn Owens studies the decline of the Amsterdam squatters movement as a specific contribution to social movement studies, which has been dominated by resource mobilization and political process approaches that focus on how social movements originate. Rather than a broad sociological analysis, Owens analyzes the emotions in narratives of squatters in reaction to high profile events that he argues are crucial to the development and the eventual decline of the movement. (These events are identical to those that Mamadouh and Duivenvoorden highlight.) Owens presents a multi-layered narrative in which he emphasizes the individual voices and diversity of opinions of squatters to these events.

Duivenvoorden's text, *Een voet tussen de deur* (2000) recounts a popular history – the result of meticulous archival research, intended for an audience of members of the educated Dutch left who possess considerable knowledge of major figures in Amsterdam politics since the 1960s. Focusing on 1964 to 1999, Duivenvoorden traces how the movement began, how it grew, and its relationship to the Amsterdam municipal political machinery. He describes the movement's activities, methods, its internal subcultural institutions, the social profiles of the participants, and a number of mediagenic riots that he contends, impacted the movement's development.

These three texts as well as the entire documentary collection on the squatters movement of the Staatsarchief (approximately 250 hours' worth of video) provide the data for the historical narrative that I present. The documentary footage display a range of images: from hours of footage of riots, interviews of squatters by mainstream news programs, videotapes of satirical performances by squatters, to hour-long documentaries by non-Dutch filmmakers. In addition, many of the videos repeat footage. Without describing each video in detail, the cumulative effect of these documentaries provides a sense of the subculture's presence as a protest movement and a countercultural lifestyle in the 1970s and 1980s.

Historiography

Presenting the history of a squatters movement proves challenging because the act of squatting is often clandestine. Thus, most squatters go to great lengths to ensure that no written trace of their activities exist, leaving no record available from which to construct a historical narrative. With this in mind, the history of the Dutch squatters movement is primarily a chronology of certain types of people who squat through public occupations and who identify as being members of a social movement. Such a classification excludes people who squat outside the movement, for which only one article exists (Diepen and Bruijn-Muller 1977), and people within the movement who squat but do not engage in the movement as activists. Duivenvoorden transparently discusses his exclusionary focus (2000: 52):

> Young people occupy a house and sooner or later have to deal with an eviction threat from the government and/or the owner. In the overwhelming majority of cases, the squatters leave silently. In the following story, the only squatting actions that are described are the ones that contribute to a better understanding of the history of the squatters movement. And there are plenty of these stories. (my translation)

Describing "actions that contribute to a better understanding of the history" means concentrating on a minority of politically well-organized activists articulating themselves in a manner that Duivenvoorden and others recognize as a legitimate form of squatter activism. Duivenvoorden writes that between 1964–99, approximately 45,000 to 70,000 people in Amsterdam had some involvement with the squatters movement, the overwhelming majority of whom were not activists and whose participation derived from a diversity of motivations. Consider, for example, that in this movement, there were macrobiotic squats, vegan squats, feminist squats which prohibited the presence of men, as well as squatters who only sought free housing and lacked interest in politics. For squatters embedded in such households, the actions and conflicts that Duivenvoorden highlights as instrumental were most likely far removed from their social worlds.

By focusing on self-identified political activists and on mediagenic actions, the historical record gives excessive attention to branches of the movement that produced written text while failing to consider whether such texts resonated in the informal, verbal, non-written discourse and debates of the movement. The most textually verbose groups are those most often quoted, leading to a distorted view of movement discourse and giving excessive importance to texts with disputed relevance or may have been only one voice among a cacophony.

By focusing on actions, riots, and evictions to tell the story of the movement, these texts create an impression of artificial linear progression and only narrate its front stage. In this book, I argue that the movement's internal and external faces are circular and repetitive rather than linear and progressive. Rather than viewing violent actions as events that transform history, an overly simplistic teleological narrative, I assert that riots, evictions, and actions are not as instrumental for so-called larger movement goals. Instead, these events serve to compile squatter capital on the movement's back stage as well as advance towards a vision of self-realization of the ideal autonomous activist.

Furthermore, the historical record emphasizes discussions in reaction to actions, but none consider the intricacy behind organizing these actions, which masks these actions with a doubtful coherency. To illustrate, a number of squatter documentaries repeatedly present one action in which squatters in 1978 took over a city council meeting. In this clip, a group of young, white squatters in their early twenties storm the meeting. One young man, tall, blond, wearing glasses, grabs the microphone from the chairperson, stands on a table, and makes a speech. A few documentaries feature this clip because it portrays various facets of the front stage of the squatters movement: spontaneous direct action, anti-parliamentarism, lack of respect for authority figures, articulate public speaking, and bravery.

This clip, repeatedly featured in the documentary collection, gives cause for reflection on how an action intended to give the impression of spontaneity must have, in actuality, been planned with incredible attention to detail in order to succeed. What was the brainstorming session that eventually led to this action being chosen as the one to pursue? How many meetings did the group hold to plan it? Who wrote the speech? Why did the group decide to pick this young man in particular to give the speech? How did they manage to videotape it? Did they invite the press? What were the hundreds of small details that they had to address to produce this action? These questions illustrate the contradiction between the necessity to intricately plan with the desire to leave an impression of spontaneity. This results in the intricate construction of the front stage and the discursive invisibility of the backstage apparatus required to create that performance.

Furthermore, these texts tend to uncritically represent how authority functions in this movement as well as reify the voices of male leaders. Mamadouh and Duivenvoorden strengthen the authority of leaders by only referring to well-known, articulate men by name while subsuming the rest under the label of the group.[2] Such a practice renders invisible the participation of unnamed members who crucially enabled the production of actions. These unnamed members include people who may have been non-articulate, did not publicize their activities, or were women. Both authors fail to recognize that this method of historical narration, in which they privilege the voices of authority figures and represent actions as a consequence of their leadership, undermines their arguments that these movements were anti-hierarchical and anti-authoritarian.

Finally, if one views the history of post-war Amsterdam through the lens of the squatters movement, the texts present a misleading and nostalgic white urbanity by neglecting the arrival and impact of non-white immigrants in the city. During the period that these books and the documentary highlight, from the late 1960s to 2000, the population of Amsterdam radically transitioned from mainly white Dutch to over half "foreign" (this percentage includes certain classifications of non-white people born in the Netherlands). In 1980, the official population of "ethnic minorities" was 11 percent of the city, by 1986 it was 16 percent, 27 percent by 1992, and 32 percent by 1995 (Tesser 1995: 56). By the time I conducted my fieldwork, the populations of the major Dutch cities had 50 percent or more non-white residents who were classified as foreign.[3]

With the exception of Mamadouh briefly mentioning tensions between Surinamese squatters and white Dutch people in the Transvaal neighborhood, the texts wholly ignore the consequences of the radically changing face of the city's population. In terms of squatting, by only focusing on a particular profile of white squatter activists, again the historical texts present a misleading and distorted view. There are rumors and assumptions in the squatters movement that Surinamese immigrants squatted entire housing blocks in the Bijlmer in the 1970s, which have remained squatted until the present day. During my fieldwork, the majority of eviction notices published in the newspaper were for apartments in the Bijlmer that were squatted outside the movement. Yet, only one academic article from 1977 (Diepen and Bruijn-Muller) mentions this phenomenon. Otherwise, all academic research on squatting in Amsterdam has failed to analyze it in-depth – including my own.

In terms of contextualizing squatters in the city and their relationship with their neighbors, the lack of discussion of immigration presents a problematic Eurocentrism and limited critical inquiry. The texts habitually present non-squatter neighbors as authentic, white, working-class residents who resist their displacement by urban renewal projects. However, looking at the figures for the population of the city further complicates these assumption regarding the locations of these "solidaric" neighbors. By selectively focusing on certain sections of the city and particular types of people and lifestyle practices in exclusion of others in the immediate context, these texts construct a fantasy of urban whiteness, a mythology which impacts gravely on the movement.

With this perspective, it's possible to construct an alternate reading of the squatters archives, but such a project is outside the limits of an ethnography of a movement between 2005–08 based on interviews and participant observation. This historical background intends to demonstrate a lineage for the activities that comprise the internal movement culture as well as display the repetition and circularity of this movement over the past forty years. In addition, this background serves to contextualize the interactions between squatters and the front stage of the media, the state, and the press and demonstrate the institutionalization of the squatters movement in urban life. Last, I avoid repeating problematic aspects of the sources used to construct this narrative, such as by extensively describing violent riots and profiling male leaders.

Historical background

In post-war Amsterdam, squatting space was a fairly common practice. Families living in cramped social housing[4] apartments often took over clandestinely an extra floor in their building for more space. With the inability of the housing corporations to keep track of the empty properties, these extra spaces eventually became the possession of the "squatters." The phenomenon of young people taking over empty spaces without legal entitlement was first featured by the media in 1964 when a group of young married couples squatted in houses scheduled for demolition which had languished empty for years.[5] These couples wanted to reside independently from their parents but could not obtain social housing. In response to this action and the extensive press coverage, the state and the housing corporations offered the couples social housing.

During this same year, a university student newspaper featured an announcement that sought people to live in buildings in which a group of students had squatted. Although these buildings were evicted within a few months, there were reports of internal conflicts between the "legitimate residents," who had organized the squatting of the buildings, and "illegitimate residents," who moved in afterwards. With the exception of these two public squatting actions, squatting was hidden from the public eye until 1969, after which it has developed into a visible part of Amsterdam life through public actions with ample coverage by the media and through their spatial presence in which squatted spaces are dotted throughout the city.

The legacy of the Provos is instrumental to understand the tactical approach of the squatters movement. The Provos were an anarchist, situationist, countercultural group active between 1965 and 1967. They sought to challenge authoritarian and hierarchical social relations between citizens and the state. This attitude brought them attention in a culture, which at the time, highly valued conformity and the uncritical obedience of authority. They also attacked consumerism and car traffic in the city. The group was associated with one figure in particular, Robert Jasper Grootveld, a performance artist, who regularly staged weekly "happenings" which combined non-violence with absurdist humor to provoke the police, often ending with his arrest.

While the Provos comprised a small group, they developed a tremendous following and successfully impacted social norms. They created a space to reconsider the relationships between the citizen and the political machinery of the city. They also put forward an array of what they termed "white plans" to improve quality of life. The most famous, the "white bike" plan, proposed to ban car traffic from the city and replace it with 20,000 white bicycles unlocked for people to use freely. Other examples of "white plans," included the white housing plan, suggesting that the city council ban speculation and legitimate squatting as a means to solve the housing shortage, and the white wives plan to create reproductive health clinics which offered advice and contraception for young women. The Provos gained enough popularity to win a seat on the city council in 1966. By 1967, the members of the group declared the Provos dead and moved on to other projects.

In 1969, squatting re-emerged with three groups that publicly squatted houses to protest the housing shortage in situationist media spectacles, Woningburo de Kraker, Woningburo de Koevoet, and de Commune (The Squatter Housing Agency, The Crowbar Housing Agency, and The Commune). The participants of these groups had either been members of or were heavily influenced by the Provos. While the Provos attacked a range of social institutions, these groups protested housing shortage and, in particular, the lack of social housing for young people. In the tradition of the white plans, they painted the doors of empty houses white and declared them speculated properties. The groups engineered media spectacles around their squatting actions that lasted a few days before they were evicted. During evictions and threats by owners, the squatting groups invited the media to witness and record the violence committed by the police and the threatening behavior of the hired thugs. Furthermore, they organized a national squatting day in 1969.

Despite the media attention on their actions and their concrete target – a lack of housing for youth – the general public misinterpreted their messages. Housing seekers who visited the groups often believed that they were real estate bureaus whose purpose was to find them affordable housing. The housing seekers did not understand the "DIY" and anti-authoritarian messages that were essential to the squatting actions that the three groups organized. Moreover, due to the almost immediate evictions of the squatted houses and the police violence during evictions, the squatting actions failed to provide a sustainable housing solution.

Squatting groups that took over spaces for the sake of housing rather than to send an anti-authoritarian, situationist message were initiated by alternative youth support organizations that, ironically, received funds from the state. Recognizing that housing presented a central problem for young people, alternative youth support organizations lobbied policymakers and politicians to solve the problem by creating independent youth housing. Since lobbying had limited impact, the organizations then became involved in squatting and transformed it from a symbolic tool to a viable means to both protest and provide housing. In Amsterdam, they began a voluntary organization called the *Kraakpandendienst* (Squatted Houses Services Agency) to support the squatting of houses and the squats themselves. This organization emphasized "DIY" principals from its inception. Outside of Amsterdam, alternative youth service groups initiated squatting and the organization of the squatter groups while in Amsterdam both independent squatter groups and youth service organizations existed simultaneously. The independent groups used more radical rhetoric and promoted the use of violence more severely than the squatter groups associated with the alternative youth service organizations.

In terms of party politics, former Provos launched the Kabouter movement (the Gnomes). The Kabouters were anti-authoritarian, environmentalist anarchists, who opposed pollution, housing shortage, and car traffic in the inner city. They manifested these ideals by creating an alternative state in 1970, the Oranje Vrijstaat, which comprised of symbolic acts that served to parody the idea of states, particularly capitalist, social democratic ones. The Oranje Vrijstaat's housing policy was to squat houses, enabling the Kabouters to possess a notable presence throughout the number of squatted Kabouter offices spread around the city.

A few months after the Kabouters launched the Oranje Vrijstaat, they significantly won five of the forty-five seats in the city council elections. The Kabouters' presence in the Amsterdam city council meant that the squatters movement had allies to influence municipal policy decisions.

Meanwhile, by 1970, the three situationist squatting groups – Woningburo de Koevoet, de Kraker, and de Commune, merged into one, called Actie '70

(Action 1970). Actie '70 and the Kabouters organized a national squatting day in 1970 to take over houses countrywide. In contrast to Amsterdam, the municipalities in the rest of the Netherlands responded to the squatters' protests by creating affordable housing for young people. Between the police repression, the short amount of time a squat existed before its eviction, and the concessions by the other municipalities to the squatters' demands, squatting as a practice was waning.

Surprisingly, a higher appeals court decision reversed this decline in 1971. At the time, squatters relied on a statute from 1914 that declared that someone could occupy or use a space without having legal entitlement to it. The practice of this statute translated into the requirement to display a table, bed, and chair to the police at the squatting action, if one wanted to establish residency in a property. In 1971, the Court of Higher Appeals ruled that squatting was not only not punishable as a criminal act, but that squatters retained the rights to domestic peace in their residences. This decision meant that squatters possessed the same rights as renters and homeowners to refuse entry to anyone, including the police and property owners. Hence, only a court order, often obtained after a lengthy procedure, could evict squatters.

With these elements in mind, the squatting of houses through public take over had significant support: legally, through the change in case law; organizationally, buttressed by the state-funded youth organizations; and politically, by being embedded with the Kabouter party in the city council. They just needed houses to squat. These houses became available as a result of the large-scale remaking of the urban spatial landscape planned during this period by the city government, beginning with the Nieuwmarktbuurt.

Nieuwmarktbuurt

In the late 1960s, the city council decided to build a four-lane highway to run through the inner city of Amsterdam, and a metro. Both were intended to connect the city center with a planned middle-class community in the far southeast edge of the city called the Bijlmer. To construct the highway and metro, the city planned to destroy the Nieuwmarktbuurt, an eighteenth-century former Jewish neighborhood which had languished dilapidated since World War II, when the majority of the property owners had been deported and killed in concentration camps.

The process of drastically remaking the urban landscape involved the – at times – forced relocation of the working-class locals to other parts of the city while a small number of residents protested the demolition and refused to leave. Furthermore, once the Nieuwmarktbuurt was emptied, the bulldozing stalled for years due to political disagreements regarding the financing of the project. Meanwhile, the local council had given two recently vacated buildings in this neighborhood to former Provos who had created a non-profit

organization, De Straat (The Street) for cultural innovations, such as art pro-
jects and the experimental implementation of the "white children" plan, a
Provo idea to create child care facilities collectively run by a revolving group
of parents. The local council's endowment of the two buildings to De Straat
proved highly controversial to the remaining residents. They demanded that
De Straat's projects should derive from collaboration with the neighborhood
residents rather than vaguely on their behalf.

The disagreement between the working-class neighborhood residents
and De Straat reflected tensions that arose in the alliances of neighborhood
action groups and squatters; squatters were often ideologically romantic
while neighborhood activists were more pragmatic. For example, squatters
often sought to retain old housing at all costs and opposed the building of
new social housing; while neighborhood groups advocated for the construc-
tion of more social housing in addition to the maintenance of older build-
ings when possible.

In the Nieuwmarkt, De Straat responded by connecting the neighbor-
hood action group with people interested in squatting the emptied buildings
to protest and delay the demolition. Meanwhile the neighborhood action
group, encouraged by the neighborhood support center, lobbied politi-
cians and mobilized support throughout the city. The neighbors and the
squatters effectively worked together in the neighborhood action group
and even formed a committee that reviewed potential squatters as a way
to exclude non-political tourists who were only interested in free housing
(Duivenvoorden 2000; Mamadouh 1992).

The Nieuwmarkt campaign eventually succeeded. The city council can-
celled the highway plans and built a fraction of the planned metro beneath
the inner city. Thus, the campaign prevented a radical transformation of the
eighteenth-century center with its narrow streets and canals to a function-
alist cityscape that privileged automobile access. Such urban planning was
antithetical to a built environment that bred neighborhood cohesion and
gezelligheid, a Dutch term that vaguely translates as warm coziness, with
connotations of nostalgia and intimacy.

In terms of the squatters movement, the Nieuwmarkt campaign enabled
the squatters to transition from disparate groups that existed simultane-
ously to a network of interdependent squatters groups. The independent
squatter groups and the kraakspreekuren (KSUs, the squatting informa-
tion hour), mainly neighborhood based, formed the nodes of the network.
The kraakspreekuren held significant authority since the members of the
KSUs decided who they supported in the squatting and maintenance of a
house. The alarm list – a phone tree that squatters use to mobilize to defend
against hired thugs and police officers – was instituted during this period,
as well as the citywide and nationwide squatters consultation meetings.
In cultural terms, the Nieuwmarkt campaign witnessed the transforma-
tion of squatting from an often symbolic protest tool, to a lifestyle that

combined activism and experimental forms of New Left communal living. Owens comments on the significance of the Nieuwmarkt campaign:

> Squatting had become more than a way to simply put a roof over your head. It was a means of creating a better world, or at least a more livable city. Squatters began placing more emphasis not on the political message of squatting, but rather of the opportunities it gave to live an autonomous life, for self-development. (Owens 2004: 49)

In 1975, the city evicted the squatters from the houses that were scheduled to be demolished for the metro during which huge riots ensued between the squatters and the police.

The mythical 1980s

By the second half of the 1970s, a split unfolded in the squatters movement regarding attitudes towards the use of violence. A non-violence consensus had prevailed until a particularly brutal use of force by the police during the eviction of a squatted house on the Jacob Lennepstraat in 1978. As Erik Williams, a young squatter, who went to the eviction to film it, describes:

> Squatters from throughout the entire city were standing in front of the building … I stood there with my Super-8 camera then there came in buses of ME (riot police). Well, I had never seen such a thing, and I saw them coming towards me, and they ran towards the people and they immediately began to beat them up, and I was stunned. But I believe that everyone was really stunned, because the entire group that was standing there had also personally never experienced that before, and they stood there yelling "no violence, no violence" and the ME, yeah they began to hit them and the people were beaten away and I filmed everything from the start on in a sort of stupor. (Seelan 1996 as quoted in Owens 2004: 72)

With the shift in tactics in which squatters used violence without apprehension against the police and the hired thugs, conflicts arose between squatters who worked closely with alternative youth organizations and the squatters who considered themselves more political, who called themselves the Political Wing of the Squatters Movement (PvK) associated with the neighborhood, the Staatsliedenbuurt. The PvKers advocated for open and direct violent confrontation with the state instead of a defensive posture against police and the hired thugs.

The Groote Keyser, a squatted mansion on the Keizergracht, and the immense defense of this house against eviction symbolized the squatters movement's embrace of violence and the cultivation of a defiant attitude towards the so-called Mainstream. For most of its existence, the squatters who inhabited the Groote Keyser primarily aimed to in party rather than engage in political action. They often rented rooms to tourists and the key to the house was rumored to float around Dam Square available to anyone who sought a crash pad. When the eviction notice for the house arrived, most of the residents moved out, but ten refused to leave and instead barricaded the house to protect themselves against the eviction attempts of the bailiff and the police.

The PvKers from the Staatsliedenbuurt decided to take over the defense. They moved in, replacing the barricades of bed spirals with steel, and engineered a media spectacle around the house. They broadcast a pirate radio station from within the house (called the *Vrije Keyser* – the Free Emperor), and produced a number of documentary films that displayed the endless rows of paint bombs and Molotov cocktails that the squatters had prepared for the eviction. Countless documentaries and news clips from this period showcase tall, thin, masked, young men engaged in various activities, from debating suited news reporters to walking on the roof of the house to guard it from potential evictors. The squatters were ready to fight.

As Owens describes, "The Keyser became an armed camp, ready and waiting for the looming eviction" (2004: 74). According to Mamadouh, half of the squatters movement was willing to give up their lives for the cause of the Groote Keyser (1992: 144). Given this readiness and the emotional uproar around the building, Mayor Pollack refused to evict, claiming that it posed to be too dangerous for the public order. Instead, the city bought the building to create independent housing for young people.

The violent confrontation that the PvKers sought came unexpectedly during the attempted eviction of another squatted villa, the Vondelstraat. The three-day riot around the Vondelstraat has since defined images of squatters and Amsterdam in the 1980s. The squatters set up burning barricades and removed stones from the street to throw at the police. In reaction, the riot police attacked the house with a force of 1,200 police officers, helicopters, several tanks, and water cannons. As Owens narrates:

> Tanks rolled through the streets of Amsterdam early on the morning of Monday 3 March, 1980 ... Their goal: to break through the barricades built by a large group of squatters who had occupied the building over the weekend, after beating back the police. The streets were blocked off with paving stones and garbage. Inside the walls, squatters celebrated their strength and victory. The *Vondelvrijstaat* [Vondel Free State] was a place of joy and excitement. Never before had squatters taken the offensive, and it seemed to be working. (Owens 2004: 49)

During the eviction of the Vondelstraat, over 10,000 people demonstrated against the city's heavy repression of the squatters, in particular the deployment of tanks against the city's own population.

After the Vondelstraat, the next defining and mediagenic riot took place during the coronation of Queen Beatrix on April 30, 1980. For months, the squatters had campaigned against the coronation with the motto, *Geen woning, geen croning* (No housing, no coronation, a phrase that rhymes in Dutch) positing the use of state resources to celebrate the excesses of the coronation against the lack of funds directed to solve the housing shortage in the Netherlands.

To protest, squatters organized a nationwide squatting day during the coronation, opening hundreds of empty houses around the Netherlands. However, a group that called itself the Autonomen declared war on the Queen with a riot that lasted all day. For months afterwards, movement participants debated the riot: whether it was fruitful, who took responsibility for it, and its impact on the squatters' public image. Owens illustrates the different sides of the debate:

> Piet believed that it was the best day ever for the movement – an exciting, powerful protest against the ruling class, which managed to include not only squatters, but also many disaffected citizens, who used this opportunity to make their displeasure known. The majority, however, felt differently. They considered the day a black eye for the movement. Wietsma had only one word to describe the events: "Terrible." Most squatters believed that the protest neither represented any of the real interests of the movement, nor did it even accomplish anything for the values it did support. It was nothing more than meaningless destruction. (Owens, 2004: 78)

The coronation of Beatrix is widely considered both the height and the beginning of decline for the squatters movement. As Owens notes (2009), decline is subjective and can last for years, especially since the squatters movement continued for another thirty years after its so-called point of decline.

While at the level of public and scholarly discourse, this point may have signified the beginning of decline, culturally, this was a time of renaissance for the squatters' subculture. The squatters succeeded in realizing the absurdist, parodying goals of the Oranje Vrijstaat to create a state within a state. If one participated in the movement, one could live entirely in it without interacting with the Mainstream: one could grocery shop, weld, attend the cinema, find a plumber, and read newspapers, all from within the squatters' subculture.

Squatters boasted their own media. There were fifteen newspapers for and by squatters, including one that only related gossip, one intended for foreign squatters, and one for squatter children. The Squatters Newspaper (*De Kraakkrant*) had a circulation of 2,000. Squatters ran a major pirate radio station, a pirate television station, and regularly hacked into the city cable system to transmit. They formed printing press collectives to publish newspapers, pamphlets, books, posters, and other printed media.

The squatters' subculture featured cafes, restaurants, bars, infoshops, give away shops, bakeries, bookstores, bicycle repair shops, grocery stores, cinemas, welding workshops, dance clubs, performance spaces, medical clinics, rehearsal rooms, and a multiplicity of art initiatives and gallery spaces. An enormous infrastructure existed solely intended for and created by predominantly young people who lived on low incomes that derived from state benefits or university scholarships. Everything that could not be produced from within the movement with a combination of voluntary labor and cheap and readily available products, was stolen from the Mainstream, such as building materials used in squatted houses to renovate and barricade.

The squatters movement comprised of people involved in a wide assortment of radical left political issues such as anti-nuclear energy, anti-apartheid, anti-militarism, and anti-fascism. Many worked on solidarity campaigns with Nicaragua and El Salvador and organized attacks on the US Embassy to protest US foreign policy and the presidency of Ronald Reagan. The women's movement manifested in the squatters' subculture through a number of squats that banned the presence of men, to the point that during alarms, they permitted men to stand in front of the house but did not allow them to enter the squat to defend it from eviction.

A differentiation existed between activists who mainly identified as squatters versus activists who resided in squats but primarily invested their time and energy into other radical left issues. Mobilizing these activists for actions related to squatting was challenging since they were busy with other commitments and also because to be active in the squatters movement meant primarily participating in resistance during evictions. Furthermore, in the left activist community, squatters had the reputation for being violent, confrontational and extremely rude.

Violence on the front and back stages of the movement

The internal disagreement regarding the use of violence came to a head in 1982, with the riot during the eviction of the Lucky Luijk. The Lucky Luijk was a villa in which hired thugs had evicted the squatters in 1981. Despite the squatters' legal right to domestic peace, the police refused to help the squatters retake the house. The squatters then organized a massive action to violently evict the hired thugs and re-squat the space. With the media and political attention obtained from the squatters' campaigning, the city decided to purchase the house and convert it into social housing.

The city's decision proved controversial within the movement. A number of squatters felt content to leave the house because of its eventual conversion to social housing rather than remaining an unused object of speculation.

However, the PvKers from the Staatsliedenbuurt refused the offer, demanding that the city give social housing contracts to the house's squatter inhabitants since their efforts led to the house becoming social housing in the first place. Owens describes the feelings of Piet, who was involved in the negotiations around the Lucky Luijk:

> Piet felt torn during the negotiations process over the Luijk. He believed that, even if the building was not going to end up in the hands of the squatters, it could still be put to use, because it would help working people, "families with kids, bus drivers, taxi drivers, it doesn't matter." On the other hand, he saw some value in confrontation and keeping the building. Both sides tried to seek his support. The hardliners "made me out to be a traitor, because I'll talk to the council, but on the other and, they were trying to appeal to me." (Seelan 1996 quoted in Owens, 2004: 130)

Despite the internal debate, the PvKers' stance was the answer to the city council's decision, who responded by evicting the squatters. Again, an enormous riot ensued during the eviction, during which the squatters set an empty city tram, Tram 10, on fire. The media coverage, and in particular, the image of the blazing tram, led to the squatters' losing public support in Amsterdam. Owens comments on how this image led to the loss of public support, "Whatever the actual cause of the fire, the image became forever associated with out-of-control, violent squatters willing to sacrifice the public safety for their own private gains" (2004: 123).

The internal debate that followed from the riot calcified existing tensions in the squatters movement. The PvKers, who were associated with the Staatsliedenbuurt neighborhood, had for years advocated for more radical and violent confrontations with the state. This group also organized the most successful squatting actions and choreographed violence during evictions. Such tactics often led to material concessions from the state in the form of legalized squatted houses and social housing. The views and actions of the PvKers and *kraakbonzen* (squatter bosses) contrasted sharply with non-violent squatters and those who squatted for the cultural opportunities enabled by the practice and the movement. They often critiqued the PvKers as authoritarian and for undermining the consensus-based decision making of the citywide squatters' consultation meeting. "The bosses, the men of the movement, hid a great deal of information just for themselves." (Seelan 1996 as quoted in Owens, 2004: 129)

Meanwhile, the PvKers considered squatters who failed to attend squatting actions and evictions as parasites. This was particularly aimed at artists who only wanted free space but lacked interest in the political activity that enabled the spaces to exist.

Despite the sizable resentment of the kraakbonzen, those who opposed the PvKers lacked their strategic acuity and skills. For example, deciding to eschew the authority of the PvKers who dominated the *kraakspreekuur*, one group squatted a building on the Prins Hendrikskade. When a vast police force arrived to evict the house, broadcast live on radio and TV, no squatters responded to the Prins Hendrikskade squatters' alarm. With the media spectacle, the PvKers became involved. They succeeded in organizing a riot by mobilizing hundreds of squatters to fight the police, a deed that the anti-authoritarian squatters who resided in the house had failed to accomplish.

The burning of Tram 10 and the condemnation of the Lucky Luijk riot as a failure shifted the movement's consensus regarding the use of violence to favor pragmatic negotiation with the state instead of confrontation. The PvKers retreated to the Staatsliedenbuurt neighborhood and fortified it into a bulwark of the squatters movement, which featured five hundred squatted spaces. A member of parliament who visited the neighborhood in 1984, proclaimed:

> The Staatsliedenbuurt is actually no longer a part of the kingdom of the Netherlands. Authority has ceased to exist there; the laws of the squatters reign. Because of safety concerns, the police no longer patrol. What I experienced there was, in fact, an American situation. There are places in New York where the police are afraid to get out of their cars. They are afraid someone will be armed, and people on both sides will be killed. (Duivenvoorden quoted in Owens 2004: 182)

The police did not enter the neighborhood and the PvKers had developed strong relationships with the renters. Furthermore, the PvKers held strict standards for acceptable behavior of the squatters in this neighborhood, to the extent in which they evicted those who they considered problematic.

Isolated from the rest of the squatters' subculture, the PvKers in the Staatsliedenbuurt became more militant and extended their gaze beyond empty houses, hired thugs, and police officers, onto other squatters. During a number of violent evictions, a few arrested squatters had identified other squatters. Informing on other activists is taboo since its customary for activists in custody to remain silent for three days until their release (an expectation that continues today). To condemn this behavior, the PvKers formed a research organization to find the "traitors" – those arrested who identified other participants – then published posters with the names, photos, and addresses of these individuals. The PvKers' methods became even more draconian. They chased "suspected traitors" through the streets of Amsterdam with cars and searchlights. They beat up and threatened to torture another squatter with electric shock. In the film, *The City Was Ours*, Theo van der Gijssen dismissed the violence of this act, "He was well treated and those electrodes are irrelevant. It only counts if you use them" (Seelan

1996).[6] The PvKers' tactics proved intolerable for a number of squatters. They decided to eject one of the main PvKers from the movement, Theo van der Giessen, by going to his house and beating him to the point in which he was hospitalized. After this attack, the rest of the PvKers retreated, leading to the squatters group in the Staatsliedenbuurt falling apart.

The historical treatments of the squatters movement conclude with the defeat of the PvKers and dissolving of the movement as a result of intense internal conflict. However, a number of consequential changes occurred that impacted the decline in participants in the movement. First off, two laws changed the legal landscape for squatters. In 1987, the first law, The Empty Property Law allows owners to take squatters to court anonymously, whereas previously, the owner had to know the name of one inhabitant in order to sue and evict. This meant that as long as the owner did not possess the legal name of any of the inhabitants, the residents of a squat could potentially remain in a house indefinitely. Second, in 1993, article 429 went into effect, declaring that only houses that are factually empty for a year could be squatted, further reducing the number of spaces available. As a result, squatters had to prove with some form of documentation to the police at squatting actions that the space had been empty for at least a year, a practice that was not necessary prior to this law.

In addition, the availability and quality of potentially squattable spaces had reduced considerably. In the 1970s and 1980s, most squatted buildings were massive warehouses located in the city center. These houses had been legalized into social housing and simply were no longer available to squat. Much of the abandoned properties that dominated the urban landscape were renovated and rented or sold. Anti-squatting was introduced in 1990, an arrangement in which an agency contracts people to "guard" a space, which is essentially a temporary rental agreement without Dutch tenancy rights (described more in detail in Chapter 1). The anti-squat system took care of the housing needs of young, single people, often students, the constituents who the squatters movement had previously attracted en masse.

Moreover, the social system that supported a squatter's lifestyle radically changed. The squatters in the 1970s and 1980s lived in a social welfare regime where the only preconditions to receive an unemployment allowance were to be sixteen years old and older and the ability to articulate one's incapacity to work. The preconditions became stricter, determining that one had to be twenty-three or older to qualify for public assistance and that the state could force someone to take a job in lieu of unemployment benefits. Also the system of university scholarships had transformed, limiting the number of years one could study and receive a living allowance. Last, during the 1970s and 1980s, one could fulfill study credits through activism, while in the 1990s, being an activist was seen as a diversion rather than a part of one's education.

.io-political context during fieldwork 2006–10

ıe overwhelming majority of contemporary squatters are unaware of this brief history. A continuum of knowledge exists, from a vague awareness that "the squatters movement was big in the 1980s," to a wider group of people who have seen the film, *De stad was van ons*, out of curiosity and interest, to a handful of Dutch activists who have written about the history of the squatters movement for university courses, a Bachelor, or a Master's thesis, in which they read Duivenvoorden and possibly Mamadouh, both only available in Dutch.

Despite the general lack of knowledge about the history of the squatters movement, the idea of squatters "being big in the 1980s" casts a shadow on the much smaller, but still persistent squatters movement in the 2000s. Surprisingly, this sentiment within the movement of being a shadow of its former greatness is a constant in the movement's discourse. In the documentaries which featured interviews with squatters, they often expressed a heavy nostalgia concerning a mythical heyday. In the 1970s, they referred to the late '60s; in the late 1970s, the early '70s. In 1981, they extolled 1980 as the moment of authentic activism, and in the mid-80s, the early 1980s was

Figure 0.2 Graffiti against the squatting ban circa 2006: "Fight for your housing rights. Stop the squatting ban"

the high point. By the 1990s, this sentiment became "the '80s," a mythmaking discourse which continues up to the present.

Although this nostalgia seemed timeless, during the period in which I conducted my fieldwork, this sentimentalization about the movement was repeated in political debates about squatting and became embedded with dominant xenophobic discourse. In reaction to mediagenic violent evictions or in discussing the issue of squatting, the main media message as well as the reaction of white, middle-class, and left-leaning Amsterdammers can be summarized as, "Squatting was widespread in the 1980s when it was idealistic. Now it's done mainly by foreigners who do it for free housing rather than out of ideals." I have encountered this sentiment an innumerable amount of times, such as whenever I have told people the topic of my research, on television news, and in the newspaper.

Consequently, the Amsterdam public has a conflicted view on squatting. On one level, they generally support it due to the housing shortage and the exploitative market conditions. On the other hand, this support is damaged by nationalistic and xenophobic sentiments that resent foreigners for exploiting a Dutch protest tactic. These feelings resonate with larger antipathy towards non-white immigrants, particularly working-class Turkish and Moroccans, in the Dutch public sphere. Last, the reasoning that the squatters movement has been taken over by foreigners was one of the main justifications for the passing of the national law that forbid squatting and criminalized squatters in 2010 (see conclusion).

In addition to a conflicted relationship with the "public," a number of structural factors impacted the squatters movement in the second half of the 2000s. As already mentioned, anti-squat hugely undermined the squatters movement since the types of people who had squatted en masse in the past – white, middle-class students – instead house themselves as anti-squatters.

Moreover, the system of social housing has been in the process of being slowly dismantled. That is, the federal government decided to convert Amsterdam from a city of majority renters to majority owners by emptying social housing blocks of their renters, relocating the tenants, renovating the buildings, and then selling each unit one by one. During the emptying and relocating process, buildings often were squatted. However, the conversion to condominiums meant that social housing corporations were unwilling to give rental contracts to squatters. They could also more aggressively and quickly evict squatters in this political climate since judges were less likely to rule in favor of squatters than in the past. Consequently, while in the 1980s and 1990s, with sufficient preparation, squatters could expect to live in a building from five to ten years, during the period of fieldwork for this study, squatters could be evicted anytime within the first two weeks to a maximum of two years if they were lucky. Most squatters only spent a few months in a space.

Social movement literature review

There are no academic studies of internal dynamics of hierarchy and author-
ity within social movement communities that engages with social movement
theory. The neglect of internal dynamics and social movement performances
and habitus, exists both in classical social movement literature and its
recent culturally oriented scholarship, including those that result from eth-
nographic research and participant observation. In this section, I will first
provide an overview of classical social movements literature and discuss its
subsequent "cultural" turn. I then review recent studies of social movements,
in particular, the alter-globalization and social centers movements and how
these texts have summarily ignored internal dynamics in their analysis. Last,
I situate this book within social movement studies.

Overview of the field of social movements

My approach to this study has been influenced by urban anthropology in
both methods and theory (Caldeira 2000; Goddard 1996; Hansen 2001;
Holmes 2000; Mitchell 2002; Pardo 1996) and the literature on global cities
(Appadurai 1996; Hannerz 1996; Harvey 1991; Hayden 1997; Ong 1999;
Sassen 2001; Zukin 1996) rather the field of social movements. Working in
the anthropological tradition, my intellectual interests were straightforward.
By living and working in this community, I was investigating the people who
participated in this movement, where they were from, what they did every
day, how they narrated their lives, and their ideological motivations.

In contrast, social movement literature is dominated by a series of recur-
rent theoretical questions, which are fairly removed from actual dynamics
within social movements themselves. Analyzing culture in social movement
communities with an anthropological perspective is highly difficult since
social movement scholars investigate social movements as organizations
rather than in seeking to understand the motivations of people who com-
prise these movements. Since the abstract concept of culture is itself difficult
to engage with in this field, situating a study of micro-social internal dynam-
ics and questions of hierarchy, authority, performance, and habitus poses a
considerable challenge.

Neil Smelser, in *Theory of Collective Behavior* (1962) considers social
movements as an example of collective behavior. He categorizes social
movements as norm-oriented and value-oriented. Norm-oriented move-
ments primarily seek social reform while value-oriented movements are "a
collective attempt to restore, protect, modify, or create values in the name
of a generalized belief" (Smelser 1962: 313). The critique of Smelser and
the collective behaviorist approach to social movements is its implication
that individuals participate in social movements only in reaction to crisis

and social marginalization (Della Porta and Diani 2006: 6, 12; Diani and Eyerman 1992: 5; Melucci 1989: 18).

The resource mobilization approach (Freeman 1979; McCarthy and Zald 1973, 1977; Zald and McCarthy 1987) is a response to the collective behaviorist approach, with its emphasis on rational and strategic choices of social movements to achieve their goals in relation to larger social and political structures (Della Porta and Diani 2006). Resource mobilization theorists suggest that social movements develop when structural conditions are conducive to their growth and that they decline when the political climate changes to their detriment (Whittier 1995). Whereas the collective behaviorist school emphasizes that feelings of unease, conflicts of interests, and oppositional ideologies are fundamental for collective action, resource mobilization scholars claim that such tensions are always present, and hence, cannot be the only conditions to explain the reasons that underlie when and why people collectively act for social change.

As a result, resource mobilization scholars concentrate on analyzing the social and political context on a meso and macro level that undergird the emergence of a social movement and how it succeeds. They attempt to understand the broader conditions in which discontent translates into collective action. It is an approach that heavily depends on tracing the interactions and impacts of the relationships between social movements, formal organizational structures, and the state. It relies on empirically observable events recorded in written texts such as newspaper reports and public records (Melucci 1989: 44).

Political process theories (Gamson 1990; McAdam 1982; Piven and Cloward 1988; Tarrow 1989; Tilly 1978) concentrate on the relationship between institutional political actors and protest. They examine the "political opportunity structures" defined as the external environment in which a social movement exists. Examples of political opportunity structures include whether the local political system is open to social movement concerns and grass-roots initiatives in general, electoral instability, whether influential allies are available, and if the elite tolerate protest. A movement's ability to negotiate resources and the political playing field leads to the successful achievement of its goals.

In resource mobilization, the main subject of analysis is "the social movement organization" rather than participants. In political process theories, individuals exist but as "social movement actors." "A social movement actor" is a rational person who carefully calculates costs and benefits of collective action, such as the presence of resources which support the movement and strategic interactions which develop the movement. In this area of literature, there is no description of the types of people who participate in social movements. There is no analysis of who they are, the different perspectives that they bring to the movement communities in which they become embedded, the variety of motivations that drive people to engage in collective action, and the dynamics that arise from the interactions due to the multiplicity of locations of individuals who comprise these communities.

In the 1980s, European sociologists and political scientists performed a "coup" on the American dominated social movement literature and its emphasis on the resource mobilization approach, called the New Social Movements Approach (Eyerman and Jamison 1998). Instead of concentrating on rational and strategic tactics of social movements on a meso and macro level, European social scientists, as characterized by the work of Alberto Melucci, emphasized instead the values and meanings of collective action. They draw attention to how the symbolic values of actions that challenged the dominant political order created new forms of collective identity. The spotlighting of new forms of identity and space as being one of the many diffuse and non-material goals of collective action contrasts sharply with the analysis of the rational interest and strategic interactions on the part of the singular movement. In his critique of resource mobilization approaches, Melucci states:

> Participants in collective action are not simply motivated by "economic" goals – calculating costs and benefits of their action – or by exchanging goods in a political market. They also seek goods which are not measurable and cannot be calculated. Contemporary social movements ... have shifted towards a non-political terrain: the need for self-realization in everyday life. In this respect social movements have a conflictual and antagonistic, but not a political orientation, because they challenge the logic of complex systems on cultural grounds. (Melucci 1989: 23)

Melucci argues that contemporary movements do not express themselves in instrumental action, operating instead as signs in which their actions serve as symbolic challenges to dominant codes. He further explains that social movements serve to renew cultural outlooks of dominant institutions and select new elites for the mainstream (Melucci 1989: 12).

With this European "coup," culture was put on the table of social movement literature and was seriously considered by a number of American social movement scholars, including those who had specialized in resource mobilization and political process analysis (see edited volumes: Johnston and Klandermans 1995; Larana 1994; Meyer *et al.* 2002). Where the Europeans considered collective identity and the symbolic meanings attached to collective action by creating spaces away from a state that encroached on every possible intimate space, American scholars who analyzed the culture of social movements did so by focusing on the process of "framing," (Snow and Benford 1986, 2000), the creation of expressive culture from within social movements and movement's channeling of cultural traditions from the past for emotional resonance in the present (Eyerman and Jamison 1998), the impact of informal movement communities on movement longevity (Rupp and Taylor 1999; Taylor and Rupp 1993; Whittier 1995, 1997), decision-making processes (Polletta 2002), as well as collective identity (Whittier 1995). Therefore, culture in social movement studies is often constructed as rational and instrumental and never a question of habitus, which is subconscious and habitual. In addition, there are no examinations of the possible disruptive clashes that occur from the intensive interaction of diverse backgrounds.

To research framing is to understand how social movements present themselves discursively to communicate to potential participants and motivate them to engage in collective action. According to Benford and Snow (2000), who founded frame analysis in social movement studies, "Collective action frames are action-oriented sets of beliefs and meanings that inspire and legitimate the activities and campaigns of a social movement organization." Eyerman and Jamison critique the excessive focus on framing in social movement studies, charging that they are methods for studying social movements as texts and discourses for social scientists and not an active component of social movement activity (1998: 19). Furthermore, they argue that the emphasis on frames belittles social movement actors' perspectives and the meanings that they bring to their actions by investigating primarily how these discourses successfully bring about social change.

In *Music and Social Movements*, Eyerman and Jamison argue that social movements often have a greater impact culturally than politically because the reflection on habitual mores and the reconstitution of culture that occur during times of social change eventually seep into the culture of everyday life after the political uproar has simmered down (Eyerman and Jamison, 1998: 6, 11). Versus the dominant mode of analyzing social movements in instrumental terms, Eyerman and Jamison argue for the crucial role of culture within social movements to address its neglect in the literature and further connect cultural studies with social movement studies.

Nancy Whittier, in her book *Feminist Generations* (1995), used interviews and participant observation in a Midwestern radical women's community to consider questions of diversity of the collective identities of radical feminists in the 1970s and 1980s. The radical women's movement in the United States serves as an interesting counterexample from which to compare the squatters movement in Amsterdam since they share ardent anti-hierarchical and anti-authoritarian ideals. Furthermore, the "personal is political" ideology of American feminism – one that intends to de-construct gender norms on the level of practice and annihilate the boundaries between the private and public spheres – lends itself to the policing of habitus as a marker of conviction in new social movements where collective identity reigns.

Whittier argues that participants in the women's movement had varying experiences based on the social and political context of the group with whom they were associated – what she terms micro-cohorts. She explores, first, how radical feminists identified themselves in relation to liberal

feminists and then, how each generation of radical feminists developed dis-
tinct identities based on the specificity of the social and political context of
their activist participation. Engaging with social movement literature, she
contends that social movement communities are political and serve move-
ment goals by sustaining movements during periods where the state and
dominant cultures are hostile. Whittier defines the alternative women's cul-
ture primarily as institutions for expressive culture – music, art, bookstores,
record companies, music festivals, and publishing houses.

Throughout the text, Whittier refers to a number of dynamics within
the movement that fit into broader anthropological notions of culture but
fails to examine them in more profound ways. She refers to women being
"trashed out" of collectives, but refrains from explaining the term. What
does it mean to be trashed? Who trashes and who is trashed out and what
types of power relations exist between them? She mentions the conflicts
between women identified as "bar lesbians" versus "political lesbians," but
again, does not discuss the tensions more in-depth – one that at first glance
seems to reflect class differences. She alludes to the symbolism embedded in
the decision on whether or not to shave one's legs, but again fails to explore
the meanings that underlie such negotiations.

Taylor and Rupp utilize the tools of social movement literature to analyze
how and why the women's movement continued during times of abeyance
to contribute to debates within women and gender studies (1993). Taylor
and Rupp, scholars of the American Women's movement in the twentieth
century, use analytical frameworks from social movements literature to
reconsider debates in women and gender studies about "women's culture"
and "cultural feminism" as the antithesis of radical feminism in the second
wave of the American Women's movement. Cultural feminism was posited
as a countercultural retreat which ultimately betrayed radical feminist goals
to eliminate capitalism and patriarchy.

Rupp and Taylor shift their focus away from the debates around the ideol-
ogies of these feminisms prominent in women and gender studies, and instead
concentrate on the actual participants in the communities of the American
Women's movement. They contend the practices of lesbian separatism, which
highly valued investing in an alternative "women's culture" actually enabled
radical feminist culture which, in turn, promoted feminist activism.

Like Whittier, a number of scholars obliquely mention the subcultures
of social movements yet abstain from a more intensive analysis, especially
around questions of habitus which require participant observation to collect
data. Eyerman and Jamison refer to a:

Habitus of protest and rebellion as embodied in the ritualized practice of
individuals and groups. Such practices help to personify the movement
among individual activists and serve to shape preferences and tastes in
much the same way that the conspicuous consumption of classical music

or champagne reflects reproductive strategies of certain segments of the middle class. (Eyerman and Jamison 1998: 28)

Nick Crossley calls for a further examination of a "radical habitus" in social movement studies. Crossley states that class-based skills exist and that social movement participants often feel pressured to conform to a particular type of dress code and lifestyle, dynamics that are ignored in the resource mobilization paradigm (Crossley 2003). In *Freedom is an Endless Meeting* (2002), Polletta focuses on how participatory democracy in decision making further promoted leftist social movements goals. In her examinations of a number of American social movements, she remarks on the habitus of activist culture. In the New Left, for example, despite the discourse against hierarchy, a masculinist mode of being dominated in what she describes as a "competitive intellectual bluster" (Polletta 2002: 157) of the New Left's man of steel and his tough, sexual posturing.

With a focused investigation of these monographs, one can compile different taste choices and performances which accumulate to Crossley's "radical habitus." For men, this radical habitus comprises a range of different styles: wearing beards in the New Left of the 1970s (Crossley 2003), to being soft spoken in the meetings of the Direct Action Network described by Polletta; a style which is in itself a reaction to the machismo of the American New Left of the 1960s and 1970s. For women, radical habitus extended to the policing of conviction in the American Women's movement. Such policing included noting whether or not a woman shaved her legs or, in the case of the "bar" versus "political lesbians," how a consumption practice then becomes a code word for a whole set of assumptions regarding a woman's class and political affiliations. The hesitancy by which these performances and habitus are explored reveals the limits of this scholarship. Such boundaries exist either because scholars lack the data to further analyze these lines of inquiry or and are committed to represent them uncritically despite having knowledge that contradicts their movements' front stage self-representations.

A range of academic literature on the women's movement (Freeman 1972; Gordon 2002; Polletta 2002; Rupp and Taylor 1999; Taylor and Rupp 1993; Whittier 1995) describes the internal tensions and conflicts that result from the anti-hierarchical, anti-authoritarian organizing model that privileged friendship groups. Polletta and Freeman charge that the friendship group model is inherently problematic because it creates bonds based on trust that simultaneously exclude. Whittier explains such tensions through her concept of "micro-cohorts," stating that the level of experience and seniority of activist women leads to differential power dynamics. Only Gordon examines internal power dynamics as partially arising from class, noting in particular which activists were considered qualified to act as media spokespersons. However, when Gordon discusses the impact of activists' class backgrounds on internal dynamics, she relates it as a personal account, not academically. The scholarship on the women's movement examining tensions around hierarchy all conclude that they arise from dynamics of seniority and friendship groups, and in doing so fail to examine how more pervasive structural differences between participants are the source of differential status hierarchies.

The alternative globalization and social centers movements

The alternative globalization and social centers movements have been the subject of recent ethnographically informed scholarship that engages with social movement studies. Maeckelbergh (2009) and Juris (2008) focus on decision-making processes, interactions, and networks; Scholl (2010) examines tactical interactions between protesters and authorities in summits in Europe; and Avery Natale (2010) considers how participants in black blocs conceptualize themselves as "queer."

These scholars have chosen to highlight decision-making processes, interactions, networks, and symbolic aesthetics rather than portraits and analysis of social movement communities and the people who comprise them. They neglect to answer basic questions such as:

- who are these people?
- where are they from?
- what motivates them?
- what are their personal circumstances?
- who depends on them?
- what are their backgrounds: class, race, ethnicity, etc.?
- why do they have the time, energy, and resources to travel all over the world, going back and forth between meetings and riots?

The nature of the alternative globalization movement lends itself to a focus on processes rather than communities as the movement only becomes visible during protests of intergovernmental summits that last approximately two weeks a year. This means that communities are not defined by sharing physical space but are more diffused, interacting mostly digitally until the time of the protests themselves. As a result, there is a focus on processes and aesthetics rather than the people who make up activist communities, leading to an absence of discussion on internal movement dynamics.

Moreover, the absence of critical inquiry into the structural locations of activists mars the literature with a perspective of white myopia. For example, by focusing on protesters' dress and their symbolic messages, the studies present a homogenized, ahistorical vision of "the activists" and "black bloc" that fails to elucidate or challenge stereotypes of the compositions of the protesters.

The literature neglects to address the presumption that the protesters are entitled citizens of liberal democracies who are demonstrating their rights to protest and that the types of violence against them is fairly limited. The literature fails to question the supposition of who comprises the protesters, and how the state's response varies accordingly, for example, states with a history of violent repression of protests or where the state is a liberal, Western European democracy, but the protesters are less privileged citizens, such as members of minority groups. The literature assumes the structural locations of these activists – which is highly educated, middle-class, privileged, white, and often European or American but never explicitly speaks to these conjectures and how the authorities' response to protesters differs vastly if they were not assumed to be privileged whites (take, for example, the civil unrest in Paris suburbs created by working-class Muslim immigrant youth in 2005, to which the French state reacted by brutally policing the residents of these neighborhoods).

The literature promotes a mythic erasure of protesters' identifications through their wearing a particular black bloc uniform. But they fail to recognize that it's impossible to erase privilege, especially when confronted by the state's apparatus of violence. Hence, rather than solely framing anarchists' participations in black blocs as representing a liberatory future, it would be helpful for the literature to consider how this participation is a demonstration of white privilege and as a result, reinforces hegemony rather than liberation.

Research on the European social centers movement (Guzman-Concha 2008; Martínez 2007; Membretti 2007; Mudo 2004; 2005) similarly neglects internal movement dynamics. Similar to the writing on the women's movement, the literature classifies tensions that arise from hierarchy and power relations that often contradict the ideal of direct, participatory, egalitarian democracy, as the result of seniority (Piazza 2007). By lumping all status tensions as a consequence of seniority, more prominent factors such as skills and habitus arising from class, gender, and race are ignored.

In general, with some ethnographically informed exceptions (Crane 2012; Portwood-Stacer 2010: 13; Rouhani 2012), recent social movement scholarship has suspended critical perspectives towards social movement communities and consequently rendered internal movement dynamics invisible.

Ethnographies of social movements

Interesting analysis on social movement culture has emerged in studies stemming from traditional ethnographic methods, in which researchers

systematically study and observe the groups they write about. Since anthro-
pological approaches do not view movement cultures instrumentally but
examine them on their own terms and seek to map the hierarchical dynam-
ics of the social "field" as Bourdieu recommends, they often shed a light on
internal dynamics that social movement literature does not. Interestingly,
none of these ethnographies situate themselves within the theoretical field
of social movements or the assumptions of emancipation being the natural
telos of movements that informs this literature.

Thomas Blom Hansen's ethnography of the Shiv Sena (2001), a Hindu
fascist movement in Bombay, India, for example, examines how the dissolve
of traditionally class-based affinities leads to the emergence of disturbing
fascist identities founded on the construction of previously non-existent
language-based ethnicities, wreaking havoc on a multi-lingual and multicul-
tural urban landscape. A discourse interpolating fragile Hindu masculinities
and a vilified Muslim "Other" bolsters the group's membership and discur-
sive authority in Bombay. The room and legitimacy for the articulation of
popular resentment and discontent in all its facets, Hansen contextualizes,
is created by democratic politics.

Sociologist Michael Schwalbe's (1996) ethnography of the American
men's movement focuses entirely on the identity and masculinity concerns
of the participants. According to Schwalbe's research, informed by years of
participant observation in the 1990s, participants of the men's movement
consist of highly educated, upper-middle-class men in their late forties and
early fifties, who have mainly succeeded professionally in feminized social
service professions (education, social work, counseling, non-profits). Using
Victor Turner's ideas about communitas, Schwalbe argues that the men par-
ticipate in the men's movement to reaffirm a fragile sense of masculinity and
create a spontaneous communitas based on their mutual anxiety. In particu-
lar, Schwalbe contends that the participants actively avoid discussing poli-
tics and collective action because it may impede the sense of communitas.
Thus, the unspoken goals of this movement are to serve the unmet identity
needs of this particular profile of manhood rather than to change culture or
society in any profound way.

David Graeber (2009), published a sprawling ethnography of his experi-
ences as an "observing-participant" in the alternative globalization move-
ment, specifically detailing the period leading to the protests of the World
Trade Organization in Quebec City. Graeber argues that the practice of
non-hierarchical decision making defines its political participation. The ide-
ology of the antiglobalization movement is embedded in what he refers to as
the practice of new forms of democracy via a different structure of decision
making. In contrast to the other monographs on the alternative globaliza-
tion movement that I highlighted earlier, Graeber actually discusses, albeit
in a general way, what structural traits (class, educational level, race, gender,
ethnicity) comprise the activists.

In his discussion of activist culture, Graeber distinguishes between two types of revolts which underlie people's motivations to participate in leftist collective action: the revolt against alienation versus the revolt against oppression. In the American context, these motivations separate into lines of race and class. Thus, highly educated people, mainly – though not exclusively – white, are compelled by the antiglobalization movement's promise of a social world that combats the alienation that they find in the "Mainstream." By claiming a hippie or a punk identity, such people participate in a mass movement of bohemianism that, paradoxically, creates the very space to live as an oppositional, critical, anti-mainstream/mass thinker.

According to Graeber, activists who participate in collective action as a revolt against oppression, however, are often people of color and/or immigrants who do so through hierarchical organizations that combat specific discriminations. Thus, the difficulties that these groups have working together derive from wildly divergent underlying motivations. Furthermore, Graeber contends that the racial and class privileges inherent in the lifestyle choices, clothing styles, and consumption practices of self-identified hippies and punks who constitute the antiglobalization movement often offend activists who revolt against racialized and class oppression, since they would never be permitted to engage in practices such as "dumpster diving" or fighting in a black bloc without far more severe and violent reactions from the state. While Graeber still tends to romanticize activists and promote the movement in the style of the alterglobalizaton ethnographies that I described earlier, Graeber's explicit analysis of race and class dynamics reflects his focus on American-based groups in the alterglobalization movement in which such issues are more openly discussed than in Europe.

Social movement studies and this book

This study contributes to the work of a number of more culturally oriented social movement scholars by matching their theories with ethnographic situations within a social movement community, thus fleshing out abstract ideas.

Using Francesco Alberoni's theory of non-reciprocal love between authority figures and participants in social movements (1984), the present study demonstrates how in this particular movement community, non-reciprocal love has to be expressed via a negation of that love, that is, through hostility manifested in horrendous gossip, as well as aggression towards the lovers of authority figures (Chapter 2). Nancy Whittier (1995) argues that the collective identities of social movement participants vary according to both the micro-cohort and the political generation of which an activist belongs. I further explore this dynamic, arguing that activists who are culturally central eventually leave the movement, partially due to the presence of culturally marginal people who are unable to function outside the movement's subculture (Chapter 4). As a result, for activists, micro-cohorts impact not only one's identity, but also the concrete length of time that one spends in the movement.

I engage most often with Alberto Melucci (1989; 1996), whose writing, though often abstract, most helpfully elucidates many of the contradictory dynamics that I witnessed. Melucci argues that in new social movements, participants primarily seek ephemeral symbolic gains instead of material conquests. Such an approach illuminates how the squatters movement can discursively claim that its main struggle is for housing but how at the practice level, participants are more interested in pursuing a radical left bohemian, communal existence than to fight for affordable housing.

Taking Melucci's classification of the types of social positions of participants in social movements, using ethnographic examples, I elaborate on the concepts of culturally marginal and culturally central and demonstrate how these terms constitute each other and what types of tensions occur when culturally marginal and culturally central people work together and seek recognition and authority (Chapter 2). Furthermore, to comprehend how authority works in this anti-authoritarian community, one must understand how a person's centrality or marginality in the mainstream contributes to their stature and ability to function within a movement subculture.

Melucci's writing on the participation of youth in social movements clarifies the role of social movement involvement in the biographies of culturally central, middle-class activists. He describes participation as a fake rite of passage for "youth", assuming that youth are privileged, highly educated, white, European, and entitled to the welfare state. Hence, on the one hand, social movement communities serve to enact liminality before entering into more adult lifestyles that require more responsibility. But on the other, social movement communities function as a space to act out an eternal youth, at worst, developing into retreats from the mainstream. Melucci's theories on youth participation in social movement communities helpfully illuminate the assumptions and contradictions around the *bildungsroman* of the left activist self that I saw in the squatters movement. However, the main bulk of my observations and reflections are borne directly out of my intense ethnographic and personal encounter with the world of the squatters in Amsterdam.

Methodology

Data collection

Prior to my fieldwork, I spent two summers in 2003 and 2004 (three months each) conducting pre-dissertation fieldwork in Amsterdam. I conducted informational interviews with members of *kraakspreekuren* (squatting information hours) throughout Amsterdam, attended squatting actions, and generally hung out in the public social spaces of the squatters' subculture. In 2003, I attended a citywide squatters' meeting of approximately a hundred people. Upon introducing myself as a researcher, one of the attendees publicly interrogated me about my values and my choice of residence, ending his speech by saying: "I went to university where I studied sociology and I learned a method called participant observation (he enunciated the last two words slowly). This means that if you want to study squatting the real way then YOU SHOULD BE SQUATTING" (caps indicate yelling). Despite this experience, I continued pre-dissertation research the following summer.

I began my official fieldwork in the fall of 2005. Through the fall and winter, I conducted interviews with informants who I found through snowball sampling. I visited kraakspreekuren and squatted social centers, where I introduced myself and asked for interviews. Through these contacts, I arranged additional interviews. People who I had interviewed often then invited me to other squatter social events, where I met more squatters to interview. In the spring of 2006, I began a period of participant observation. I worked nights in the kitchen of a squatted social center as the second cook of one of two *vokus* (short for *volkskeuken*, people's kitchen). The collective of the social center then asked me to serve as the main cook for the second night. Cooking in the voku completely changed my fieldwork because I transitioned from a position of interviewing squatters to becoming a member of the collective of a squatted social space. Also, it proved an effective means for meeting people since people who attend vokus often feel grateful to the cook for the long hours and effort of cooking and seek to socially connect with the cook. On my cooking nights, I hung out with squatters for hours afterwards.

These experiences originally formed the basis for my ethnography. However, at the point where I began to write my dissertation, I found myself without a place to live and without enough money to rent a flat in Amsterdam. Since I already possessed the contacts, I moved into the living group of a squatted house in the heart of a squatters' community in a neighborhood in Amsterdam. I had sincerely believed at that point that my fieldwork had terminated; looking back, I realize that it had just begun. I eventually lived as a squatter for over two years.

I resided in the first house for about a year and a half and plunged myself socially and politically into this community. I continued cooking in the kitchen of the squatted social space as the voku coordinator. With the help of my fellow squatters, I installed a heater in my room and did physical repairs to my house. I actively participated as a member of the social space's collective. I took part in every squatting action in the neighborhood. Every weekend, I attended parties throughout the squatters' scene in the city. When my house became threatened with eviction, I worked with my housemates and other squatters in the neighborhood on a campaign to defend it from

Figure 0.3 The author cooking in a squatted restaurant, 2006

eviction by developing strategy, organizing actions, lobbying politicians, and writing press materials. The campaign successfully prevented the house from being evicted for over a year.

After being evicted from this first house a year later, I moved into another squatted house for two months and then onto a block of squatted houses where I had my own apartment. I felt happy living in this block of houses because I had the comfort and privacy of my own apartment but could easily visit the living groups in the block when I wished. I had avoided the violence of squatter life up until that point, but the seemingly utopic living arrangement was disturbed one night when I was woken at 4 a.m. to the sound of people screaming and police sirens. Police had responded to a noise complaint due to a party and the situation escalated. To the surprise of most of the veteran squatters involved, the police evicted the block of houses, arrested all fifty of the inhabitants, and impounded all possessions, without an eviction order. This event proved shocking in its brutality, particularly because the police behaved outside the institutionalized set of rules and behavior that police and squatters expect from each other.

The fear of seeing the police surround the house and arbitrarily beat random pedestrians on the street, managing the hysterical reactions of the people around me inside the house during the siege, the brutality of the eviction, the claustrophobia of sitting in jail, and then, after being released, not knowing if or when I could obtain my possessions from the police were traumatizing features of this experience. Although I wanted to stop squatting, I still could not afford to rent.

After this eviction, I moved into my fourth squatted house. Still recovering from the police eviction, I interpreted the unstated codes of the living group who had invited me (see Chapter 3 on living groups). In exchange for the colossal room and high status in the living group, the group expected me to develop the campaign for the house's defense. I fulfilled the expected role to the best of my ability and managed a coalition of squatters, renters, undocumented immigrants residing in the building, and the renter's union in the neighborhood. Although this campaign was also fairly successful and brought me further squatter capital (see Chapter 1), I realized after a few months that the cost of squatting had outweighed the benefits and moved to rental accommodation to finish my dissertation.

These experiences provided the data for this ethnography. My fieldwork experience was fairly intense, dramatic, and traumatic. However, methodologically, I learned the value of participant observation. If I had not lived in this community as a squatter instead relying only on the interviews, I would have had a much more limited and idealized view of this community. By becoming a squatter, I could understand clearly the gap between how my informants talked about their lives in interviews versus how they practiced their lives.

My researcher positionality

In order to further explore my position in relation to this community, it's best to understand it as a relationship that changed during the three-and-a-half years that I lived and worked in a squatters' community. Furthermore, the fairly intimate relationship that I had with members of my neighborhood community differed substantially from how I interacted with squatters in Amsterdam from outside this neighborhood.

From August 2005 to November 2006, I introduced myself to every squatter I met as a researcher and was known primarily as a researcher who was working at a squatters' social center. In November 2006, I moved into a squatted living group. All of my fellow squatters in my neighborhood community knew me as a researcher but upon moving into this community, my relationship changed with them. My squatter housemates and I interacted with each other as people living together, cooperating on chores, and sharing private space. The term "sharing private space" refers to the intimacies resulting from living with people as well as the types of close bonds one forms when residing in a semi-legal housing situation where one is under constant threat of eviction. I overheard the arguments between my housemates and their lovers. My housemates also knew minute details about my personal habits such as what I ate for breakfast, how many times a month I took long baths, and my various experiences negotiating Dutch residence permits and scholarly affiliations. I participated in discussions about the mundane tasks of daily life, from washing the dishes to scolding each other about forgetting to lock the door.

My other fellow squatters in this community knew me as one of the members of this community who worked at the social center and participated in its mutual aid and its social life. The squats were located anywhere from half a block away to a fifteen-minute walk from each other. The social life was comprised of eating together at the voku twice a week and then hanging out for hours afterwards, drinking and talking. Members of this community commonly ate at each other's houses. Most of the squatters in this community had flexible schedules since they either lacked paid employment (including myself during the initial year and a half that I was a squatter), were students, or worked part-time. This meant that people spent hours hanging out, drinking, using soft drugs, until three or four in the morning during the week, either in the social center, or in each other's houses. During the weekend, there were parties in squats throughout the city. On Friday and Saturday nights, a whole group from this neighborhood often went out together to party and bar-hop. On Sundays, active members of this community met again to squat houses. I lived this lifestyle for approximately one year.

In May 2007, my participation in this community changed when I became involved in the campaign to defend the squat where I resided for which I eventually earned "scene points" (see Chapter 1). My squatter capital from the campaign of this first house and my work in the social center led me to be invited to live in my third and fourth squatted houses. During the last year that I resided as a squatter, from January through December 2008, almost no one in this community identified me purely as a researcher. My squatter friends all knew that I was writing my dissertation on the squatters movement but none asked me about its content. People who joined the subculture after I had assumed that I was a fellow squatter without knowing more detailed information about me. In the squatters' subculture, people generally do not ask personal details about each other's lives, such as their education and their professions. Of the few who asked me more detailed questions after knowing me superficially for years (questions such as, So, what do you do? Do you have a job? Are you studying? Are you thinking of going to university?), almost none asked details about the content of my writing.

I suspect that the reason why most squatters had almost no interest in my research or my writing was due to the fair amount of researchers who regularly present themselves in the squatters movement. Thus, most squatters, especially those who work at kraakspreekuren or in social centers, are accustomed to interacting with researchers, ranging from undergraduate students writing a paper to tenured academics. Moreover, a number of squatters write about the squatters movement academically at an undergraduate and a postgraduate level. As a result, my role as a researcher did not particularly distinguish me. I believe that my reliably working in the social center as a cook, and then, my conforming to the role of a "good squatter" set me apart from other researchers who often limited their contact with the squatters movement to analysis of websites, indymedia articles, books, and at most, one visit to a kraakspreekuur or by attending a squatters' demonstration.

I find it difficult to assess how much status I had in the community for "non-movement" parts of my life that earned me prestige in Amsterdam outside the squatters' subculture, specifically, doing a PhD, being a student at Yale, and being American. Despite the discursive rejection of academic status, university education and in particular, working on a PhD, holds value in the squatters' subculture. Once again, I was not unique since other squatters in this community also have PhDs or were in the process of writing their dissertations. My position as a Yale student may have brought some prestige when I initially began fieldwork.[7] As I developed relationships with fellow squatters, I believe that this prestige subsided. Being an American in a radical left activist community did not earn me estimation especially in the context of the Iraq war and the widespread international hatred of George W. Bush. Ultimately, my American citizenship and my position as a Yale PhD student had a subconscious rather than a transparent impact on my relationships with members of this community because these privileges demonstrated to them and to myself that I always possessed opportunities to leave this subculture at will (see Chapter 4 about entrapping marginality).

Outside of the squatted neighborhood where I lived and worked, Amsterdam squatters mainly related to me as the girlfriend of a *kraakbonz* (squatter boss). The number of times that squatters approached me merely to ask questions or make comments about this kraakbonz is too numerous to recount although I discuss the phenomenon of gossip, sexuality, and authority more in-depth in Chapter 2. The combination of my being a non-white, non-punk, American and in a romantic relationship with an authority figure led me to have a reputation on the level of the Amsterdam squatters movement. However, I do not classify this reputation as "capital" because it is not composed of a background of skills and achievements, but from the sexist perspective of being attached to a male authority figure.

My clarification on my own position in this community can only be partial and subjective since it's impossible to objectively analyze oneself and one's impact on others. I believe that I earned the respect of my fellow squatters according to the internal values of this movement, but that I was also subject to the same scrutiny, distrust, and violence that underlie how this community operates. Due to the legal liminality of squatting, I was structurally at risk and suffered as a consequence. However, methodologically, these vulnerabilities were apparent to my fellow squatters who decided to share their lives with me, both formally via interviews and informally through the practice of community living.

My personal circumstance is important for understanding my position in relation to this community. The squatters offered me a large room – a physical space – and an emotional space in their community. I was factually interdependent with the squatters. I needed them beyond the data that they provided through the interviews and the observations. They helped me in the minute details of squatter life, such as with installing heaters and toilets. I dedicated myself to the campaign to defend my first house not to have the novel experience of working on a squatters campaign but because I simply did not want to be evicted from a beautiful house. After this house was evicted, I spent a year living nomadically as a squatter, moving from house to house, which I found overly stressful due to lack of stability

I clearly mark quotes from interviews. All other quotes originate from casual conversations and were recorded in my field notes. I changed the names and identifying details of informants to the best of my ability.

Participant observation versus militant ethnographer and observing-participant

My researcher positionality differs from the ethnographers of the alternative globalization movement who classify themselves as "observing participants" (Graeber 2009, Scholl 2010) or "militant/engaged ethnographers" (Juris 2008, Maeckelbergh 2009). This self-characterization creates an intentional distance from the ideal of objectivity in more positivist social sciences, which dominates social movement studies, and emphasizes that their commitment to their activist identities is equal to or greater than to their academic production.

I consider my work in the anthropological tradition of ethnographic fieldwork comprised of systematic, long-term, participant observation and my intended audience wider than only activists. In contrast to many movement researchers, I did not begin as an activist and then decide to write a dissertation about a movement to which I was emotionally and politically committed to; rather, I began as a researcher and then became an activist in the squatters movement. Although my positionality in this movement is complicated, my writing does not seek to promote the squatters movement in Amsterdam but to analyze it by systematically measuring the practices of the participants by the movement's dominant internal discourses and ideologies.

As mentioned above, a number of movement researchers feel their academic production serves as an extension of their activism. I do not share this approach. The role of researcher and of activist demand varying skills and modes of operation that at times may or may not overlap. To successfully produce academically, one is required to be diligent, to have the capacity to spend hours at a time reading texts and taking notes, to possess a good memory, feel comfortable with a certain amount of isolation, have copious amount of self-motivation, and a commitment to maintaining a peaceful and stable life that enables the conditions for writing and analysis. To be a capable activist in a radical left community that defines itself by committing direct action against the state, one should be fearless during acts of violence, detail-oriented, reliable, communicative, enjoy working intensely and collaboratively with others, and accept a certain amount of instability and chaos in one's life.

Although it's possible to possess all of these skills, in the year and half that I lived in a squat while writing my dissertation, I found it challenging to combine writing with the nitty-gritty of an activist's life. This separation failed because the pressing tasks of my squatter's life, from managing the details of an eviction court case to strategizing on how to react to the threats of the thugs sent to harass me and my squatter housemates (we cut off their water supply and they responded by throwing plastic bags of their feces into our backyard), often overwhelmed me and prevented me from having the peace of mind to analyze and write. It comes as no surprise that I wrote the majority of my dissertation after I stopped squatting.

Since these two roles require divergent sets of skills, I do not see my writing as an activist act. As a squatter, what "counted" for myself and the other members of my community were the daily tasks that enabled the continuation of a squatted community in the face of constant threat. If I had failed in the thousands of tiny details that constituted a squatter's life, such as making sure that the door was closed to thugs, police, and owners, my writing would ring hollow and meaningless even if it were full of praise.

I understand that social movement scholars often refrain from critically analyzing internal social movement dynamics due to a reluctance to put pressure on activists who are already contending with vast challenges, from repression to organizing against increasingly neoliberal regimes. My critique does not condemn this movement without empathy for its struggles and aims. Rather, the critique I offer is a tool arising from years of meticulous participant observation research from someone who sympathizes with this movement.

My hope is that activists can use this critique of internal dynamics to rethink how to overcome such persistent contradictions and problems. I have presented my work to numerous audiences of squatters and received a range of reactions. Some have supported the analysis positively – finding it refreshing – while others have been offended, not by its content but rather fearing that a critique from a movement "insider" could damage the movement's strategic goals. Ultimately, I hope this critique promotes transparency rather than denial in order to avoid reproducing the very dynamics that autonomous activists find oppressive in the "Mainstream."

Chapter summaries

Chapter 1: squatter capital

This chapter introduces a number of classifications and theoretical concepts. It presents a matrix of the types of skills and the style of the identity-making performances necessary to enable one to inhabit the ideal of the authentic squatter. Squatter capital, that is, specific skills and the differential prestige that one gains by excelling in such skills, describes the unspoken value system of the internal social world of the squatters movement. Furthermore, to achieve a sense of authenticity, one must demonstrate that one has mastered and rejected tastes and values, both mainstream and those associated with the radical left; as well as performing an inculcated middle-class value orientation to render invisible and natural a long, arduous and self-conscious processes of socialization and skill acquisition.

Chapter 2: the habitus of emotional sovereignty

This chapter explores how authority functions in this community. Specifically, the types of habitus and skills possessed by those who hold authority in the movement. I examine the consequences of participants' backgrounds on the activities of the movement and the invisible logic of why and how more culturally central people, who have a number of resources needed by a movement, accumulate capital and become authority figures.

Chapter 3: "showing commitment" and emotional management

This chapter presents a cartography of internal power dynamics within the intimate space of squatted houses. Squatted houses comprise the fundamental basis of the structure of the squatters movement in Amsterdam. Communal living groups within squatted households both reflect and refract larger movement dynamics of hierarchy and authority. They reflect larger movement standards in the sense that one's squatter capital contributes to one's status position within a squatted household. They refract in that within a household, the highest values are to maintain a lively and peaceful group dynamic, silently maintain the unspoken hierarchies within a group without challenging them, and to avoid tension and conflict.

Chapter 4: liminal adolescence or entrapping marginality?

In this chapter, I consider why social movement subcultures often serve as a form of youth culture. This leads to a number of activists constructing their involvements in social movements as a liminal, youthful stage in their lives before they transition to so-called adult lifestyles which require long-term commitment and responsibility, such as by dedicating themselves to a career and/or a family. Moreover, someone who has already transitioned into an adult lifestyle can then enter a movement subculture and revert to a youth culture's way of living defined by changeability, temporariness, and lack of responsibility.

Conclusion: the economy of unromantic solidarity

I conclude by reflecting on how this movement reproduces two social profiles of centrality and marginality and its economy of unromantic solidarity.

Notes

1   I capitalize Mainstream in order to convey that this is an ideological classification of the world of "normal people" against whom squatters are identifying themselves.
2   Owens analyzes each step of decline in-depth, with quotes from interviews of twenty-eight different squatters, many of whom are women.
3   The shift in the composition of the urban population results from a number of factors. In the 1970s, the Netherlands had a guest worker policy leading to a substantial migration of laborers from Turkey and Morocco. The Dutch state intended this policy to be temporary and never expected these workers to settle in the Netherlands. Regardless, the workers remained and reunited with their families, who immigrated to the Netherlands and began their own families. Furthermore, Suriname, a former Dutch colony, achieved independence in 1975. Consequently, a huge influx of Surinamese immigrated to the Netherlands between 1975–80 (after which, Surinamers could no longer claim Dutch citizenship).
4   Social housing refers to low-cost rental housing, the vast majority of which was originally built by a variety of associations (Communist, Protestants, Catholic,

Socialist, etc.) for their members. From the post-war period through the 1980s, one became a member of a particular housing association and waited for several years to receive an apartment. Eventually, in the 1990s, the distribution system radically reformed so that all social housing was available through one database. By the time of my fieldwork, the average waiting time in Amsterdam was fifteen years.

5   During this period, single people under the age of twenty-seven lacked the right to access social housing. The housing policy privileged people with more years on the social housing waiting list. This system automatically discriminated against young people and expected them to live with their parents, even if they had started their own families. Duivenvoorden recounts a story of a young man who was on the verge of committing suicide because he lived in a tiny one room apartment with his wife. His two children were placed in state child care because the state had deemed his housing unfit for the children to share the space with the parents. Helpless and frustrated, the young man literally was on the verge of killing himself before the housing authorities allocated him adequate housing for his family to live together.

6   I once met a member of the PvK at a squat party in 2006. I asked him about the torture and the electric shock threat from the film. He responded nearly identically as Theo van der Giessen, "Well, it's not torture if you say you are going to use electric shock on someone. Its only torture if you actually use the electric shock."

7   During two separate conversations with squatters working on their PhDs, when I informed them that I was studying at Yale, both responded, "What are you doing here with us?"

1

Squatter capital

Excerpt from interviews:

> Frederick: In the beginning it's restricting [not being Dutch]. It's hard to say where it comes from but in general, new people have to prove themselves in the activist community, I mean, you don't get a place like this, you know, it's not for free. When you want to come into a certain group, you need to do stuff for this group that the rest appreciate. It depends on which collective you are working with. Just being there also for a long time and showing that you are constantly interested and that you are willing to do the shittiest jobs in the beginning and then starting to do more pro-active organizing projects by yourself, or whatever. You need to come in and that takes time and it is certainly restricting if you are a foreigner, not knowing a lot of things, not knowing a lot of codes. Not understanding how people communicate culturally cause it's sure, another culture, but there is a big difference between activist culture where I'm from and the activist culture here, which is not the same as the normal culture or the hegemonic culture or whatever you want to call it.

> Dirk: The second time I ran away [at age sixteen], I went to Den Haag where there was a guy from my village who had been squatting there since he was fourteen. I thought, I am young, can I live here? Which is not how it works, of course. It's not how it works. Of course people give you shelter for a while but that's not the same as just joining living groups. It's not that easy. So they advised me to go to Amsterdam to get my act together.

Despite their differences in class, education, and their structural locations in the world, both of these squatters agree that one must prove oneself to be accepted in an activist community and that activist culture has its own set of standards that are difficult to understand and fulfill at first glance. Frederick, employed as a strategic planner in an environmental non-governmental organization (NGO), came to Holland from Denmark in his early twenties to study intellectual history, bringing with him a background in radical left activism in Copenhagen. Dirk, who works for an organic produce distribution company, grew up in a deeply religious, conservative, Catholic family in a village in the south of the Netherlands, and ran away from home as a teenager to find himself squatting in Amsterdam. While Frederick clearly articulates what he perceives as the hidden codes and expectations of activist culture, Dirk refers to the same set of hidden codes by emphasizing, "it's not how it works … it's not that easy," and that he had to get his "act together" before he could be accepted as a member of a squatters' community.

What does it mean to prove oneself as a "real" or authentic squatter? What are the practices, conventions, and actions that constitute this fragile authenticity? Authenticity is complicated and fraught because it is a double process of inhabiting a location, whether that is a claimed and performed identity or a seemingly natural "habitus," while simultaneously being recognized by others as authentic. Thus, the process of being named as authentic is constantly in flux because it depends on the actors involved: those who are or consider themselves authentic and those who then recognize (or do not) that authenticity. I argue that the act of living in a squat is not enough to be recognized as an authentic squatter. Authenticity is, rather, a status that one achieves through a lengthy process of practices, actions, and lifestyle performances that must then be evaluated by the squatters movement as authentic.

Achieving the status of authentic squatter requires, first, the ability to demonstrate a complicated mix of functional skills and activist performances with a sense of naturalness and ease – which I term squatter capital.

The second characteristic of authenticity is how a squatter defines themselves in hostile opposition, to a series of imagined Others: from the most external, such as the police, to internal squatter communities within the movement. Activist squatters share animosity towards various groups of imagined Others who are part of "the Mainstream" and perform a stance of hostility, which alters in intensity depending on whom this aggression is waged against. However, activist squatters feel restricted and are unable to display hostility during interactions with particular groups classified as "neighbors," immigrants, and undocumented people. When interacting with these groups, squatters tend to feel uncomfortable because they are excessively authentic. As a result, squatters feel challenged in their oppositional identities by becoming aware of their privileges. This sense of restriction and paralysis results in moments of rupture. I will further explain this dynamic in the last part of the chapter.

To help analyze how squatters negotiate authenticity, I will use the work of three scholars, Pierre Bourdieu, Sarah Thornton, and Howard Becker. According to Bourdieu (1984), class is not merely an economic phenomenon, but one that is exhibited culturally and socially through taste and "habitus."

Habitus is a set of subtle micro-behaviors that derive from a common historically produced set of dispositions of a particular social or ethnic group. It is the result of one's family, class position, status, education, race/ethnicity, gender, and ideology (Behler, n.d). Habitus includes how one stands, moves, dresses, eats, and smiles – micro-behaviors that communicate one's history and status. Hence, class and social position are reproduced through subtle, unconscious recognitions of affinity that are demonstrated through habitus and taste.

This understanding of habitus is essential to how Bourdieu distinguishes between various forms of "capital," looking beyond monetary wealth to larger cultural and social articulations of class and social position. He classifies economic capital as one's amount of financial wealth. Cultural capital refers to the amount of cultural and educational knowledge demonstrated through habitus and taste that is often associated with wealth without requiring actual finances. Finally, social capital is the strength of one's social networks.

In the book of essays, *The Field of Cultural Production* (1993), Bourdieu builds upon these formulations of capital to discuss spaces in social life that have alternative definitions of capital that may superficially reject those valued in the Mainstream but actually refract them. Using the art world as an example to elucidate this process of refraction, in the essay, "The Production of Belief," Bourdieu discusses how the financial success of an artistic product, which has value in capitalist social worlds, is inverted in the art world whereby commercial success actually has a lower status than more subtle, exclusive means of valorization among those in certain elite sections of the art world. For those within these alternative milieus, the values within the subculture dominate and those values considered external are rejected. Thus, there is a subtle process of mastery and rejection in which one understands the values of the Mainstream, masters them, and then rejects them to both conform to and reify the values of the alternative milieu (Bourdieu and Johnson 1993).

To complement Bourdieu's more theoretical work, Howard Becker's study of jazz musicians (1963) and Sarah Thornton's study of ravers in the UK (1996) use ethnography to describe the social worlds of subcultures, their particular values, the process of hierarchical stratification within subcultures, and how subcultural participants define themselves oppositionally in relation to others within their social worlds. Heavily influenced by Bourdieu, Thornton appropriates the term "capital" and modifies it to apply to social worlds within subcultures:

Subcultural capital would seem to be a currency which correlates with and legitimizes unequal statuses ... Subcultural capital is the linchpin of an alternative hierarchy in which the axes of age, gender, sexuality, and race are all employed in order to keep the determinations of class, income and occupation at bay. (Thornton, 1996: 104–5)

Thornton critiques how the literature of subcultural studies often focuses on how people in subcultures identify themselves in relation to an overwhelming Other that they call "the Mainstream." First, she states that researchers mirror subcultural participants' characterization of themselves and their worlds uncritically. Second, researchers often reveal a bias through their representations. That is, researchers often reify subcultural participants as resistant and avant garde versus an imagined Mainstream that both researchers and subcultural informants regard as banal and conformist.

She further charges that such classifications have a hidden classed and gendered disdain, since many of the subjects of subcultural research tend to be articulate middle-class men, hiding behind a classless subcultural guise. In Thornton's research of ravers in the UK in the 1990s, clubbers, who considered themselves heterogeneous and difficult to stereotype, uniformly classified and disdained the "Tracys and Stacys dancing around the handbag;" that is, an imagined Mainstream female Other who attended dance clubs that were not considered as hip and exclusive as the carefully marketed rave parties that ravers proudly attended.

In this instance, the Mainstream Other is a denigrated working-class female. The handbag signifies a mature woman – "the symbol of the social and financial shackles of the housewife" who exemplifies, therefore the anti-youth who "do not enjoy the classless autonomy of "hip youth"" (Thornton, 1996: 101).

Thornton analyzes the codes behind the term "Tracy and Stacy dancing around their handbag," to exemplify what she refers to as the "social logic of subcultural capital," which reveals more about subcultural participants by who they define themselves against than how they define themselves.

Becker's study of jazz musicians reveals similar insights. Jazz musicians seemed preoccupied by the decision to either play as a jazz musician or a commercial musician. Working as a commercial musician meant that one could earn a living but also signified losing the respect of one's peers for "selling out." Meanwhile, to work as a jazz musician demonstrated a musical conviction that exceeded material concerns. Yet, this option resulted in a hand-to-mouth living. Beyond the distinction between jazz and commercial musicians, musicians viewed the audience as the third Other. They tended to feel contemptuous of their audiences who, in their eyes, lacked sufficient and knowledgeable appreciation for their music.

Furthermore, the musicians tended to feel disempowered by the audiences because of their request for music that the musicians considered commercial and vapid. Hence, the jazz musicians divided their social world twice: first, between musicians and the external world of the "squares" – all those who lacked musical knowledge; and second, the distinction continued within the intimate world between commercial and jazz musicians.

Using these ethnographic examples, Thornton and Becker demonstrate that the participants' way of classifying their particular Others reveals more about themselves than about the people who they imagine. The contempt that Becker's jazz musicians have for the "squares" reveals the squares' power over the musicians. The musicians desire recognition for their talent and their hard work, yet despise the audiences precisely for acknowledging these qualities. The anguish with which Becker's musicians contemplate going commercial versus continuing with playing jazz provides a similar model for how squatters negotiate internal identities within the movement, as I shall argue. Equally, Thornton emphasizes that clubbers identify themselves in a negative relationship to the Mainstream; "Interestingly, the social logic of subcultural capital reveals itself most clearly by what it dislikes and by what it emphatically isn't" (Thornton, 1996: 105). In *Art Worlds*, Howard Becker similarly notes that the best way to find out information about conventions and practices that are considered normal is through the complaints of informants:

> Fieldworkers know that complaints are especially good data about organizational activity. Why? Because organizations consist of ... regularized ways of interacting, ways known to everyone taking part as the way things are done. Participants take these ways for granted ... and are upset when others do not behave as expected. And they complain, their complaints making clear what had been taken for granted as "the way things are done here," which is, after all, what a sociologist wants to know. (Becker, 2008: xv)

In the squatters movement, I found that squatters rarely articulately illustrated who and what the authentic and ideal squatter was. Instead, by labeling someone as "not a real squatter," they easily articulated what they disliked and disrespected about others in their community. By participating in countless conversations and listening to gossip in which squatters mainly talked negatively about each other, I acquired a sense of what kind of actions activist squatters valued and what types of skills they respected. In addition to listening, long-term participant observation that documented the discrepancy between how squatters represented themselves versus how they practiced their lives forms the basis of the composition of the ideal of the authentic squatter. This chapter relates what informants actually do, not what they claim to do, and describes how their practices reveal the values of the movement in contrast to how the movement represents these values.

I appropriate Thornton's term, "subcultural capital," and alter it to "squatter capital." In Thornton's definition, subcultural capital refers to ephemeral qualities such as hipness, which is carefully manufactured through a strategically marketed exclusivity in the dance worlds she describes. I do not deny the hugely subcultural stylistic elements of squatter capital. Many squatters dress alike, listen to similar music, and hold an ideal of "anti-consumption" while consuming identically to other squatters.

However, I prefer to emphasize the non-leisure aspects of squatter capital when describing its building blocks.

Squatter capital comprises a combination of complicated practical skills that are discursively naturalized as "easy" but are not discussed openly, as well as performances of conviction through confrontations in political actions. These skills are valued in the squatters movement as different indicators of prestige and competence. After presenting a composite of the ideal squatter and the skills which are valued in this community, I explore authenticity among squatters as an ideal, negotiated in relation to external and internal Others. I further argue that inhabiting the ideal of the authentic squatter is defined more by what one is not rather than what one is. I locate the community of activist squatters where I conducted my fieldwork in relation to their internal and external imagined Others and to how they perform their identity primarily through hostility. In the last section of this chapter, I consider moments when this fragile authenticity is ruptured during interactions with "neighbors," immigrants, and undocumented people both within and outside the squatters movement.

Squatter capital

Squatting a house

The ideal of a good squatter is someone who is well organized, responsible, trustworthy, committed, critical, outspoken, articulate. They should confront state authorities and demonstrate a willingness to fight violently if necessary against the state, property owners, and those considered political adversaries such as fascists. The first action that reveals if someone is a "good squatter" is if they have successfully squatted a house. Such an act comprises a number of complicated and challenging tasks.

A squatter should have research, communication, and observation skills. First, the squatter has to thoroughly research an empty space, its history, and status bureaucratically, compiling information from the space's neighbors, as well as watching the house to check signs of habitability. In addition to searching for information on the internet, a squatter should call various municipal agencies about the site. In terms of communication skills, the squatter should feel comfortable approaching strangers and asking them deceptively about their neighbors' house without revealing clues that they intend to squat it. With regards to observation, a squatter should diligently keep track of a certain location and consistently check if it's inhabited over a long period of time.

Once the *kraakspreekuur*[1] that the squatter has consulted with has determined if the house has been empty for a year or longer, then the squatter has to show organizational skills. They should assemble a number of elements. First, a "squatting kit" of a table, a chair, and a bed to establish occupancy – by searching throughout the city's bulk trash nights for the items. Second, barricading material, by collecting items from squats, warehouses, and construction sites. Third, an attorney for the action – by obtaining recommendations from other squatters for which attorney to use and then assertively communicating with this attorney to retain their services. Fourth, a squatter should compose a letter to the neighbors – which means finding a model for a neighborhood letter and help from a Dutch speaker to translate the letter. Last, the squatters should publicize the action to ensure a large enough group to enable its occurrence, which means that the squatters have made tiny flyers and distributed them throughout squats and social centers since squatting actions cannot be publicized over the internet due to fear of police surveillance. All of these elements have to be in place before the actual squatting of the house.

The group meets at an assembly point and once enough people arrive, someone briefs the group about the location of the house, its history, and the plan of the action. During the squatting action, everything comes together: the door has to be broken open quickly before the police are called by the neighbors, the squatting kit of table, bed, and chair are placed

Figure 1.1 Breaking open a door during a squatting action, 2008

in each floor (for houses of more than one floor), enough people should be inside the squatted space before the police arrive, the door must be barricaded strongly enough to keep the police and others (such as the owner's hired thugs) out who may want to evict, and enough people should stand outside the space to block the door to convince the police that they will violently resist if the police attempt to evict. Meanwhile, a member of the kraakspreekuur negotiates with the police as the official spokesperson for the action. Assuming the action is successful, everyone who participated drinks beer together or more elaborately, shares a meal provided by those who squatted the house. After everyone has left, ideally, the newly squatted house should have an occupation schedule to ensure that the house is continually occupied in case of visits by the police or the owner during the first week.

Dirk, who has been part of the movement for over ten years, describes squatting actions as primarily "social, in crowd scenes." He characterizes squatting actions as tedious and predictable. He connects his boredom with squatting actions as one of the reasons he stopped being active in the movement:

> I am bored with it. It's always the same, you go to an action, wait for half hour, decide if you have enough people, go there [the space to be squatted], kick open the door, and wait for the police. There is lots of waiting. The police say it's fine or not fine, sometimes with a little fight or at least an argument, and then they leave or they don't leave and they evict you or they don't evict you the same day. It's always waiting. Every squat action is the same. I'm done with it. There are other people who can do it.

The predictability and the ease with which most veteran squatters describe squatting actions masks the number of details necessary to execute the action and the amount of pressure felt by the squatters and the members of the kraakspreekuur planning the action to ensure its success. Before I became one, squatters often encouraged me to start squatting. When I told them that I was afraid, I received nonchalant responses about how squatting was "easy," "not-a-big-deal," and "anyone can do it."

This is not true. If one detail is missing, there are dire consequences – immediate eviction, arrests, and violence. If such consequences occur due to a missing and foreseeable element, it's considered embarrassing and shameful for the kraakspreekuur that organizes it since they could easily have prevented this problem. In contrast, unforeseen problems are considered an acceptable risk.

At one squatting action I attended, all the elements proceeded as planned. However, the spokesperson of the kraakspreekuur (who may have been drunk at the time) told the police that the house had stood empty for less than a year. In consequence, the police decided to evict. At the time, I stood outside with the group guarding the outside door of the house, but found myself moved with the entire outside group to crowd around the newly squatted flat and line the staircase inside the house to scare the police from evicting. Instead, the police called for backup, who, finding no squatters outside the building guarding the door, surrounded the building and gained control of the entrances and exits. The kraakspreekuur then negotiated intensively with the police and decided to leave the house because the police could have easily tear-gassed the inner staircase, arrested everyone, and evicted. Plus, the squatters for that house comprised a family with a small child who the kraakspreekuur wanted to protect from the possible violence.

Immediately after the retreat, the squatters at the action met to discuss why it had failed. The spokesperson was conspicuously absent at this meeting. After a long discussion, the most experienced squatters present, who also spoke the most, decided that the combination of the lack of a *bouwstempel*[2] propped against the outside building door, that the outside group had entered the building, and the spokesperson's error led to the failure. Except for one experienced female squatter, Dana, who criticized the spokesperson, the rest of the group of experienced squatters speaking in the meeting emphasized other missing elements over the spokesperson's error. For the next couple of days, I heard different members of this squatters' community who had not participated in this action, criticized the tactical mistakes of the kraakspreekuur during the action, disdained the squatters of the action for having bad luck and their disorganization, and derided the spokesperson as an irresponsible drunk.

Another example of a failure was a house squatted by two immigrants with the kraakspreekuur. Although the action itself proceeded without incident, the two immigrants failed to continuously occupy the house during the first week. During a time when neither was home, the owner reclaimed the squat with the police's help. After this occurred, I ran into Dana, who confided to me, "I feel sick about it. I can't even sleep knowing that they just left the house like that. They didn't have electricity for one night, so they slept somewhere else and now the house is lost."

Both of these examples show the tremendous effort and attention to detail required to successfully squat a house and how a few missing details can lead an action to failure. Also, in both of these situations, news of the failure resonated after the action and circulated as gossip about the involved squatters. The impact of failure on the squatter capital of those involved depended on the position of the person in the community and the expectations of this person. In the case of the first example – with the spokesperson and the missing bouwstempel – the actual squatting group comprised a family who lost a possible home for themselves. In terms of squatter capital, their status as a family meant that the squatting community expected less from them than if they were young single punks, for example, and so they did not lose any capital by this failed action.

The members of the kraakspreekuur, and especially the spokesperson, felt the embarrassment of this failure because with planning, they could have easily prevented and avoided such mistakes. Although I never spoke with the spokesperson about this event, I imagine that he left immediately after the action rather than participate in the meeting to analyze its failure because he felt humiliated and wanted to avoid criticism. Yet, during the meeting itself, most of the veteran squatters discussing the failure took great care to avoid criticizing the spokesperson despite his absence. The veteran squatters in this case, all who knew each other for at least five to ten years, protected the spokesperson from criticism, a consideration that they most likely would not extend to squatters with less capital than the spokesperson.

These cases reveal the socialization process of the movement in which through the gossip around failures, one learns what not to do in order to learn what types of behavior and actions the movement values. One can therefore see that squatter capital is compiled not through explicit language of validation but from organization and participation in successful actions that are deceptively construed as effortless and quotidian. The fragility of that success is masked and unacknowledged by everyone who works together to enable the action. Bourdieu comments on "the paradox which defines the "realization" of culture as *becoming natural*" (my emphasis). He elaborates that:

> Culture is thus achieved only by negating itself as such, that is, as artificial and artificially acquired, so as to become second nature, a habitus, a possession turned into being ... so little marked by the long, patient training of which it is a product that any reminder of the conditions and the social conditioning which have rendered it possible seems to be at once obvious and scandalous. (Bourdieu 1993: 234)

Bourdieu discusses how art competence is class based and how such a seemingly innocuous detail of cultural capital participates in a process of domination. Oddly enough, a parallel exists between the naturalization of the skills of appreciating art to the point of invisibility and how squatters deny the difficult and complicated production of squatting a house by either naming the tasks as "easy" or by not discussing them at all. By masking the challenge and the level of skills necessary to accomplish the tasks required to squat a house, squatters exclude others from openly discussing the complications and learning how to overcome them. Therefore, the many who either feel too afraid to squat their own house (including myself) or who had tried and failed, are left with a sense of inferiority for never having mastered this basic task of squatting competence.

The ability to consistently squat a house and master these details builds credibility and reputation, the building blocks of squatter capital. As noted, it is extremely challenging and complicated to successfully manage all the elements for a squatting action. Nonetheless, some squatters lack the capacity to execute the number of details; yet so often, a combination of luck, random circumstances and the assertiveness of others in the squatting community who intervene, enable the success of action. For example, in the squatters' community where I lived, resided a group of three Eastern European men. None spoke Dutch and could barely speak English. In my experience with them, they were always either drunk or high from a cocktail of drugs that ranged from marijuana (commonplace for squatters) to heroin (taboo). Despite their language handicaps and their addictions, they managed to eke out a living in Amsterdam by playing music and performing on the street for tourists. To squat their flat, they required tremendous assistance from the members of the kraakspreekuur who performed the research, organizational, and communication tasks on the squatters' behalf without being explicitly asked since these men lacked even the capacity to ask for such assistance.

Although these men could not fulfill many of the tasks to plan a squatting action, once inside the house, they had the construction skills to make the house habitable and no longer depended on others. In this case, these men's squatter capital comprised entirely of their building skills and the fact that they did not pretend to have skills in other areas – such as research, communication, or organization, and thus, felt content to have others do such tasks on their behalf. They did have pride, however, in their construction skills. In the months before their house was evicted, a female squatter colleague approached them and offered to help with barricading, to which they responded, incredulous, "You're going to help US barricade? No. WE are going to help YOU barricade."

Beyond the basic skill of squatting one's own house that forms the basis of squatter capital, an unstated hierarchy of skills valued by activist squatters also contributes to the accrual of squatter capital. These skills include breaking, building, organizing, strategic manipulation (a term that includes the skills of campaigning and research), and acts of bravery.

Squatter capital has two elements: competence and prestige. Different types of competencies give different types of prestige. Moreover, there is no direct correlation between competence and prestige. Breaking and campaigning seem to be more prestigious than building and organizing skills, which I conclude based on two observations. First, breakers and campaigners tend to be arrogant about their abilities, which indicates that these skills are considered scarce and desirable. Second, squatters who are esteemed as breakers and campaigners are often criticized for being egomaniacs, correlating with my observation that people with the most authority are also subject of the most gossip and criticism (see Chapter 2 for an elaborate discussion of this dynamic). Third, I've watched squatters demonstrate their appreciation of these skills during discussions of actions and campaigns, in which they nod their heads, expressing "yes," and purring admiringly, "cool," or "*stoer*" (tough/cool).

Breaking skills

Breakers – the people who break open the door during squatting actions – are well-regarded for their skills. Knowing how to break doors has its range of intricacies from the most "brute" – breaking it down with a crow bar – to its most complicated, involving special tools and an in-depth understanding of how locks function, including tools to open specialized and expensive locks. In general, the more specialized one's knowledge is, the more prestigious.

Women who seek to contribute to the movement and quickly earn squatter capital often decide to become breakers. During a conversation with Sjaak, a member of the squatters' research collective, I asked why there were only men in the research group. He answered, "When women want to do anything in the movement, they go for really macho things, like being a breaker. Research is really important but it's not macho and cool like breaking."

Whenever I have attended squatting actions where a woman broke the door, afterwards, I spoke to the breaker about her experiences. One woman, Marjoleine, commented, "Breaking is easy and women need to see that everyone can do it." Again, this is not true. Breaking is extremely difficult. It requires skills, concentration, knowledge, and the ability to perform under pressure since the breakers must open the door as quickly as possible

Figure 1.2 Breaking open the door during a squatting action

(average time is eight seconds) before the police arrive while ensuring that the door remains intact to effectively keep the police out if necessary.

Women breakers charge that while they break, men often interfere and take over, believing that the women are not breaking skillfully or quickly enough. Women must then manage this extra pressure of male distrust in their abilities. Once, I watched as a small, French woman squatter was in the middle of breaking open a door when an enormous Dutch male squatter took over without her asking for his help. Startled, she tipped the crowbar backwards, hitting her face, and cutting open her eyebrow. In addition to the pressure of the police arriving before she opened the door, she found herself bleeding and injured.

Once again, this language proclaiming ease denies the difficulties of the task. To break efficiently, breakers require a "long and patient training" as Bourdieu had described in relation to art appreciation skills. But the investment of time and energy to train as breakers is not discussed openly. Joseph, a former squatter who retired from the movement, told me that he spent months studying locks to become an effective breaker. Stijn, a nineteen-year-old squatter who told me several times that he wanted to be "a professional squatter," dedicated himself to practicing how to pick locks. Both of these young men privately revealed how they taught themselves to break. In contrast, Laura, a Slovenian woman who became involved in squatting through the alterglobalization movement,[3] approached Joris, a well-known male breaker to teach her how to break. During the action in which they had agreed that she was to break open her first door, she arrived at the location to find that Joris had already done so despite his promise to help only if necessary. Frustrated, she stopped trying to learn and never explained why to Joris. Apparently, learning how to break must be done in secret.

Building skills

Building skills such as knowledge of how to work with electricity, gas, plumbing, carpentry, and general construction are highly respected. The squatter capital of being a builder translates into material advantages. Such people are sought as housemates in squatter households because their skills contribute significantly to the quality of life within a squat – details as basic as having running water, a working toilet, a shower with hot water, indoor heating, better locks, to more aesthetic details to improve the interior decorating of a squatted house. Accordingly, squatters with building skills often have a higher position in these living groups due to their skills and the fact of their being invited. Plus, builders often exude an air of autonomy because they have the capacity to squat their own house and renovate it independently without assistance from others.

Regarding building skills, the squatting movement's ideology is "Do-It-Yourself" implying that everyone has the capacity to learn these skills and that plenty of people will teach those willing to commit the time and energy to learn. Jenna, an "authentic squatter" who embodies this DIY ideal, shared her frustration with me about her housemate, Dora, who "does nothing. The water heater has been broken for two days and she waits for me to either fix it or ask someone else to fix it for us. She tells me that she doesn't know how. Well, she should learn. That's what we all do. We learn how to fix things."

Despite this DIY ethos, building skills are difficult to master. They require significant investment of time and energy into learning; well-known squatter builders are often asked to do the actual construction work in squats rather than teaching others these skills to enable them to build independently.

In terms of gender, the ideology of the movement rejects traditional gender roles and promotes women's equality with men. Consequently, women are expected to learn building skills, as Jenna's comment illustrates. In practice, the builders in the movement are overwhelmingly male due to gender roles in which construction is still regarded as a male profession both in the movement and in the discursive Mainstream. While a number of capable women builders are in the movement, men are asked more often for help. Furthermore, female builders' squatter capital is often not comprised of their building skills in contrast to male builders.[4]

As a result, squatter women invoke gender roles through an ironic prism of double rejection: first, the rejection of how the imagined Mainstream constructs gender roles, and second, the rejection through mockery of the expectation in the radical left of an independent, feminist, squatter woman who inhabits the DIY ideal.

When discussing building and renovating, squatter women often refer ironically to the contradictory requirements of the imagined Mainstream and the radical left. They reject the Mainstream construct of gender roles which denies women's ability to build. Simultaneously, they mock the movement's countercultural expectation that squatter women should be comfortable DIY builders in order to express feminist ideals. Marina, a Romanian squatter, told me that one large house that she had originally squatted with a group, lacked indoor heating because her housemate, Felipe "was too depressed to do the "man jobs." He wouldn't fix anything." I once told Alexandra, a young, attractive, female, veteran squatter that I felt afraid to live in a *krot* – a house that requires extensive renovation – because I lacked building skills. She slowly eyed me from head to toe and joked, "That's what your tits are for." I overheard another conversation where a male squatter teased his girlfriend for receiving help from male builders to repair her house, "Look at you, with all of these guys hanging around because you are a cute girl." She replied, "They don't help me because I'm cute, they help me because I'm a good comrade." To which he answered, "Well, you are a good comrade, but they help you because they think you're cute."

These examples demonstrate an ironic awareness on the part of the female squatters. They understand the expectation to master these skills to further accrue squatter capital as independent feminists who reject the stereotype that women cannot build. Instead, they opt to manipulate the unstated but ironically acknowledged practice of a number of male builders who seek female companionship. Thereby, these female squatters receive help with their repairs without learning the skills. I suspect that other than the assumption of male competence in building, women builders are not called upon for help because they most likely would force female squatters to learn the skills themselves. In my experience of receiving assistance from male builders, they rarely tried to teach me how to "do-it-myself," because they could install and repair quickly and efficiently and my efforts to learn only delayed and frustrated them. I was also conscious of the loneliness of these builders and knew that afterwards, I was expected to hang out with them for hours, chitchatting, eating, and drinking, as a subtle and tacit way to demonstrate my appreciation. No one ever articulated this expectation but I clearly understood it.

Organizational skills

Organizational skills also contribute to the accrual of squatter capital. In contrast to breaking, building, and campaigning, organizational skills are mostly associated with women, as in the case with many skills associated with details and facilitation in "the Mainstream." The social and political life of the movement can function only if there are people who pay attention to details and carry out tasks to ensure that political actions actually take place.

Germaine is a Belgian woman who has been involved in the squatters' scene for over ten years. While she lacks nearly all the other skills listed in this section, her squatter capital is entirely comprised of her organizational skills, which have enabled well-known, politically active squats[5] where she has resided in the past to function. One squat was an enormous warehouse that was well known in Amsterdam for hosting multiple, public cultural events every week, providing rehearsal and atelier space to artists, in addition to housing a living group. Her coordination of these events in this house and the reputation of the other houses where she has lived as "active and political" led her to gain substantial squatter capital.

Germaine moved to Amsterdam from Flanders to attend university. To combat the loneliness and formality of university life, she participated in student leftist politics. Through this circle, she eventually became involved in the squatters' scene. Her living situation has varied in the past few years in which she alternated between living in squats and sublet rooms. Despite having accrued a significant amount of squatter capital, Germaine has a quiet, shy, and socially awkward demeanor in contrast to men with similar squatter capital who tend to be loud, arrogant, and dominating. She doesn't discuss the squats where she lived and how she successfully managed them. Instead, I found out about her role through others. She enjoys organizing large events such as benefits for different leftist political causes, parties as well as actions. In contrast to skills such as breaking and acts of bravery, Germaine's skills lack luster. By investing her organizational skills in the squatters movement, Germaine finds emotional satisfaction from working with others in group projects rather than being recognized as a courageous activist.

Strategic manipulation

Another set of skills that boosts squatter capital are grouped together under what I refer to as strategic manipulation. Strategic manipulation encompasses a number of activities that intend to maneuver legal, administrative, and political procedures to enable squatters to retain their houses for as long as possible. To describe strategic manipulation, squatters use military language, such as "campaign," "defense," "economic warfare," and "being strategic."

There are a range of levels of strategic manipulation. Else's case exemplifies a basic level of strategic manipulation. Else lived in a squatted house for three years. The owner, a housing corporation, sued to evict her. In preparation for her defense, she thoroughly researched the house itself, its history of renters, and the housing corporation's plans for the renovation of the house through the municipal archives. She found that the owner had lacked building permits to renovate the house and neglected to submit future renovation plans to the neighborhood council. Based on her research, she proved that the owner did not intend to use the space and thereby won her court case. Else's case exemplifies basic strategic manipulation in that she used research to win her case but she limited her defense to a legal one without constructing a larger political narrative, which would have required a higher level of strategic manipulation.

A number of examples exist of strategic manipulation that similarly use legal and administrative means to retain squatted houses. One group of squatters delayed their eviction by working with a foundation that seeks to place monument status on nineteenth-century Amsterdam buildings. The series of court cases to determine the monument status sought to delay the inevitable eviction of the houses to enable the squatters to possess them for as long as possible. Another group of squatters postponed its eviction administratively by using municipal environmental clauses to protect the breeding places of bats in their house. Just as in Else's case, these squatted houses limited their tactics to administrative and legal ones without constructing their house defenses into larger political campaigns.

Campaigning is strategic manipulation at a more intensified level in which squatters publicize a house in local political bodies, the press, and the neighborhood by constructing it as a symbolic object of urban policy meas-ures which lead to gentrification and the displacement of low-income people from Amsterdam. As a squatter, I worked on two campaigns to "defend" the houses I lived in, and so much of this description derives from the experi-ence of campaigning.

To be strategic is to plan actions with an eye to manipulate political and legal processes. It requires understanding that these processes are not fixed but flexible and that with enough public and private pressure, whether it is administrative, legal, or political lobbying, one can influence such processes. Jansen, a member of the squatters research collective, referred to campaign-ing as "creating a reality" to describe this process of manipulation. Jansen elaborated:

> You create reality because it's not possible to actually know what is happening with these houses. These are all speculators and mafia in Amsterdam real estate and they are doing shady and criminal things with these houses. You can't find proof so you make the truth. The truth is not found but made.

When the owner of the first house where I resided attempted to evict us, we embarked on an aggressive campaign to discredit him to pressure the neighborhood council to block his efforts to evict us. This campaign successfully delayed our eviction for a year. We "created the following real-ity" based on existing narratives regarding the relationship between hous-ing speculation, empty properties, and money laundering: that our owner served as a more legitimate front man for the former owner, who laundered money through real estate for the mafia. In order to "create this reality," we produced a website for the house and posted a story on indymedia (the news media website of the radical left in the Netherlands), alternative news networks, and internet squatter forums publicizing the history of the house in which we strongly hinted that the owner laundered money. We spread flyers throughout the neighborhood publicizing this story. We lobbied the members of the housing committee, and sent press packets to the neighbor-hood council members. We organized actions at the neighborhood council itself, in which a representative of the squatters group declared the owner a mafia figure from whom the neighborhood council should withdraw sup-port. We cooperated with the elderly woman renter in the house, who had a forty-year history of tenancy, publicized her support of the squatters, and prepared her to speak at the neighborhood council.

For the campaign, we courted the support of this elderly renter for stra-tegic reasons. As a working-class and elderly Amsterdammer, she seemed more authentic and vulnerable compared to ourselves, the squatters, who we believed appeared to the Mainstream as self-serving in our manipula-tions to stay in the house. These tactics intended to create the house into a news item because once the house developed significance in the political and administrative consciousness, we could then exert pressure on the neighborhood council to act more carefully, and thus, postpone the eventual eviction. "For squatters, delaying is winning," comments Jantine, a squatter with campaign experience.

After a year of campaigning, we received notice that the police planned to evict us in the next eviction wave. In the last few days before the eviction, we tried numerous tactics to pressure the neighborhood council and the mayor's office to cancel our eviction, including meeting with the chairperson of the neighborhood council in the home of our elderly neighbor. We impressed upon the chairman that the squatters served as the only force to protect the neighbor from the bullying new owner who wanted to pressure her to leave her flat so that he could renovate and sell her apartment. We then organized an action on the city council in Amsterdam in which we occupied the main hall with hundreds of squatters and police sirens, surrounded by press, and demanded an audience with the mayor.

Despite the squatters' interrogating the mayor and the elderly neighbor pleading the mayor for protection from the speculating house owner, he decided to evict our group of five squatters the next morning, with twenty police trucks, a water cannon, and a remote flying robotic device that cost the Dutch taxpayer several thousand euros. Meanwhile, our group of five stood outside the house and watched the police evict "us."

Figure 1.3 Eviction of a squat in Amsterdam, 2008

These campaigning tactics are well within the repertoire of squatter campaigning for the past forty years. Talking about the mafia and its use of real estate to money launder and constructing narratives which play on populist Amsterdam sensibilities that hate real estate speculation has proved relatively successful for those who campaign by leading to either the legalization of their squat or being offered low-cost rental housing.

Despite the possible gains of campaigning, compared to building skills, a relatively small number of activist squatters engage in strategic manipulation and even less campaign. I found it puzzling that most squatters who I knew would rather move out of their house, find a temporary place, store their belongings, search for a new house to squat, squat that house, and then make their new house habitable, all under the threat of eviction, rather than campaign to remain in a house. When I have asked squatters why they prefer to move than campaign, I received answers such as, "It's too much work to campaign," and "Why bother, we'll get evicted anyway." Why do squatters consider campaigning as too much or relatively more "work" than moving from place to place under tremendous insecurity with the additional time and energy investment of rehabbing one's house?

Despite the discourse that squatting is a solution to the lack of affordable housing, a number of squatters do not campaign because they are simply not interested in the material rewards of a legalized low-rent house that results from campaigning. Based on my observations, many squatters choose, rather than are forced, to squat. I have sat in numerous meetings where the possibility of "getting legalized" has arisen. I have found myself one of the few interested in an affordable, low-rent apartment. Without concrete material benefits, campaigning is merely a way to earn squatter capital, which is not rewarding enough for squatters to actually engage in the politics of housing in Amsterdam despite the movement's political rhetoric that squatting arises out of housing shortage. It seems that in the social logic of the movement, campaigning is unnecessary and potentially a waste of time and energy due to the potential of failure.

As a result, little social pressure exists to campaign in comparison to activities considered necessary, such as rehabbing one's squat. For example, I once had dinner with a squatter, Jacob, who discussed forming a new group to squat a large space. He mentioned his friend, Ernst, who was about to be evicted and also seeking a group but with whom Jacob did not want to share space because, "Ernst is a crust. He's lived in his house for over a year and never installed hot water. He washes himself in the backyard with a cold water hose and the [non-squatter] neighbors complain about him." (There is a section on "crusty" punks later in this chapter.)

In addition to being "a crust," Ernst also did not engage in strategic manipulation. He did not defend his house during his court case. Instead, he simply left after receiving the eviction notice. While some members of the kraakspreekuur criticized Ernst's neglect of his court case, such actions are normal for the majority of squatters. Since most squatters do not engage in strategic manipulation, it seems unlikely that they will criticize others for similarly not doing so, and therefore minimal social pressure exists to campaign. Yet, Ernst's inability to arrange for basic repairs in his house crossed a line and decreased his squatter capital, marking him as "a lazy crust."

Hence, more community pressure exists to acquire building skills and demonstrate them through rehabbing one's squat than to campaign, which is considered simultaneously prestigious, impractical, and unnecessary. Building skills lead to a concrete result: a toilet exists where there was none. With strategic manipulation, the result is more nebulous. Squatters can invest time and effort into campaigning without gaining the desired result, only earning squatter capital through their efforts.

Regarding the long-term investment of time and energy, squatter capital is overwhelmingly instrumentalist in which practical gains reign over symbolic ones. When examining the practice of the movement versus its rhetoric, the community networks and solidarity economy are invested in helping people squat houses to live in them rather than squatting houses as a means to protest against the housing shortage.

A key difference between campaigning and building is that squatters regard campaign skills as more elusive and associated with particular people who successfully campaign rather than as skills that can be learned. Campaigning is in fact difficult and complicated but not any more so than other squatter skills. To campaign successfully requires having knowledge about housing, legal, and administrative procedures that squatters can use to their benefit. It means understanding the court system, the rights of owners, and analyzing larger housing policies and trends in Amsterdam as well as understanding that, with enough pressure, one can manipulate any legal, political, or administrative procedure.

From my observation, squatters – especially men – seemed reluctant to take the position of learning from someone more experienced in campaigning. Because squatters categorize this skill as cognitive rather than hands on, on a subconscious level, it seems to reveal someone's personal capabilities in a more crass and naked way than building skills. In that vein, I often heard others describe Jansen, an experienced campaigner with a number of successes, as arrogant. He was, in fact, arrogant, but not any more so than the breakers and the builders training others.

Some women who attempt to engage in strategic manipulation find that men silence and trivialize them. They connect these feelings of marginalization with machismo in the movement. Jenna, a young Dutch woman who worked on a number of high profile squatter campaigns, charged that Jansen and David, two well-known campaigners, dismissed her ideas when she once worked with them on a press release. "Everything I said, they told me was stupid and didn't make any sense. I just felt like I was fighting the entire time, so I gave up. I will never work with them again," she confided to me once over coffee.

Based on my observation, however, it seems that these male campaigners treat everyone badly without targeting women in particular. The difference is that these women feel comfortable articulating this treatment as sexist, while men, who most likely feel similarly disregarded, do not articulate it as such. Instead, they refuse to engage and code these feelings under the term, "It's too much work to campaign." Therefore, the unwillingness to engage in strategic manipulation indicates a larger discomfort in acknowledging differential strategic capabilities, knowledge, and the resulting hierarchies. While squatters deny that such hierarchies exist, the hierarchical process of knowledge transference explicitly reveals status differences that squatters prefer to avoid.

Non-instrumental acts of bravery

Squatters who seek to gain squatter capital through symbolic actions do so by participating in actions which require confrontational and illegal activity that usually target the Dutch government, foreign states, or a range of multinational corporations. Squatters refer to these acts of bravery ironically as "scene points." In contrast to the overwhelming instrumentality of skills that accrue squatter capital, the skill of acting courageously during direct actions is mainly symbolic and has almost no functional practicality.[6] Alberto Melucci (1989) explains that to analyze political activity that is primarily symbolic in terms of efficacy misunderstands the nature of new social movements. He elaborates, "Contemporary collective action cannot be assessed only in terms of instrumental rationality ... When considering this type of collective action ... the conflicts within the realm of collective action take place principally on symbolic grounds" (Melucci, 1989: 75)

Rather than connecting such acts of bravery in political actions with an efficacy that may or may not exist, I classify such symbolic acts as fundamental to accruing squatter capital and whose value then serves to increase the status of the activist in the squatters movement. The other skills that I have described require investment of energy and time to learn and develop and must be demonstrated reliably over a period of time to accrue squatter capital. In contrast, acts of bravery visually perform a genuine and non-instrumental conviction quickly and dramatically. The utter impracticality of these acts demonstrate the sincerity of the squatters' convictions. As Jeffrey Alexander elaborates when exploring authenticity:

On the level of everyday life, authenticity is thematized by such questions as whether a person is "real" – straightforward, truthful, and sincere.

Action will be viewed as real if it appears *sui generis,* the product of
a self-generating actor who is not pulled like a puppet by the strings
of society. An authentic person seems to act without artifice with-
out self-consciousness, without reference to some laboriously thought
out plan or text, without concern for manipulating the context of her
actions, and without worries about that action's audience or its effects.
(Alexander, 2004: 548)

In the case of squatters, it seems that the very lack of strategic practicality of
an act of bravery constructs it as more honest, and ergo reflects the deeply
held convictions of the activist who performs them.

I have witnessed countless acts of symbolic, non-instrumental bravery.
During a noise demonstration[7] in front of a police station to support peo-
ple arrested during a political action held earlier that day, Christophe, a
Greek squatter, spray painted "Fuck the police" (in English!) on the wall of a
police station. This led to a riot between the people attending the noise dem-
onstration and the police, and eventually several more arrests. As a result,
Christophe's act portrayed a bravery and conviction without practicality.
The resulting lack of strategic consideration was harmful, yet its "bravery"
led to an increase in Christoph's squatter capital. As Karl, a German squat-
ter, commented, "Christophe's scene points went up."

At another eviction, Dino, a Portuguese squatter, was part of a group
blocking the police from the squat. Everyone in the group sat down and
locked arms. When it became clear that the police intended to charge the
group to disperse it, all except Dino left the area; the police pulled him away
from the building and broke his arm. After Dino returned from the hospital,
I watched as others gave him special treatment for having his arm broken.

Once, while I worked as a cook at a squatted restaurant (*voku*), Edwin,
a former Dutch squatter who has been active in the scene for nearly fifteen
years, walked into the kitchen and screamed at me because he felt that he
had waited too long for his meal. Shocked, I was on the verge of screaming
back when Jillian, an Australian squatter, pulled me aside and whispered,
"Don't get into a confrontation with him. He's got a bad temper but he's
a really good activist. He's been to tons of actions." In this case, Edwin's
squatter capital as "a good activist" protected him from being held account-
able for abusive behavior.

In general, the more arrests squatters have from political actions, the
more squatter capital they accrue. Although squatters generally do not dis-
cuss this openly, activist squatters feel pressured to perform acts of brav-
ery to maintain their squatter capital, despite their other capabilities. At
a noise demonstration to support forty people arrested en masse during
the eviction of a well-known, politically active squat, I spoke with Jenny, a
respected squatter who has successfully squatted and legally defended sev-
eral houses. In response to my asking why she had decided to participate in

the mass arrest, she confided, "Well, I've never been arrested and I really felt like I had to at least once." Despite her numerous skills and achievements that made up her squatter capital, Jenny still felt that without an arrest, she lacked authenticity in the eyes of the community.

How to be an authentic squatter

Sarah Thornton, in her ethnography of ravers in the UK, writes, "Interestingly, the social logic of subcultural capital reveals itself most clearly by what it dislikes and by what it emphatically isn't" (Thornton, 1996: 105). With this negative identity formation in mind, this section describes how the manner in which subcultural participants create their social world and their identity in relation to others, reveals more about themselves than about those who they imagine. The descriptions that follow of the social world are based empirically on my observation and from how activist squatters talk about their imagined Others within and external to the movement. This means that the social world I describe is partial, describing only those against whom activist squatters find it relevant to compare themselves.

I use the term "activist squatter" to describe squatters who identify themselves ideologically as squatters (whether or not they live in squats), see themselves as members of a social movement, take responsibility for the movement by contemplating strategies and its future, have expectations for how others in their squatter community should behave as an extension of one's identity as a squatter, and feel a sense of solidarity and commitment to their squatters community.

In *The Presentation of Self in Everyday Life*, Erving Goffman argues that people constantly perform roles during micro-social interactions in daily life. He uses the metaphor of the theater to explain how every person sends two signals, those they give intentionally and those they give unintentionally (Goffman, 1990: 2). In order to manage the impression of oneself that others have, the "actor" is aware of one's role and intentionally alters one's behavior depending on the audience and on how one wants to influence this audience. Even in situations where an actor is convinced of one's performance, this conviction cannot be sustained and the actor moves back and forth from being cynical about the requirements of the performance and being moved by it.

Goffman argues that the front stage is a fixed presentation or performance involving performers and an audience. While the backstage is the space where the performers are present without an audience, and thus without the need for the performers to maintain their front stage facade. He contends that the relationship between the backstage and the front stage is pragmatic. The front stage, in which the audience is the outsider, is much more self-consciously performative, while the backstage is a place where, supposedly, more trust exists between the performers, as there is no need to disguise themselves among each other. The backstage enables the front stage because it is a place of rest, trust, and bonding between all those who perform on the front stage.

Borrowing from Goffman, I divide activist squatters' imagined Others into two modes of performance: the front stage and the back stage. For squatters, the audience of the front stage consists of those who are deemed external to the movement. It's the Mainstream with a capital M which mainly consists of the police, the state, the owners, and the press. The front stage is also significant because it's the performative realm during which squatters form a united front against the Mainstream. The internal differences within the squatters movement disappear to create an impression of unity on the front stage. I use eviction waves to discuss how squatters self-consciously perform for the police, the press, and the Mainstream via these spectacles. I then consider the foil of the discourse of hatred of anti-squatters and how this contempt reveals an uncomfortable intimacy on the part of activist squatters.

I then describe the back stage of the squatters movement, which is the internal social world that squatters refer to primarily as "the scene." Again, I do not claim to fully represent the numerous groups that comprise the heterogeneity of the squatters movement. Rather, I relate how activist squatters, primarily the campaigners, classify other groups in the squatters movement. Within the back stage of the squatters movement, I note a further division between activist squatters whose identity is based in the squatters movement versus student squatters and "hippie activists", who invest their energies into other activist realms and whose participation in the movement is openly transient.

Performing hostility

According to a number of squatters, a culture of hostility dominates the social world. Jennifer, from Canada, left the squatters' scene early upon encountering it because of this anti-social and unfriendly atmosphere. She notes, "I never felt like I fit in. I have never met so many hostile people in my entire life." Margit, a Dutch squatter who is an actress, describes how she deliberately behaves more reserved and less sociable when she attends squatting actions and *vokus* (squatted restaurants):

> People are often very grumpy, wearing black clothes, that's obviously because of their political ideas, I think they want to communicate something with it. I don't find them very social often. Not so expressive; sometimes I come in somewhere and … everyone is sitting there very quietly looking like this [she makes a face], and I come in like, hey hello [in a

loud voice] and I am about to introduce myself, but apparently it's not a habit to do that; I learned pretty quickly that that's not the way to go and now I go in like this (makes a face) ok (we both laugh). And I see someone I know and I go straight to the people I know and it's like, Hello (in a loud voice); it's kinda, I don't know, kinda strange, not so cozy, *gezellig* [translates as cozy]. You don't fit in because you are too social [we both laugh] and you're laughing too much.

[In response to my question, why do you think people act like that?] I don't know, the first reason that pops in my mind is that it's this kind of social group that is not used to communicate that way. It could also be that I'm extraordinary in this. I don't know if you notice but I'm pretty quiet there, when I go into this voku and I also adapt a little bit and go a bit lower than I normally do; like for example when I meet my art school friends, it's more like waah [makes a number of exuberant sounds] everything is more like bursting, but there no one is going to react if you do that. Maybe they are kinda outside of society sometimes. Maybe that is also why they join in the squat scene because it's kind of a place where it doesn't matter if you are not so social; because the link between people is political either it's more because of ideas that you share, it's not because you have a social same level to talk about things. You can only have to talk about housing if you want to. If you don't want to talk about other things, it's ok. For me it's a bit strange.

Margit connects the politics of squatting with what she considers as an anti-social behavior that dominates in the culture of squatters. She further hypothesizes that squatters internalize the aggression of their political posturing into how they interact with each other within the movement. The voku and squatting action meeting points are back stages for the squatters movement, and yet the pose of hostility continues in these intimate spaces despite the absence of the front stage of the external Others.

To continue this point of connecting squatters' behavior on the front stage to communicate political ideas to "the outside" with dominant social norms between squatters within the movement, I will locate squatter hostility onto a range of posturing in relation to a continuum of Others from the most external to the most intimate. In relation to each imagined Other, squatters have different registers and intensities in which they demonstrate hostility: open warfare and hatred of the police, manipulation and disdain for the press and the Mainstream, hatred for anti-squatters and disgust of yuppies, dismissal of wild squatters and crusty punks, and mockery of baby punks. At the most external end of the continuum, the hostile pose is intact and can be expressed easily because these enemies are determinate. However, as the Others become more intimate, as is the case with internal Others within the movement, the pose becomes more ambivalent and fraught. In the last section, I consider the relationship that activist squatters have with the so-called neighbors, immigrants, and undocumented people within the movement. In terms of the continuum of Otherness, these groups are indeterminate and thus, the most problematic because they paralyze activist squatters' sense of authenticity by disrupting the normalized pose of hostility.

Eviction waves

Eviction waves occur approximately three times a year and they constitute the ultimate form of the front stage in the squatters movement because squatters consciously treat these events as performative rituals to communicate with the police, the state, and the imagined Mainstream. The city contracts the riot police to evict all squatted houses with eviction notices on the same day to avoid the costliness of evicting on a more frequent basis. The "riot" between squatters and police is highly institutionalized since it has occurred frequently during the forty years of the movement's history. As a result, the primary performers comprise the squatters and the police, and the audience consists of members of the activist community, random observers, neighborhood residents, and the press, who expect particular types of performances. I base these observations on having witnessed a number of eviction waves and having been evicted by riot police twice, once as part of an eviction wave while the second surprised me and the other fifty people evicted and arrested.

To begin with, the squatters stand either on the roof or inside the squatted house. The press expects the squatters to throw Molotov cocktails or stones at the police although usually they have paint bombs. Because normal police are unprepared to handle the resistance expected from squatters, riot police evict them. Before the riot police vans arrive, the area fills with plainclothes policemen who photograph people in the area. My fellow squatters and I always easily recognized plainclothes policemen because they dressed like football hooligans. To mock them, we often waved and smiled at them while they filmed us.

Soon after, the riot police arrive with fifteen vans, including a truck with a water cannon to high pressure spray the squatters to subdue them. The riot police wear shields and helmets, and wield batons. They clear the area, block a wide circle around the squat, and violently charge anyone standing in front of the house attempting passive resistance. The police trucks surround the house and order the squatters to leave the house with a loudspeaker three times. Then the riot police leave the trucks and walk towards the house on foot, covering themselves with their shields to protect themselves from projectile objects. They then spend an inordinate amount of time and effort breaking through barricading to enter the building. Once they enter the building, they ascertain if squatters remained inside hiding or have locked their bodies structurally into the house, called a "lock-on," which then

Figure 1.4 Plainclothes police officers attempting to look casual prior to a squat's eviction, 2006

requires more time and excessive physical force from the police to extract the squatters. Eventually, the police announce that they have cleared the building of squatters and return it to the owner.

Squatters openly view this ritual as a performance. I heard Darrel, a squatter in the movement for nearly fifteen years, complain about a photographer who asked to shoot the squatters on the roof during an eviction in which Darrel threw paint bombs at the police. When the photos were published, the caption stated that the squatters had thrown stones. Darrel felt angry about the misleading inaccuracy of the caption because, he emphasized, "it's all just a show."

Both Darrel's remark and the photographer's misrepresentation of the squatters demonstrate an awareness of and investment into the fantasy of violence and the compulsion to portray it theatrically. The squatters are aware that both the press and the squatters' scene expect violence at evictions. They negotiate these expectations by performing a fiction of violence that it is not actually dangerous by using paint bombs instead of stones. The photographer also seemed aware of the audience's fetishistic need for violence and so he misrepresented the squatters to make them appear more violent. The police perform "uber-toughness" in this interaction as well. They

sport new gadgets, enormous trucks, and align themselves in military forma-
tion, with shields, weapons, and helmets. Each eviction wave costs thousands
of euros for the city.

The press and the squatters compete with each other to control the rep-
resentation of the squatters movement. Once the city announces an eviction
wave, journalists often call the squatters' press group to tape the preparation,
interview the squatters, and film the resistance of the squatters against the
police from inside the house. Members of the squatters press group attempt
to control the press's access by having them communicate with articulate,
strategically minded squatters who choose their words carefully. Before one
eviction, journalists from a national news program negotiated with the press
group to embed a reporter in a house during a wave. The press group had
chosen an articulate, reasonable, strategically minded student squatter to
interact with the journalists. Instead, the news program pursued a tall, sexy
punk with a working-class Amsterdam accent to interview. When the punk
pulled out, the journalists expressed disappointment.

During another incident involving arrests of squatters on a street where
I lived, reporters from a local news show camped in front of my house to
interview squatters. Because of my utterly un-punk demeanor, the squatters'
press group asked me to grant an interview not as a member of the squatters
group but as a respectable, expat neighbor. The reporters sought informa-
tion about the foreign background of the squatters which I carefully avoided
disclosing.

During my experience preparing for the eviction wave of my first squat,
I encountered a number of surprises. All of us in this house were conscious
of the expectations from the larger squatter community to resist the eviction
with violence since the house had a reputation as "active and political" due
to the success of the campaign defending the house from eviction. Based on
the discourse within the squatters community about evictions, I had assumed
that most squatters resisted during eviction waves. Yet, when we met as a
group to plan the eviction, almost none of the veteran squatters in the group
had ever "been inside," (the term for being inside a house while the police
try to evict from the outside). Knowing that none of the veteran squatters in
the group had resisted in the past nor felt a need to resist this eviction, I felt
less pressure to engage in violence. As one member of the group confided to
me privately, "There is no point in resisting. The police are going to get in no
matter what. What's the purpose of sitting in jail for three days?"

Stijn, a member of the group, disagreed with the rest. At the age of nine-
teen, Stijn was a veteran squatter, having squatted and having been evicted
from countless houses all over Europe. He proposed to create a "lock-on," in
the form of a giant block of concrete molded into the attic that would lock
his body into the attic and make it impossible for the police to remove him.
In comparison to the other members of the group, Stijn was unconcerned
about sitting in jail and looked forward to the opportunity of locking himself

into the house and confronting the police. Despite his enthusiasm, our group decided against violent resistance. Instead, knowing that the police feared that our group had created booby traps throughout the house against the police (we had graffitied the word booby traps outside the house to advertise this impression), we engineered what is known in Dutch as a *ludiek actie*, an action which intends to mock rather than result in violence. Instead of violent resistance and booby traps, we filled the house with hundreds of balloons that the police deflated before they could declare it clear of squatters. The press's coverage of the eviction wave highlighted the balloons.

In instrumental terms, squatters who resist during evictions serve a purpose for the movement. If regular police and bailiffs can evict squatters easily, the city will stop conducting eviction waves. Eviction waves serve squatters because with sufficient calculation, squatters can reside in a house for at least three to four months – that is, if one squats a house immediately after an eviction wave, one can expect to reside there until the next wave four months later. My observation, however, revealed that instrumentality was not forefront in the minds of those who resisted during eviction waves. Rather, the resistance existed in its own right as a performance of hostility against squatters' ideological enemies: property owners, the state, and the police.

However, as a performance of hostility, the eviction waves prove unsatisfying in their lack of drama. First off, they proceed extremely slowly. The first time I was evicted, I spent hours waiting with my housemates for the police to arrive since they toured the city to evict squats. We listened to the squatters' radio station that reported on the police's movements, read the updates on indymedia, and received phone calls and visits relating various rumors about the location of the riot police.

Approximately half an hour before they arrived, the atmosphere in the neighborhood seemed to electrify with excitement. I cannot explain why this happened, since this sense of anticipation reached beyond the squatters in which non-squatter neighbors gathered in the area around the squat and waited for the police. While the arrival of the riot police with over twenty trucks and their army-like presence proved dramatic, the whole scene was markedly subdued with an eerie quiet during the actual eviction. In many ways, the drama of the event was constructed by the press through clever and strategic editing of photographs and video footage and in the gossip and descriptions of the evictions among squatters afterward. Even during evictions with extreme resistance, in which the squatters barricaded every square inch of the house and the squatters inside threw objects at the police, the whole event is quiet and slow, lasting hours with long pauses in between movements.

Despite the careful preparation to perform for the front stage, the backstage of the squatters movement also serves as a more relevant audience for squatters invested in the community and who seek to obtain "scene points" and the prestige of squatter capital. In my experience preparing for the eviction wave, all of us in the house had different feelings about each member of the audience. My housemates, who had organized the balloons and had graffitied the word "booby traps" outside the house, had considered how to communicate this aggression to the police and the press. My other housemate, who talked to me about the futility of resistance, mainly reflected on the reaction of the backstage of the squatters' scene and his lack of interest in scene points. I also felt the pressure to resist more for the performance than for the utility and was relieved that the veteran squatters in the group lacked interest in doing so, thus removing the obligation to resist and go to jail on my part since I had the least experience in the group. Stijn, although aware of all of these elements, was compelled by resistance for its own sake, disregarding scene points, and enjoying the idea of building his first lock-on in a squat with youthful exuberance.

Barricading

An institutionalized legal procedure precedes an eviction wave. To evict squatters, an owner must take squatters to court and prove that he (owners are nearly always a he) plans to use the space. The overwhelming majority of owners win their court cases and, eventually, the squatters receive an eviction notice that announces the date from which the bailiff can evict. As I stated earlier, the state organizes eviction waves based on expectations that squatters will violently resist all evictions. Consequently, to continue the eviction waves and the delicate calculation of timing involved in living around eviction waves, squatters have to create an impression through barricading that they will violently resist if the bailiff or the police attempt to evict.

Barricading reveals a similar negotiation between utility and squatter capital. Instrumentally, squatters barricade to physically prevent the owner, the bailiff, and the police from entering the squat and to maintain a perception that they will act violently if anyone attempts to evict. As a result, a range exists between barricading that factually prevents entrance and "symbolic" barricading which communicates a message of resistance to the police and the owners.

In the first squat where I lived, my housemates described the barricading as "symbolic." Additionally, my housemates contended that by symbolically barricading, they provided the police with the justification that released them from the responsibility to evict outside the waves.[8]

I have heard squatters describe the police in two ways: first, as "pigs" who they hate; and secondly, as "lazy workers." During negotiations with the owner of my first squat, we learned that our court case was scheduled after the June eviction wave, the last eviction wave before the summer. During the negotiations, my housemates felt that they held an advantage over the owner because they knew that our group could remain in the house for another few months until the next eviction wave. I asked my housemates, "How do you know that the police will not try to evict during the summer?" My Dutch housemates responded incredulously, "Do you think the police want to organize eviction waves and do heavy stuff during the summer? They don't want anything to jeopardize their vacations."

Each type of barricading emits different symbolic meanings and communicates messages about the squatters to the backstage of the squatters' scene. To enact the ideal of "defending a house until the end," is to barricade a house in a way that factually prevents entrance, notify the squatting community to prepare themselves to be on "pre-alarm" in case of an attempted eviction, and to maintain an occupation schedule to ensure that the squat is never empty. Such preparations lead one to accrue squatter capital.

Hermance, a veteran squatter, believes that such barricades give the movement a tactical advantage, "Barricading is important for the movement because it forces the police to work hard to take a house back." When I asked Maartje why she had invested time and energy to barricade and defend until the end, she said with conviction and passion, "I'm not going to give one inch of this house back to that fucking owner. He'll have to take it from us." I decided to barricade and stay until the eviction of my first squat for practical reasons: I found it more stressful to move out of this house, live as a guest somewhere else, and find a new house to squat than barricade and time my residence around the eviction wave.

Defending a house until the end is unusual for squatters – most squatters leave a house shortly after receiving the eviction notice. Although this is common practice, it is less respected than staying until the eviction wave. A group of student women who squatted a house agreed to leave on a certain date, months before the eviction wave. I heard much criticism of their decision, so I asked them why they left. Alicia, a German squatter, told me that everyone in the group had various vacation plans which they did not want to alter in order to defend this house.

In contrast to the practices of barricading and resisting during eviction waves, squatters identify themselves against anti-squatters discursively rather than through a performance. The anti-squatters are equivalent to Thornton's "Stacy and Tracy dancing around the handbags," of UK ravers because the discourse around anti-squatters reveal more about squatters themselves through their way of classifying than about the empirical reality of who anti-squatters are and what anti-squatting is.

Anti-squatters

Squatters generally position anti-squatting as the opposite of squatting and taboo in the movement. Calling someone an anti-squatter is an insult.

Within the movement, different understandings exist for what it means to anti-squat. Depending on the definition, anti-squatting can encompass nearly every form of housing outside of squatting and legal, permanent rental contracts. In addition, squatters imagine themselves in relation to one stereotype of an anti-squatter but also acknowledge the diversity of what it means to anti-squat and who is an anti-squatter.

The dominant definition of anti-squatting is that to prevent a building from being squatted, owners contract people – known as anti-squatters – to live in their properties who they generally find through anti-squatting agencies. Anti-squatting agencies abound in the city and target mainly white, Dutch, higher education students. To anti-squat, one undergoes a screening process by the agencies and pays to place oneself on a list of potential anti-squatters. Samuel, a former Dutch squatter active in housing politics, comments that to be an anti-squatter, "You need to be in a network of white families to get into them [anti-squats]. You must be in a social network and introduced to become an anti-squatter, which means that you must be middle class."

People who anti-squat live a nomadic life in which they move from anti-squat to anti-squat. In order to prevent anti-squatters from claiming extensive Dutch tenancy rights, their contracts define them as guards rather than tenants. Lifestyle clauses that prohibit smoking, posters on windows, and parties, feature prominently in anti-squat agreements. Anti-squatters can be asked to move with little notice, residing in a space from two months to years, depending on the space and its owner's intentions such as whether the owner plans to demolish, renovate, or keep it "vacant" until it's sold. The fee one pays as an anti-squatter also varies from the cost of utilities to the equivalent of market rent.

Squatters display a continuum of feelings about anti-squatters. Damien, who identifies himself as an ideologue, calls anti-squatters "strike-breakers and scabs." I have heard others mock anti-squatters with vicious pleasure, criticizing their lifestyles and how they dress. Joris, a Dutch squatter, told me, "You can always tell an anti-squatter by how he dresses. Just look at his shoes. Only anti-squatters spend so much money on shoes. The fuckers." Other squatters defend them. Thijl, a veteran squatter of fifteen years, says, "The movement should be more open and try to understand the position of anti-squatters. They are doing their best. We are all victims of this [housing] situation." Hermance similarly criticizes the overall movement's disdain of anti-squatters, "Not everyone can handle squatting. It takes a lot of psychological strength and if you are weak, you can't handle it." Although she dislikes the movement's stance, I have heard Hermance curse, "these fucking anti-squatters," a number of times.

Beyond competing for the identical empty spaces, one reason for this overt hostility is that anti-squatters' reasons for choosing anti-squatting over squatting seems hypocritical, since anti-squatters cite insecurity and nomadic living as reasons for not squatting. According to Gerd, a German student squatter:

> Anti-squatters have fewer rights than squatters. An owner can ask anti-squatters to leave without legal protection while with squatting, there is a legal process that owners must use to evict. Anti-squatters say that squatting isn't stable. Meanwhile they are moving every few months, sending SMSs to everyone they know a week before they have to leave to find a new place.

Furthermore, Samuel contends that "anti-squatting is popular being its considered more civilized than squatting. It has a contract without rights while squatters have rights without a contract."

Generally, squatters imagine anti-squatters to embody a middle classness that they reject. Thus, the hatred of squatters towards the imagined anti-squatter – a white, Dutch, middle-class university student – stands in for all that squatters find repugnant about middle-class life. Based on my observation and countless conversations, here is a composite of all that anti-squatters represent: compliance, a desire to choose what is easier, comfortable, and socially accepted over what is oppositional, defiant, and difficult since anti-squatting has the appearance of a more legitimate industry with agencies and contracts; conformist, uncritical, yuppies-in-training, naively believing in "the system" as something that they can eventually use to their advantage, and cowardly participating in their own exploitation.

The unrestrained hatred for anti-squatters reveals an uncomfortable intimacy on the part of squatters. Samuel comments on the history of squatting and anti-squatting and how the current anti-squatter fits the profile of the Dutch squatter during the movement's height in the 1970s and 1980s:

> Squatters at the end of the '70s have the same profile as the current anti-squatters. Back then, more people got housing through squatting than official means. Now it's easier to find anti-squat. During the '70s and '80s, squatting wasn't subculture, but Mainstream, so that it attracted middle-class people who are now currently anti-squatting. Current squatters are marginalized groups such as immigrants and poor people.[9] The middle-class who do squat do so because it's fashionable and a wild adventure, while for marginalized groups, it's difficult to get power, legitimacy, and influence.

Beyond the uncomfortable intimacy that some squatters share with anti-squatters, the contempt for anti-squatters is ironic considering the superficiality of the anti-squatting/squatting opposition. In actuality, many squatters have anti-squatted in some form. They may have illegally sublet or had a temporary contract or even been an anti-squatter. After losing a court case, a number of squatters sign a temporary contract, agreeing to leave until the owner needs the space, converting the squatter into an anti-squatter.

Squatters who can anti-squat openly without being labeled as such have significant squatter capital, are well-liked, or are deeply embedded in movement and community networks. Those who lack such squatter capital then hide their anti-squatting past to avoid community judgment that they are weak and have compromised on their ideals. Anja, a German squatter, signed an anti-squat contract after she received an eviction notice to stay in her flat. She kept this a secret. Through interviewing and socializing, I met a number of squatters who had signed anti-squat contracts but hid this information to avoid being criticized. Also, they knew that the kraakspreekuur would most likely refuse to help them squat again with the rumor of an anti-squat contract in their past. On the other hand, squatters with tremendous squatter capital can sign an anti-squat contract or make an anti-squat agreement without receiving harsh criticism. Maaike, a veteran squatter who has squatted a number of houses all over the Netherlands independently and has accrued enough squatter capital as a resourceful and responsible person, openly admits to having signed an anti-squat contract in the past to prolong her stay in a squatted house rather than get evicted.

How the squatting community judges anti-squatting is also mixed with the perception of the anti-squatter. If it's someone who is capable and "empowered" such as a middle-class, emotionally stable (not drug- or alcohol-addicted), white, Dutch person, then they are harshly judged. The assumption is that such a person has enough internal and communal resources to draw upon so that they are not forced to anti-squat. Internal resources include one's own conviction in oppositionality, a critique of the state and the housing crisis, and one's emotional strength to manage the stresses of squatting. Such a person has the strength, the energy, and the skills to find a housing arrangement other than a temporary contract. If the anti-squatter is structurally underprivileged – by being poor, undocumented, or is a mother with children – then such people receive more sympathy and are not as harshly judged because they are seen as compromised structurally rather than internally. In such cases, the act of anti-squatting is separate from being labeled an anti-squatter.

In fact, one can be labeled an anti-squatter without actually being an anti-squatter. Once, I was drinking in a squat bar with some squatters before going to the birthday party of Jonas, a young, Dutch man who socialized in "the scene" but was not a squatter. When I told the squatters where I was going, they identified Jonas as "that anti-squatter." Jonas had a permanent and legal rental contract but the squatters labeled him an anti-squatter based entirely on his non-punk style of dressing and his mannerisms. Ludwic, another Dutch squatter who was often ejected from squatter living groups, once called his ex-housemates of a squat, "a bunch of anti-squatters." The group of four occupied an enormous building and hesitated to accept new housemates, which Ludwic considered equivalent to anti-squatting since a small number of anti-squatters often occupy entire buildings. Janneke, a female Dutch squatter, frustrated with her housemates, told me that they were "weird. They're not real squatters. They're more like anti-squatters. They party all the time and go to Mainstream bars. They don't do anything for anyone."

Within the movement, the negative identification continues in which different groups of squatters identify themselves against other groups of squatters, whose differentiations are based on a complicated matrix of style, ideological commitment, and expression of political conviction. In addition, the community where I conducted my fieldwork had its own peculiarities and identity in relation to other activist squatter communities in Amsterdam. This community, identified primarily by its neighborhood as is customary for squatters' communities, has a reputation for conducting campaigns by engaging in local housing politics and for "being older and not so punky" as described by Laura, a squatter who is politically active in a more punk-oriented squatters' community. For the purposes of classification, I refer to this community as "the campaigners." Although a number of activist identified squatters in other communities refer to this group disparagingly as "the social democrats," because they engage with political parties. It is from the perspective of members of this community from which I classify other squatters within the scene. Based on the discourse of the campaigners, activist squatters classified themselves mainly against wild squatters, crusty punks, and baby punks. They also mentioned hippies and student squatters but discussed them with a higher sense of respect. Similar to how squatters imagine anti-squatters, these various classifications reflect more about how activist squatters imagine themselves than about the empirical reality of the people who they classify.

Methodologically, this means that the description of these groups are not articulated by squatters, but rather I have compiled and distilled these descriptions from prolonged observation and listening to how activist squatters described these groups in casual conversations. The following conversation between myself and Dana, a veteran squatter, about Bonnie, a twenty-year-old Portuguese squatter, illustrates the types of conversations from which I drew conclusions:

Dana: Where does Bonnie live now?

Nazima: I think she's staying at the Marcusstraat.

Dana: Why isn't she living at the Transvaalstraat? (a squatted house where Bonnie resided for months).

Nazima: I don't know. I guess she moved out.

Dana: She didn't move out. She was KICKED OUT. She's just a little punk.

By calling Bonnie "a little punk," Dana legitimated her dislike of Bonnie and referred to a set of behaviors known as punklike: to constantly party, spend most of the time drunk or high, lack financial responsibility, neglect repairs and household chores, and lack reliability. Lastly, by emphasizing that her housemates kicked her out of the house, Dana showed that Bonnie's behavior was so problematic that it forced them to kick her out, an act that is generally avoided in squatter households. Another example is a conversation that I had with a housemate about a squatter neighbor who had been an adolescent punk but saw himself as an adult bohemian artist well integrated into society:

> **Nazima:** David is worried because Matthijs didn't show up for work today. He called asking about him. Have you seen him?
> **Mindy:** Well, he's probably passed out drunk somewhere from a party last night.
> **Nazima:** That doesn't sound like Matthijs. He always shows up to work.
> **Mindy:** Well, not really. You never know. At the end of the day, he's a punk.

In this case, by referring to Matthijs as a punk, the term encompasses behavior such as unreliability and irresponsibility (not showing up for work) and excessive drunkenness (passing out). Mindy also suggests that despite Matthijs's adult identity, beneath the exterior, lies a punk. The following descriptions of internal others within the squatters movement is information that I have deduced from countless conversations such as these.

Wild squatters

Wild squatters are squatters who do not consult with a kraakspreekuur before squatting a house and who locate themselves outside the movement. The stereotype of wild squatters are that they are not Dutch and originate mainly from Eastern Europe. Activist squatters see them as marginal, often alcohol or drug addicted, and disorganized. Once, immigrant youth hired by the immigrant owner attacked a house taken over by wild squatters. The wild squatters went to an active and political squat for help who refused to assist because they were wild. The situation escalated, leading to the wild squatters fleeing the building, a riot between the police and the immigrant youth, and the police arresting the youth and jailing them for several days. When describing the incident, Maaike, an activist Dutch squatter, commented, "The whole incident was very shameful for us, the squatters in the neighborhood." Maaike's shame derives from a discursive solidarity that activist squatters have with people who live in a neighborhood where they squat, especially immigrant neighbors.

Wild squatters are seen as not active in the political spectrum of the movement. They do not campaign nor do they resist evictions, which in practical terms means that wild squatters occupy a space for as long as possible, but leave as soon as pressure arises. They are not considered a part of the solidarity network in the squatters movement. Yet, wild squatters often use the squatters alarm phone tree for emergencies and organized squatters equivocate on helping them. Although wild squatters are absent in the political life of the movement, they participate in its social life. In the north of Amsterdam, there are massive industrial buildings and warehouses that are wild squatted, known as party squats that host enormous techno party featuring prodigious amounts of drugs.

Crusty punks

Crusty punks are in a separate category from wild squatters because although activist squatters imagine that all wild squatters are crusty punks, a significant number of squatters within the organized squatters movement are also crusty punks. Activist squatters use the word "punks" as a short-hand to refer to squatters as a group, although they distinguish between who and what behaviors are authentically punk. Being punk refers primarily to a clothing style and attitude, such as wearing all black, sporting a number of piercings, tattoos, and wearing ripped clothing. "Squatters with dogs," a term used by the Amsterdam media to describe crusty, foreign squatters is another synonym for crusty punks.

To be crusty refers to being dirty on a bodily level by showering infrequently, laundering rarely, and residing in filthy spaces. Often punks are crusty but some people who look *netjes* (decent) are quite crusty without appearing dirty. The term summarizes a whole set of assumptions. Crust, crusty, and sometimes, punk, are synonymous for someone who is generally seen as lazy, disorganized, and irresponsible (see earlier story about Ernst who bathed himself –infrequently– with a hose in the backyard of his squat). A crust is most likely an alcoholic and possibly some type of drug addict, exemplified by waking up and spending the day drinking, partying all night, and intermittently earning a salary through wage labor. Crusty punks are defined by how much they do not care.

If punks live in a group, they hang out together and feed themselves by skipping food and dumpster diving. They frequent squatter bars and cafes to eat and drink because these spaces are cheap and depend on voluntary donations for food. Crusty punks can easily succeed in not paying for their food in squatter cafes because people who run the kitchens rarely ask them to pay. If the cook regularly requests payment, they stop patronizing such spaces. I know this from having worked as a cook at a voku in which I witnessed how crusty punks avoided paying and how they reacted when I asked them to pay.

Despite the lack of responsibility and accountability of crusty punks, many manage to organize themselves to squat houses with a kraakspreekuur.

As noted earlier, squatting with the kraakspreekuur means that comply-
ing with the multiple requirements to gather sufficient information before
squatting a house. Kraakspreekuren are neighborhood based and one in
particular works best with crusty punks. This neighborhood squats the
most in the city but also has the most evictions, which some squatters cri-
tique is the consequence of lack of adequate preparation. Although crusty
punks have a reputation for lacking interest in campaigning or research,
many crusty punks have substantial squatter capital through formidable
building skills, their efforts in creating social spaces (especially bars), and
by their solidarity with other squatters through mutual aid and sharing
resources. I lived in a community of crusty punks and although my style of
dressing and habitus characterized me at best as a student, and at worst as
a yuppie, my punk neighbors treated me kindly and were available to help
when I needed it.

Crusty punks who are recognized by others as political and see them-
selves as political activists are known for their willingness to participate
in potentially violent actions, their enthusiasm for rioting, and the pleas-
ure that they experience in fighting the police. The skill to riot is one that
is highly valued, as noted earlier, and leads to increased squatter capital.
However, for people who organize violent actions and riots, relying on the
participation of crusty punks in an action proves challenging, so that their
lack of dependability diminishes their squatter capital.

Baby punks

Baby punks are yet another group of punks, some of whom are also crusts.
The difference between baby punks and crusty punks is that baby punks are
defined by a combination of their lifestyle and their identities as political
activists in the movement while crusty punks are mainly known for their
lifestyle. Crusty punks may be identified as crusty out of laziness. For exam-
ple, by failing to connect the water pipes and build a shower due to a lack
of interest or energy. In contrast, a baby punk may claim to be crusty out
of political conviction by stating that it's unhealthy to shower frequently
and environmentally irresponsible to waste water. According to Jurgen, a
veteran Dutch squatter, "The term baby punk arose because all of a sudden
in the scene, there was a flood of young punks who were very politically
active. The next generation that followed are called embryo punks." Jurgen
also claimed that the term intends primarily to name this specific generation
rather than a style of being punk. I have encountered the term to reflect a
combination of age, attitude, and lifestyle.

Baby punks refer to people who are young, either adolescent or barely
adolescent, and have chosen to become squatter punks. Baby punks express
enthusiasm about fighting, learning, and inhabiting the tropes of the squatter

world, and then reifying this identity in a confrontational way to the rest of the squatters' scene. This attitude, often called dogmatic by squatters who were not baby punks, is compared to punks who feel more comfortable in their identity without feeling a need to prove themselves. Being a baby punk is a life of evictions, squatting actions, anti-fascist and other political actions, noise demonstrations, getting arrested during actions, the labor and time intensive process of squatting a house and making it livable, parties, vokus, information evenings, giveaways shops, and day cafes. It's a life entirely in the movement with its waves of stability and instability.

I encountered the term "baby punks" in a number of contexts. The first time was at a party where I sat with a group of squatters inhaling speed. Since I felt nervous, one woman present joked to the rest, "She's like a baby punk." This comment refers to a bundle of meanings. First, to the naivety and lack of experience of baby punks shown most in how they first react to the quotidian act of drug use. Second, to the incongruity of the image of the baby punk in contrast to myself, an utterly non-punk PhD student in my thirties.

Another time, I sat with a former housemate, discussing Geert, a Dutch squatter in his thirties who often lectured us on how he enjoyed attending anti-fascist actions to beat up fascists. Maaike commented, "He's so annoying these days. He's like a baby punk." In this case, baby punk indicated the banality of someone who finds violence pleasurable and uses it to show his toughness to increase his squatter capital. Maaike mocked Geert as well since the term baby punk connotes a temporary phase that eventually should end for someone to develop and mature in the movement and that Geert, a man in his thirties, should have overcome such a stage. Once, I drank coffee with Stephen, a punk neighbor (not crusty or baby). I handed him a coffee with milk and he said, "Oh no, you have infected my coffee with that disgusting cow's milk." I replied, "I didn't realize you were vegan. Do you want coffee without milk?" He then said, "I'm just kidding. I don't care." His joke was intended for those inside the scene, mocking dogmatic baby punks. To act "dogmatic" means to express a particular form of zeal in which one verbally criticizes those who do not share consumption decisions that symbolize political convictions (vegetarianism, veganism, animal rights, environmental protection).

Last, baby punks are well known for their enthusiasm for potentially violent actions. This love for violence is also a trait of crusty punks, but baby punks are more reliable. For example, in 2007, radical left youth from all over Europe participated in riots in Copenhagen, Denmark about the upcoming demolition of a social center. At the time, I noticed that almost none of the campaigners had gone yet the riots were full of Amsterdam squatters. I asked why and received the two word answer: "Baby punks." The campaigners discounted the baby punks' participation because they saw it as a phase of expressing the fury of youth that they had already overcome.

Hippies

Hippie activists and student squatters are members of the activist and squatters' scene but have higher statuses because of their openly transient participation in the movement. The stereotypes that campaigners hold of hippies are that they tend to originate from outside the Netherlands, that they attend political and squatting actions regularly, are primarily active in the radical environmentalist movement, and actively promote vegetarianism or veganism. Hippies often display a "hippie" fashion style that is not punk, Mainstream, or yuppie. This fashion style refers to wearing loosely fitted clothing with bright colors in an Indo-West cut, possibly with dreadlocks. The classification of "hippies" include people who work at direct action-oriented, small NGOs based in Amsterdam, such as ASEED, a European environmental action group, and EYFA, the European Youth For Action. Such organizations offer low-paid or stipend-based volunteer positions. As a result, internationals who work for them often live in squats and then integrate into the social scene of activists.

Traveling is a constitutive aspect of being classified as a hippie. They often travel to attend action camps, such as a climate camp or a no-border camp, or to riot in large-scale alterglobalization actions such as the G8. They travel widely, connecting with other activists and often visit regions in the Global South – which the radical left laud as autonomous, such as Oaxaca, Mexico – and the squatted, organized areas of post-economic crisis Argentina. Although hippies form part of the squatters movement because they often squat for housing, squatting does not define their activist identities. Squatting had not brought them into the international, leftist, alterglobalization movement; that network led them into squatting. Regardless, activist hippies play important roles in the scene, organizing benefit parties for various autonomous groups in the Global South in squatted social centers, attending parties, working in social centers, and regularly attending vokus.

In addition to clothing style and their way of participating in the squatters movement, activist hippies tend to have a gentler and kinder demeanor than squatter punks. Hippie activists tend to act more physically affectionate, smile more, and attempt to treat others more inclusively.

Miles, an Irish squatter who originally moved to Amsterdam to work for a grass-roots NGO and then became gradually more involved in the squatters' scene until he left the activist hippie network completely, commented, "When I first became a squatter, I was shocked by how mean everyone was. The antiglobalization scene is much nicer. The Dutch squatters are more macho. It took me some time to get used to it." The activist hippies are almost entirely women. Although activist hippies behave as violently in riots and actions as squatters, they refrain from discussing this behavior. They generally are arrested but downplay the experience as quotidian rather than a way to accrue squatter capital.

The term hippie activist includes those who participate in direct actions for refugees, international human rights, and environmental issues. People who regularly participate in actions and are part of such networks but do not squat often refer to "the scene" as the activist scene or activist community rather than the squatters' scene. Although the activist scene and the squatters' scene socially seem to comprise "the scene," a division exists. The activist scene is more international in addition to the core of Dutch people. It is also more transient. The Dutch squatters' scene (versus the Polish and Spanish) is more stable. Those in the former (which includes non-Dutch people) have long histories together built through the intense cycles of squatting a house, living together, creating communities, campaigning, and getting evicted.

Student squatters

Student squatters belong to the second category of openly transient members of the movement. A separate student kraakspreekuur serves the university population. A squatter is classified as a student due to their style and habitus more than the actual fact of being a student since many punks also study in the Dutch higher education system. Student squatters who function as activists in the movement are perceived as squatting to solve their housing problem and out of a sense of conviction equally. The perception of student squatters is that they are ambitious and by default, in the movement temporarily since by studying, it is assumed that they will move on to another phase of professional life. Despite the fact that for most squatters, their involvement in the movement is a phase, student squatters are characterized by the transparency in which squatting is short term in their biographies. Yet, this transience does not diminish their squatter capital. Student squatters who are activists are taken seriously and seen as valuable members of the movement versus those who squat for housing but do not contribute to the movement. Student squatter activists do not need to constantly perform their conviction because the mere fact of participating in the movement attests to their conviction since the majority of students choose to anti-squat over squatting.

Yuppies, neighbors, immigrants, and undocumented people

The final section of this chapter regards activist squatters' relationship with the people with whom they live side by side in a neighborhood. I hesitate to call them "neighbors" because squatters imagine "neighbors" differently from those they classify as "yuppies" who are also factually their neighbors. Squatters consider yuppies nearly identically to how they imagine anti-squatters, that is, white, Dutch, middle-class, university educated, working professionals, and Mainstream, except that yuppies are older homeowners who often have families. Squatters despise yuppies, viewing them as agents of gentrification who push low-income people, including squatters, out of the city. This feeling of threat derives from the Amsterdam municipal policy to transform the city from a majority of renters to a majority of owners by selling a substantial percentage of social housing as private condominiums. Although squatters articulate this hatred of yuppies within a context of urban policy, squatters mainly express their quotidian repulsion in relation to micro levels of consumption characterized as "yuppie."

For example, Jens, a Dutch squatter, once mentioned to me that he works full time to support his "yuppie lifestyle." This code referred to a lifestyle in which he regularly consumes in Mainstream restaurants and bars. This behavior contrasts with how squatters are expected to consume in the movement by eating, drinking, and partying entirely in squatter bars and cafes while simultaneously articulating an anti-consumption and anti-capitalist rhetoric. By openly admitting that he lived a yuppie lifestyle, Jens demonstrated his ironic awareness that other squatters judge his preferences. He also attempts to prevent a critique of his lifestyle from the person with whom he speaks, in this case, me.

This conversation reveals how every expression, whether it's overtly political or on the minuscule level of consumption, becomes fraught because it's always measured against an invisible but ever-present subcultural public opinion. While I was a squatter, I regularly went to a cafe well known in Amsterdam for being beautiful and relatively expensive. Squatters considered this a "yuppie cafe." Once, I ran into a few squatters in front of this cafe. As I was about to enter, they said, "What are you doing here? Are you actually going in there (pointing to the cafe)?" I genuinely felt embarrassed since I was aware that I should not frequent yuppie cafes.

Versus the threat of the white, middle-class, yuppie, the discursive "neighbor" is thoroughly working class and can be either white Dutch or working-class immigrants mainly from Turkey or Morocco. While calling someone a yuppie is an insult and a term of contempt, referring to them as neighbors reflects a relationship of attempted solidarity – whether or not such solidarity exists. Squatters who communicate with the neighbors and work with them together on campaigns receive respect and accrue squatter capital. As in many aspects of squatter capital, this valorization signifies that it is generally unusual for squatters to put energy into creating good relationships with their neighbors.

Squatters often mythologize "the neighborhood" as the honorable working poor or the unfairly marginalized immigrants. They idealize "the neighbors" as people with whom they purport to share the same financial, housing, and labor struggles. Yet this presumed solidarity is fragile because working-class people and migrants jolt squatters into an uncomfortable self-awareness. Their structural marginalization leads squatters to feel guilty in the awareness that their oppositional identities and marginal living are acts of privilege. As a result, the presumed solidarity usually only exists in an imaginary realm since it often falls apart during actual interactions with neighbors, especially when the ideologies of the neighbors clash with those of squatters.

The contradiction between who squatters classify as a neighbor versus a yuppie lends insight into the fraught nature of naming and the ease of contempt. Squatters can hate yuppies because they believe that they understand the totality of who a yuppie is and what a yuppie represents. Such a person becomes frozen symbolically as a Mainstream, consuming fiend. Neighbors, on the other hand, create problems for classification when their ideologies clash with squatters. Because the squatters idealize the neighbors, they have difficulty handling the neighbors' behavior that squatters ideologically oppose including sexism, racism, and religious fundamentalism. Regarding immigrants, a silenced tension and totalizing paralysis exists between squatters and their immigrant neighbors. The squatters realize, but refuse to acknowledge, their relative privileges of whiteness, European-ness, class, and the multiple entitlements that allow them to live on the margins to reject the Mainstream. The combination of the guilt of privilege and the ideal of presumed solidarity masks the ever-present tension and anxiety in relations between squatters and the neighbors.

Once, when I was cooking at a squatter cafe, Dino, a punk Portuguese squatter with considerable squatter capital, entered the kitchen to hang out with the cooking team. He related a story about how one day, a neighbor came to the door of his squat to complain about the noise. She said to Dino, "You squatters come here to our country, make a huge mess, and don't respect anyone. Go back to your country." Dino responded (and he related this detail to us proudly), "Look at you, with your black skin. You're not even originally from Europe." He then shut the door in the neighbor's face. The other squatters listened to this story, sat in silence, and didn't respond to Dino's racism nor the neighbor's xenophobia. The silence reflects a rupture: the squatters were disturbed by the neighbor's aggression towards the squatters; however, Dino's xenophobia was also prohibited in the movement.

Another afternoon, I sat with a few squatters on the balcony of their house. One of the squatters was black Surinamese. We watched as Moroccan Dutch boys on the street made gorilla noises at the black parking officers issuing tickets to the cars on the street. The Surinamese squatter felt offended so one of the white Dutch squatters (to support her) yelled to the boys, "Fuck off goat fuckers."

These are exceptional moments in which, in response to xenophobic and racist behavior from neighbors, squatters use the same language back to attack. However, normally, during such incidents of conflict, squatters fail to respond due to discomfort interacting with people who are in a more vulnerable structural position. As a result, they are unable to communicate directly and with hostility towards those classified as neighbors and migrants.

I have witnessed, during a number of squatting actions, working-class immigrant boys screamingly mock squatters and make sexual remarks to squatter women. With few exceptions, squatters generally respond by ignoring the boys. Once, Jop, a Dutch squatter, scolded the youth, "Why don't you bring your sister with the veil to our squat?" Afterward, squatters circulated and laughed at this comment, but in general, the anxiety producing interactions between squatters and immigrants are unacknowledged and silenced. If the people who screamed abusively at the squatters or yelled sexual comments to the women were Dutch and middle class, the same squatters who stood silent would have responded more aggressively, and then retold the incident later at squatter bars.

This paralyzing silence includes uncomfortable interactions when white, working-class Dutch neighbors express ideologies that counter those of squatters. Damien, a French squatter who, exceptionally among squatters, actively maintains relationships with his neighbors, found himself arguing with two working-class, white neighbors about an Amsterdam city policy to randomly block areas in predominantly immigrant neighborhoods and search residents for weapons and identification. The neighbors supported the policy, felt safer as a result of it, and agreed with the police's authority to randomly search people in public spaces. Damien espoused the opinion of members of the left activist community who opposed the policy as racist because it targeted immigrants, violated individual privacy, and increased the police's authority. Although Damien argued his points with these neighbors, if he had considered them to be "yuppies," he would have confronted them openly, angrily demolished their arguments and gleefully torn apart their lifestyles. Since these were white, working-class neighbors, he did not argue with them and was instead silent, dismissing their points of view as not worthy of rebuttal. Again, Damien's silence and refrain from dismantling the working-class neighbors reflected his awareness of his higher social position such as his education, his verbal skills, and his class.

In another incident, in which squatters received assistance from their neighbors while squatting a house, the white, working-class neighbor expressed racism by complaining about the dominance of non-white people in the city. Of the two squatters who heard this, one became upset and reported it to the others in the group, while the other squatter denied that the neighbor had made such statements. This was another example of a rupture. One squatter reacted within the norms of the community by reporting the neighbor's remarks to communicate her unsuitability as a partner for political actions. The other squatter's denial reflected a desire to continue working with the neighbor, with the understanding that if he were to classify her as a racist, he would no longer be able to collaborate with her due to political untrustworthiness.

The anxiety around the inability to perform hostility pertains also to legal and undocumented immigrants from the Global South within the movement.

For example, at one squatter party, I watched as Diane, a French squatter woman of Tunisian parentage, sat drunk on a table and flirted with Marcos, a Dutch squatter whose squatter capital is comprised of his enthusiasm for rioting violently against the police and beating up fascists. Squatter parties tend to have a diverse but standard mix of squatters, students, residents of legalized squats, people who identify themselves as activists, and random people who hang out in the squatters' scene.

At this party, a man in his forties, who regularly attends squatter parties, brought his friend, a Moroccan immigrant in his late thirties. This man then approached Diane to flirt with her, I presume, partially because of her looks and partially because she was one of the few non-white people present. Diane, inebriated and interested in someone else, ignored him. The man then became angry and called Diane an ugly bitch. She then turned to Marcos and told him what the Moroccan man had said to her.

I watched Marcos, who usually revels in violence, caught in a conundrum since he suddenly did not know how to behave. If he acted by telling the immigrant to leave, then he would be behaving in a way that others could interpret as macho and racist, which is prohibited by the scene. He would also be acting aggressively against one of the three non-white people at the party, which was actually a relatively high number for a squatter party. Finally, after Diane pushed him several times to act on her behalf, he then encouraged Diane to inform the barperson if she wanted to throw the man out. The barperson approached the man, who left before being asked to leave.

In this context, this was the optimal solution because it fit in with the DIY philosophy, in which a woman should Do-It-Herself and resolve a problem on her own initiative rather than rely on a man to solve a problem, especially one related to sexist behavior. Marcos avoided the macho role and the ensuing gossip that would have inevitably charged him with racism and sexism if he interacted with the man. By placing the responsibility to resolve the problem with the bartender, the situation developed into an ideological matter in which a squatted space advertises itself as promoting a woman's right to safely express her sexuality and prohibit unwelcome attention upon women by men.

Conclusion

Authenticity as a status in the squatters movement is complicated, fraught, and full of contradictions. I have posited that to understand who and what the ideal squatter is, it's important to first understand squatter capital and to explore the external and internal Others in the social world of the movement. With the external others of the police, the press, and the Mainstream, the roles are clearly performative and institutionalized, to the extent that squatters and their external Others use each other for their own means. Whether it's the police using the squatters' supposed resistance as an excuse not to spend energy in evicting or jeopardizing their vacation plans, or the press calling the squatters' press group and asking for inside information on upcoming actions on a slow news day. The hatred of anti-squatters reveals squatters' intimate knowledge of the demographic profile of anti-squatters. The ensuing revulsion of anti-squatters persists despite the myriad of contradictions within the squatter/anti-squatter dichotomy as well as the heterogeneity of anti-squatters to include people with whom squatter feel an affinity and solidarity.

The internal Others reveal similar contradictions and negotiations. Wild squatters are dismissed for their total rejection of the movement, their lack of ideological conviction in squatting, and their exploitation of movement solidarity networks for their own purposes. Crusty punks represent an uncontrolled excess of parties, drugs, alcohol, and violence and whose strengths cannot be reliably channeled to promote the movement's goals. Baby punks are too eager to prove themselves as political activists to be taken seriously and, therefore, lack the subtle habitus of mastery and rejection of radical left lifestyle choices that mark a mature and sophisticated squatter. Student squatters and hippies are not disparaged because they are transient and are not invested in being authentic squatters. Their social and professional opportunities and commitments outside the movement gloss their participation as acts of conviction, giving them squatter capital compared to those who retreat into the movement because of their inability to function in the Mainstream. The hostility towards yuppies is similar to the hatred of anti-squatters, revealing an uncomfortable mirror of squatter's tastes and lifestyle outside the movement. Finally, neighbors and undocumented people due to their excess of authenticity, disrupt squatters' constant oppositionality and thus, can never actually be taken seriously in the movement. In a movement where the performative pose is one of articulated hostility and argued dogma, the uncomfortable silence temporarily dismantles the social world.

Notes

1   A kraakspreekuur, literally translates as squatting information hour, functions as a squatters advisory service. A group of people, often squatters or ex-squatters, host a weekly drop in service at a social center located in a squat or legalized squat. Anyone who wants to learn about squatting or needs assistance in squatting a house will meet with the kraakspreekuur for information and advice. They are self-organized and not funded by an external organization.

2   A heavy and enormous metallic construction beam that squatters use to barricade doors against the police which are often "found" on construction sites.

3   The alterglobalization movement was an anti-capitalist social movement that focused on direct action and large-scale international protests at international summits from the late 1990s through the first decade of 2010. It was defined

by being loosely structured, multinational, anti-hierarchical, and in its use of mediagenic direct actions against corporate symbols, such as Starbucks coffee shops.

4   Also, based on my observation, male builders tend to be shy, socially awkward, and eager to help anyone, especially women. This reflects how the movement welcomes people, especially men, who have manual and technical skills.

5   The squats where Germaine lived had reputations for being "active." Alisa, a Norwegian squatter, knows Germaine through squatting and animal rights activism. In the following passage, she describes Germaine's first squatted house, called "the Rivierenstraat" (most squats are referred to by their street names), its reputation as an "active squat," and how the squatters community viewed its residents: Alisa: "Yes, the Rivierenstraat. It was like, oooh, the Rivierenstraat. That's what people said if you went there … Because everyone who lived there was really skilled and really active. They knew a lot. You could always ask questions about how to repair something, or how to deal with the gas company, or legal questions."

6   My argument that non-instrumental acts of bravery lack functional practicality is controversial among social movement scholars, particularly those who specialize in the alterglobalization movement. Juris (2005) argues that "performative violence" during summit protests have a number of purposes. They are pragmatic because violence attracts press coverage, which eventually brings attention to activists and their political demands. Due to the squatters movement's history in Amsterdam, the press attention to violence by squatter activists differs significantly. Juris also contends that, "Young militants … generated potent oppositional identities and communicated a radical anti- systemic critique by enacting prototypical scenes of youth rebellion against the symbols of global capitalism and the state" (Juris 2005: 15). I agree that for these particular activists, performative violence serves to generate anti-capitalist, anarchist, oppositional identities. However, I find that identities that are formed based on European and white privileges which enable such activists to, by and large, protest violently without deadly consequences – and to operate without reflecting on their privileges – to be hegemonic rather than anti-systemic.

7   A noise demonstration is an action in which a group goes to a jail and makes noise to support people who have been arrested for squatting or other political actions.

8   During squatting actions there is a dance between the squatters and the police in which the subtext plays out for whether police want to expend the energy to evict. The logic for a large crowd at squatting actions is to deter the police from evicting immediately. Squatters assume that the police are not interested in making the effort to evict in the first place and will easily allow the matters to enter into the realm of legality, courts, and paperwork. However, it's a precarious assumption that depends on the mood of the police officers. On days when police officers in training witness how to handle a squatting action, the police officers who are teaching are more violent and imposing than when they are on normal duty.

9   This statement is not true but reflects dominant discourse that claims that squatters were no longer young, white, leftist ideologically motivated, Dutch activists and that the tactic had been hijacked by foreigners and poor people.

2

The habitus of emotional sovereignty

The following conversation occurred among a small group sitting in a private bedroom at approximately 3 a.m. at a squatters' party.

> **Samuel:** Well, you know how Lianne is. She's really shallow. She's very annoying. That woman is impossible. There's something kinky about her though. I want to dominate her skinny ass and fuck the hell out of that mean bitch.
>
> **Nazima:** What is so appealing about her? What does she have?
>
> **Hermance:** Well … I asked Hans once, you know Hans, breaker Hans, with the big hands and the tools, he lives in a big legalized squat in the West. The two of them have had a thing for years. I asked him, why doesn't he let her go after all of these years? He said that she likes to have the kind of sex that he likes.
>
> **Nazima:** What does that mean? What kind of sex?
>
> Hermance shook her head in a gesture of playful ignorance along with the other two women beside her: I don't know. I didn't want to know. I just ended the conversation there.
>
> From across the small room, Lucy, a British squatter, drunk and laughing, yelled: Don't pretend you don't know what it means. You're not fooling anyone. It means she likes it fast, hard, and up the ass.
>
> We all laughed.

In the squatters' subcultures, only "real" or authentic squatters can inhabit positions of authority. Since being an authentic squatter is already fraught with unstated behavioral and stylistic expectations, I contend that to hold a position of disavowed authority, the criteria for which I will detail presently, is even more contentious. As stated earlier, achieving authenticity as a squatter is a double process of exhibiting a number of skills and competencies that accumulate squatter capital in addition to being recognized by others as "real" or authentic by exhibiting mastery and rejection of acknowledged systems of taste and values as well as by negatively identifying against various groups.

Similarly, to inhabit authority entails the double process of an individual demonstrating a set of competencies and being recognized by others as a figure of authority through a vicious and dismantling discourse. The first section of this chapter focuses mainly on the types of skills, competencies, habitus, and performances that constitute authority. The second part concentrates on how squatters distinguish authority figures by eviscerating the individuals in question through gossip, and examines the significance of the attention that is paid by squatters to the sexual practices of those in positions of authority, as illustrated by the opening anecdote.

Previously, I presented a matrix of skills and styles of identity-making performances necessary to enable a sense of inhabiting the ideal of the authentic squatter. Squatter capital, specific skills and the differential prestige that one gains by excelling in such skills, describes the unspoken value system of the internal social world of the squatters movement, what Bourdieu describes as understanding the subcategories of practice that pertain to distinctive properties of a field. To achieve a sense of authenticity, one must demonstrate that one has mastered and rejected tastes and values, both mainstream and those associated with the radical left. In addition, one should render invisible and natural a long, arduous, and self-conscious process of socialization and skill acquisition. Thus, regardless of the diversity of reasons why squatters squat, their political motivations, attitudes and their structural differences, the silent ideal of "a real squatter" exists. This archetype haunts those who are invested in belonging to the community, making many squatters feel inadequate and pushing them to perform this ideal, resulting in a social world full of discomforting contradictions.

In this chapter, I explore these discomforting contradictions further and describe how authority functions in a subculture that rejects authority. I argue that squatters who hold authority have (1) mastered over time many of the skills that comprise squatter capital, especially the prestigious skill of strategic manipulation; (2) hold positions of cultural centrality in the Mainstream; (3) should comfortably assert a persona in the movement as an articulate, assertive, and aggressive public speaker both within the movement and in the Mainstream; and finally (4) perform an emotional sovereignty and social autonomy from the movement and the community. Such a performance communicates that a person appears to sovereignly choose participating in the movement rather than being so marginal in the Mainstream that they have no other choice but to exist within the squatter subculture. With these criteria in mind, squatters who have authority often, though not exclusively, are highly educated with middle to upper-class backgrounds.

Furthermore, with the understanding of these criteria for holding authority in this subculture, I consider the ambiguity of the characteristics that comprise the position of being "cultural central." I argue that the classification of culturally central requires deeper ethnographic understandings of centrality and marginality, since the terms mutually define each other. In the context of a social movement organization, understanding the impact of participants' backgrounds on the activities of the movement allows one to examine the invisible logic of why and how more culturally central people, who possess a number of resources needed by a movement, accumulate capital and become authority figures. What Bourdieu classifies as the invisible logic of political participation, in which people who are structurally disadvantaged often abstain or delegate their opinions to those who feel more entitled to participate, is revealed when a culturally marginal person attempts to take a position of authority in a squatters' defense campaign.

To illustrate these points, I present the case of Shirin and Jenny, two "authentic" female squatters from opposite cultural and class backgrounds who were members of the same squatters group. Residing in different living groups within a squatted complex, they could have avoided each other entirely. However, due to both women's ideological commitment to fight the eviction of their house, they were forced to work together on the house's defense.

Despite the energy and extensive time that she had invested in the house's defense, Shirin, the child of working-class, Muslim immigrants lacked authority in the group due to her cultural marginality that stemmed from a lack of skills and uncontrolled aggression. In contrast, Jenny, who espoused a commitment to anti-hierarchy and anti-authority, was the de facto person in charge of the houses' legal defense. This status derived from Jenny's cultural centrality via her substantial skill-set and her sense of ease in the world, originating in part from her upper-class Dutch habitus.

To complicate Bourdieu's overly deterministic argument that fuses the ability to participate politically with one's class and gender, I also present two cases of working-class, white, Dutch, culturally central squatters who have status as authority figures in the movement. Both were socialized in the movement and mastered all elements of squatter capital. Furthermore, they mobilized their working-class Dutch habitus to form a bond between themselves and Dutch politicians as well as surreptitiously critique the tacit middle-class assumptions of the backstage of the squatters' scene.

Furthermore, in a community that rejects authority, a fundamental characteristic of having authority is to fervently deny that such informal hierarchies exist. In fact, anyone who proclaims themselves an authority is most likely a marginal figure. Authority in an anti-authoritarian community can only be acknowledged circuitously via gossip rather than explicitly and transparently. As a result, gossip is the most effective means to identify who has the most authority and serves to reify rather than undermine authority.

Gossip, and particularly gossip about sexual practices that is expressed in an anti-romantic modality, reveals a homosocial dynamic and a transaction of desire that is compelled by a habitus of emotional sovereignty that authority figures possess. This emotional sovereignty is an essential element in asymmetrical and non-reciprocal relationships that authority figures have with members of the movement. This asymmetrical relationship is characterized by the dynamic in which authority figures receive love and are needed by all members of the group but only require and express love for the total group collectivity rather than any single individual.

Moreover, anti-romantic sexual gossip enables a misogynistic homosocial dynamic. The ethnographic portraits of two so-called *kraakbonzen* (squatter bosses), Dominic and Damien, both from upper-class backgrounds, their biographies, their habitus of emotional sovereignty, the gossip that surround them, and the aggression targeted towards their girlfriends, illustrate these points.

The last part of this chapter relates the story of Ludwic who serves as an example of a failure of authority and a foil for the portraits of successful authority. Ludwic, an authentic squatter, possesses many of the skills that comprise squatter capital, but never learned to master and reject with the middle-class grace required to receive respect in the movement. Despite his squatter capital, a number of factors such as his working-class taste and habitus, his cultural marginality, his proclamation of himself as an authority figure, and his obsessive gossiping about the other kraakbonzen, reduce his credibility and prevent his recognition as an authority figure.

Figure 2.1 A squat on the Spuistraat in the center of Amsterdam, 2006

Cultural marginality and centrality

Shirin and Jenny were members of a group of thirty squatters who occupied four houses in a row, each house containing three apartments and a ground floor space, known eventually in the squatters' scene as the Motorflex block. These houses were originally social housing apartments owned by a housing corporation that had decided to demolish the houses to build more spacious, luxury condominiums. The process of relocating the original tenants to empty the houses lasted a number of years. By the time all the apartments were emptied of renters, the housing corporation covered the apartment doors and windows in metal, known as sitex, to prevent them from being squatted. They were squatted anyway.

Due to the enormity of this block of houses, the number of doors that had to be broken open simultaneously with motor flexes (handheld circular saw wheels that cut through metal), and the high possibility of police violence, the squatting action required the presence of an unusually immense group of people to protect the people breaking open the door and to dissuade the police from interfering since the majority of the apartments had been empty for less than a year (rather than for a year or longer, per standard practice). With over one hundred people present, the action succeeded smoothly and without delays. Four breakers with handheld motor flexes cut through the sitex and opened the doors within minutes. With the noise and the sparks from the motor flexes cutting through the metal, the door breaking was highly performative and, "so cool," extolled Stijn, a nineteen-year-old squatter who was learning how to be a breaker.

Three different living groups resided in the Motorflex houses. Self-identified punks who were referred to by their neighbors simply as "the punks" – both crusty and baby – resided in the two center houses. They shared a living room and kitchen between the two neighboring buildings. The members of this punk living group had considerable squatter capital. Most were veteran squatters who could build, break, and especially excelled in non-instrumental acts of bravery by enthusiastically participating in confrontations with the police and faithfully attending actions for radical left causes (anti-fur, animal rights, anti-fascism, women's rights, immigrants' rights, refugee support). The punk squatters were not expected to have organizational or strategic manipulation skills. "The expertise of the punks in the Motorflex was rioting and they did it well," joked Marie, a squatter with extensive campaign experience.

Within a week of squatting the block, the punks had built a punk bar in one of their storefronts, named "Motorflex," with lettering in the style of a 1980s heavy metal album cover. Open two nights a week, this bar was renowned for "old school" punk behavior: all night usage of drugs, drinking, partying, and among the more aggressive, crusty punks, bar fights. When the

Surinamese take-out restaurant of one of the building's storefronts vacated, the punks immediately squatted it to create a new voku, named, "Op-Roti" (Roti is a popular Surinamese take-out food in Amsterdam and Rot Op means Fuck off). According to Jop, an ex-squatter active in the scene for fifteen years, "The Motorflex house is great. It's old school. We need to have that kind of thing around these days with all the *vertrutting* going on, even in the squatters' scene" (*vertrutting* refers to gentrification as well as a larger societal shift towards more restrictive and conventional morality and behavior in the Amsterdam public sphere).

In the outer two buildings of the housing block, resided living groups whose lifestyles were decidedly not punk. One group consisted of a number of veteran squatters with squatter capital with a range of capabilities and were all known as "active" squatters. Marlous, a member of this living group, teased the punks' reputation for violent and noisy partying: "Our group lives in the building on the outer edge in order to serve as a protective sound buffer between the punk houses and those of the neighbors." Jenny, another member of the group for whom this was her first experience as a squatter, joked, "We have about six people living in this group, versus next door. I have no idea how many punks, girlfriends of punks, and random guests are living there. Its chaos over there."

Each member of this living group possessed different elements of squatter capital. Most had squatted several times in the past or at least were "active" in the scene by attending radical left political actions, parties, and hanging out in squats. The veteran squatters in the group had organized and participated in various squatter campaigns and action squats.[1] They had experience managing the press, the legal landscape of squatting and strategic manipulation, and reveled in non-instrumental acts of bravery. Despite their squatter capital, most of the group felt uninterested in investing effort into "defending the house" when it was threatened with eviction. Along with the punks, most of this group felt satisfied with allowing the lifetime of the Motorflex block to depend on a series of legal actions, understanding that eviction would follow after losing the court cases. "The people who lived in the Motorflex block were political, very political, although the house wasn't," remarked Damien, a veteran squatter from the kraakspreekuur. "The Motorflex block project was a failure," criticized Jeremy, a member of the squatter's research collective. Marie scoffed at the Motorflex block squatters:

It's fake politics. There was no coordinated defense of that block. They didn't campaign. They never worked on the actual problem of that house as a symbol of the housing corporations selling off social housing and turning them into yuppie condominiums. They depended on a series of court cases filed by a guy who has a foundation that tries to preserve working-class architectural monuments. Eviction was inevitable. That's not politics, that's laziness.

Damien explained further, "The Motorflex houses were politically useless. They were just a bunch of loud punks."

The fourth house on the outer edge of the Motorflex block was characterized by the presence of Shirin. Shirin grew up in Turkey and immigrated to Germany as a young girl. Her family had moved to Dusseldorf, an industrial city, when she was a small child. They left her in Turkey to be raised by her grandparents while they established themselves in Germany as skilled manual laborers. At twelve, Shirin reunited with her family in Germany. In the late 1970s, Turkish migrants were highly visible and unwelcome in Germany. Despite her light skin and features in which she easily passed as German, Shirin developed a strong immigrant identity.

When Shirin became older, she became involved in the emerging industry of website design. According to Shirin,[2] she burned out due to her excessive success. Eventually, she moved to Amsterdam to create a new life. She became involved in squatting because she could not find an affordable apartment and felt compelled by its alternative cultural underground. She did not look like a "real squatter." She was older, in her early forties, and she dressed Mainstream or even "yuppie" with clean and fitted clothing.

Shirin was often unemployed and struggled financially. She refused to work in her field despite her past success. Identifying as an artist, she struggled to find employment but then rejected jobs that she felt were beneath her capabilities, such as in call centers. She incessantly talked about being broke and yet, spent cash immediately upon receiving it, never saving or paying off her debts. Although physically pretty, her body language and manner of moving had a harsh edge to it that others found aggressive and off-putting.

Shirin was a "real squatter," having earlier squatted a house that had been attacked by fascists. The kraakspreekuur invited her to become a member based on her involvement in the squatting of the Motorflex.[3] Shirin felt honored by the invitation since it implied squatter capital and high levels of competence. She dedicated herself to the squatter community, dutifully attended squatting actions, and participated in strategic meetings of the neighborhood based squatters group.

Despite her involvement in the wider squatters' scene, Shirin was socially isolated from the Motorflex block. The punks resented her for not allowing more people to live in her house and for failing to develop the ground floor of her building into a social or a housing space. The punks' houses were full of residents: punks, their girlfriends (this particular group of punks were all men), plus a number of guests, resulting in eight or more people per building. In contrast, out of four floors, Shirin's house had at most three residents, and often only two, because she ritually threw guests out. Socially, she behaved unpredictably, lashing out at others.

Because Shirin was a member of the kraakspreekuur and given that no one else in the Motorflex group was interested, she took charge of the defense of the house with sincerity and dedication. However, her management of the house's defense further alienated her from the rest of the group. The attitude of the punks towards the house defense was mild interest and support. That is, they were happy that someone in the block took charge of it and would help when presented with a clear plan for their participation. According to Marlous, "The punks are sick of her. If she wants to do something, and she asks for help, they'll do it. Instead, she wants to sit all day in these fucking meetings. The punks hate that."

Shirin's style of management frustrated them because she organized endless meetings to discuss the defense but never presented coherent information or a plan of action. She often dominated in meetings and enjoyed speaking in public, but her interventions proved not pertinent to the topic of discussion. I have sat in meetings with Shirin with other Motorflex squatters in which she made random points. The punks yelled during her comments, "Irrelevant, let's move on," while everyone else in the room groaned when she began to speak. "I cringe every time Shirin speaks. I find her incredibly irritating," says Tamala, who works on a squatting group project with Shirin. After a number of such meetings, the rest of the Motorflex squatters stopped attending Shirin's meetings altogether.

In Shirin's case, having been a member of the original group that squatted the house, Shirin "belonged" automatically. But the nature of that belonging proved problematic because she lacked nearly all the skills that comprise squatter capital and was not respected by the rest of the Motorflex group. Even worse, in the area where she claimed expertise, in strategic manipulation, she simply lacked the capacity to handle the situation which included the ability to understand that, given the complicated nature of the task, it was necessary for her to ask for help from someone who possessed enough skills to assist her.

For over a year, the status of the Motorflex block's defense lay in the hands of Shirin, who busily worked on it but who could not explain its elements, status nor did she have a plan. This changed when the owner, a housing corporation, announced that they were going to file for eviction. Jenny, one of the residents of the other non-punk living group, decided to work on the defense to win the court case.

Jenny grew up in an upper-class family from one of the wealthiest sections of Holland. Conversations with Jenny revealed that she felt loved and supported as a child and continues to share a strong bond with them as an adult. She moved to Amsterdam to study Film Theory while living in student housing. Jenny became acquainted with the squatters' scene through one of her closest friends at university who was a squatter. Bored with student housing life, Jenny joined the group in the squatting of the Motorflex house. She was tall, slim, and beautiful with a simple way of dressing that was not punk nor conventionally feminine. She displayed charisma and walked with an air of confidence. Her ability to hang out with crusty punks with as much ease as with her university friends spoke to a sense of inner comfort that appeared unusual within the class landscape in Holland. Jenny enjoyed the squatters life, commenting to me once on our way to a squatting action, "I had no idea it was this much fun. Hanging out, going to brunches and parties, going to actions. It's cool, right?"

When Jenny decided to become involved in the house defense a year and a half after the squatting action, a war erupted between Jenny and Shirin. Shirin had invested time and energy managing the defense and felt territorial, resenting Jenny's interference. Yet, within a few days after taking over, Jenny – intelligent, quick-witted, analytical, and articulate – managed the whole case more efficiently and strategically than Shirin had in over a year. Once, after spending a few hours looking through the files that Shirin had compiled and organized, Jenny said to me, exasperated, "Based on what I have just seen, I fear the structure of Shirin's mind. I am very, very afraid."

Almost immediately after becoming involved, Jenny was the point person for anyone who had questions about the Motorflex defense. Jenny described the various court cases, provided summaries, analyses, legal context, and long-term strategy, all in a well-framed and logical narrative. In contrast, Shirin described the defense in a confused and vague manner that prevented ascertaining concrete facts and information. Jenny's articulate manner of speaking, her memory, and her attitude all commanded respect. She emitted confidence in her detailed knowledge about the case whereas Shirin often reacted to questions with poses that ranged from defensive, aggressive, to evasive. The Motorflex group respected Jenny and supported her leadership. When Jenny organized meetings about the defense, all the residents of the houses attended. If they had resisted her leadership, they would have dismissed her by labeling her as "authoritarian."

Clearly, Jenny possessed a number of organizational, analytical, and social skills whereas Shirin lacked capacity in these areas. Despite Jenny's relative lack of experience and minimal investment into the squatters' community compared to the sincerity and dedication of Shirin, her skills and actions enabled her to quickly accumulate squatter capital. Meanwhile, Shirin failed to accumulate any capital due to her social marginality and lack of capacity. What further differentiated Jenny from Shirin was that Jenny displayed and was recognized as being emotionally sovereign and socially autonomous in a way that Shirin was not nor ever could be.

Jenny's habitus was productive of and communicated her cultural centrality resulting from her upper-class background and her high skill level. It also conveyed a sense of social autonomy via her temporariness, that is, that Jenny participated in the movement as a phase and that she eventually would move onto another stage of her life appropriate to her class, skill, and education level. Jenny perceived and represented her activities in the squatters movement as marginal to her main interests as a student. For example, Jenny felt conflicted about the amount of time that she invested in the house defense compared to her studies, complaining to me, "I don't know why I'm even doing this. I have better and more important things that I should be spending my time on." In comparison, Shirin never complained, felt proud to handle the house's defense, derived a sense of emotional self-worth from the project, and worked on it with commitment, despite the complexity of the project being beyond her skill level. Jenny transmitted an attitude that she clearly chose to squat and could easily leave the movement for other options. If she had felt the lack of respect that Shirin had experienced, Jenny would simply have left the community.

In contrast, Shirin needed the squatters' community for social and economic reasons. Since she was unable to financially support herself, it would have been impossible for her to exist outside of the squatters' community without its free housing and its network of mutual aid.[4] Emotionally, Shirin lacked the confidence and sense of wellbeing that Jenny emanated since Jenny held a position of authority without demanding it nor even acknowledging that she possessed it. In Shirin's interactions with others and her activities within the movement, she persistently sought respect with the result that she never received it.

Shirin's self-doubt and insecurity most likely developed for a number of reasons that she revealed to me over the course of a few months: because she grew up as an immigrant in a country that detested immigrants, because she felt unwanted by her family since they left her to grow up without them in Turkey as a child, because she never began her university education, and because she could not find a job in Amsterdam despite her dream of the type of life that she felt was impossible for her in Germany. She often asked me, "Will I ever be able to "make it" here?" For Shirin, every difficulty became another rejection and then, another form of exclusion. From the rejections for waitress jobs[5] to the social snubbing of her punk neighbors in the squat, they all fit into a schema of a world that opposed her and that functioned so as to oppress her. She then expressed her insecurity and self-doubt in a socially "unacceptable" way. She treated others aggressively, rejecting others before they could reject her. She reacted defensively, acting territorially regarding issues that she did not possess and acting emotionally in situations where rational argumentation was the accepted norm.

By presenting this portrait of Shirin as emotionally dependent, I do not claim that Jenny was more emotionally independent or did not need the subculture of the squatters movement for emotional reasons. Rather, understanding the hidden codes of middle-class habitus and socialization that dominate in the squatters movement, Jenny more adeptly concealed her dependence, demonstrating her independence according to the gradations of squatter capital, and self-consciously revealing her emotions more strategically. During a private conversation with Jenny, she advised me to hide certain information because, "it makes you look really bad."

Trying to add further insight into this case with the help of social movement studies proves challenging. In social movement studies, there is a

dearth of information on micro-level social dynamics within social move-
ment communities. The writing that exists about individuals' participation
is often abstract and superficial. For example, McAdam (1986) prefers to
discuss the impact of friendship networks on political participation rather
than consider larger structural reasons that may gird their participation,
such as class or gender background.

The European new social movements approach, in contrast to the
American-dominated resource mobilization and political process theor-
ies, has been more willing to examine how larger structural issues may
attract or hamper individual participation in new social movements.
Alberto Melucci and Claus Offe consider how one's class and social pos-
ition impact one's participation in new social movements. Borrowing
heavily from Claus Offe (1985), Melucci argues that new social move-
ments are typically comprised of individuals from structurally diverse
positions which he defines as:

> (a) the new middle class or human capital class, that is, those who work
> in the advanced technological sectors based on information, the human
> service professions and/or the public sector (particularly in education
> and welfare), and who have achieved a high educational status and
> enjoy relative economic security; (b) those in a marginal position in the
> labour market (e.g. students, unemployed, or peripheral groups such
> as youth, retired people, middle class housewives) ... The core group
> of activists and supporters is to be found in the first group. (Melucci
> 1989: 53)

Melucci then considers why individuals from these locations in particular
participate in new social movements. With regard to the "new middle class,"
Melucci divides them into two groups: new elites, who are motivated to
challenge the established elites; and human capital professionals who expe-
rience both the surplus of opportunities and the constraints of the system.
The profile of the new middle class is that they are well integrated into social
activities and institutions such as households and communities. In terms of
political and social organizations, the new middle class have experience in
more traditional politics and social networks such as voluntary associations,
self-help groups, and social welfare organizations.

This type of social profile then indicates cultural centrality because it
demonstrates that these individuals identify with "modern values" and are
integrated into society regardless of their oppositional stance towards the
Mainstream. They relate to essential structures of society from a position
of substantial cognitive resources, such as educational achievement, pro-
fessional skills, and social abilities. Their skills and their "modern values"
explain how members of this group often easily shift from a position of
conflict in relation to "the Mainstream" to that of "the counter-elite."

Melucci divides "the peripherals" into two groups: the affluent and the actual marginals. Affluent marginals include students and middle-class women who work at home and therefore have access to social and cultural capital. Offe claims that middle-class housewives find themselves excluded from public spheres due to institutional sexism which then motivates participation in new social movements. Both argue that students become involved in social movements resulting from a combination of flexible time schedules and experiencing a discrepancy between the critical thinking skills that they derive from their education and the types of jobs that they can then access in an increasing limited and competitive job market. As Melucci elucidates:

> With the youth and student movements, for instance, we can see the impact of the diffusion of education, widening areas of autonomy and the extension of resources for self-training and self-determination. We can also observe that these processes are negated by the structure of the labour market and actual employment conditions, which are unable to absorb the inflated possibilities created by education. And we can see that the adult system of labour markets, career structures, and professional politics seems incapable of fulfilling the very expectations of flexibility and autonomy which it has nourished through its tolerance of a separate youth culture. (Melucci 1989: 54)

With regard to the factual "marginals" of the peripheral group, Melucci provides few details, compared to his lengthy description of the new middle-class and affluent marginals. He only states that they are comprised of unemployed and elderly people and that their motivations to participate derive in reaction to a crisis. He thus constructs a relative deprivation argument for the participation of "marginal" people. Consequently, he privileges articulate middle-class people and their ability to represent themselves in his analysis, leaving little critical analysis of such partial and privileged perspectives. The privileging of articulate voices is mirrored in subcultural studies, in which scholars have traditionally privileged the perspective of articulate, middle-class men and their experience in subcultures whose views mirror those of researchers (Thornton 1996).

Compared to the majority of social movement studies, which ignores the demographics or social position of individuals who participate in social movements, Melucci and Offe's interventions helpfully provide a broad, though abstract and slightly vague overview of the diverse populations who inhabit social movement communities. However, when trying to understand the relationship between cultural centrality and authority, it becomes clear that the concept of cultural centrality – which encompasses the new middle-class and the affluent marginals in Melucci's framework – is vague without a context to understand what conditions locate an individual as being "central." Melucci's definition of cultural centrality via a description of the "new middle class" and their "cognitive resources" is still too abstract to understand the consequences of such positions and skills on movement subcultures. One cannot understand the components of cultural centrality without having a sense of what behaviors constitutes cultural marginality.

There is a tension between marginality and oppositionality in the squatters' community. Oppositionality is a tacit value that requires a habitus of "autonomy" to be performed convincingly. Marginality is an unspoken status that should be avoided because of its dominant presence in the subculture through alcoholism, drug addiction, excess aggression, depression, and an unwillingness or inability to manage the hundreds of minuscule negotiations that constitute daily life in a wealthy, highly bureaucratized, multicultural northern European city with global pretensions.

Some squatters talk about the prevalence of cultural marginality in the "scene" openly while most avoid the topic because it is uncomfortable to articulate. Ludwic, having squatted for over ten years, said, "Anyone who has been in the community for a long time has something wrong with them. Everyone. Germaine, me, even you. Don't kid yourself." Marina, from Serbia, having squatted in Amsterdam for four years, commented, "It's hard to tell the difference between rejecting society and *being rejected* by society". Lara, a squatter with substantial squatter capital in that she possesses and masters all squatters skills and runs a successful freelance IT business in the Mainstream, told me, "Not everyone can be autonomous. The scene is full of losers. A lot of people who are losers in society come and find out, hey, I can *do* this. I can do this well. Maybe it's building. Maybe it's occupying. Whatever. But they are still losers."

Hence, the struggle between new middle class, culturally central Jenny and marginal and unemployed Shirin reveals a situation with multiple layers of conflict, on the level of habitus, group dynamics, identity, and recognition. Only by fully exploring the habitus of centrality and, specifically a sense of the behaviors that constitute marginality, can these concepts be usefully employed as interpretative tools to understand the relationship between cultural centrality and authority.

In Melucci's framework, Shirin is classified as marginal simply because she is a member of "the unemployed." Hence, her participation in the social movement is interpreted as a reaction to the crisis of structural unemployment. But in fact, Shirin's participation is as multi-layered as Jenny's. The same boredom and alienation that Jenny felt that motivated her to move from student housing to go squatting, inspired Shirin to leave her life of subletting. Despite Shirin's marginality, her choice to become a squatter was as motivated by conviction as Jenny's, and in fact, her conviction pushed her to sincerely become as involved in the squatting world as possible, even when it was inappropriate such as her work on the house defense.

Melucci and Offe present overviews of these different groups but fail to discuss the interactions between individuals from such different backgrounds and how their interactions and internal hierarchies reflect the class and structural positions of the individuals in the Mainstream. Furthermore, they fail to address whether and how mainstream hierarchies are reproduced within movement cultures. Shirin's marginality extended beyond her chronic unemployment, her unabated aggression, and her lack of cognitive skills to manage the legal defense of the Motorflex houses. Her marginality included her inability to understand that this whole terrain of skill was beyond her field of competence, and accordingly, within the norms governing proper conduct within the subculture, she should have asked for assistance or delegated the task to someone who had the capacity to handle it.

In Chapter 1, I considered why few squatters engage in strategic manipulation despite its rewards. I concluded that the hierarchical process of knowledge transference when learning strategic manipulation skills was unappealing and intimidating, leading most squatters to claim that strategic manipulation is "too much work." As a result, squatters who engage in strategic manipulation often, but not exclusively, are highly educated and originate from middle or upper-class backgrounds because they already possess and feel comfortable in skills such as research, writing, and analytical thinking. Strategic manipulation is not the only area in squatting that requires analytical thinking; other skills, such as acting

Figure 2.2 Squatted building alongside a canal in the Jordaan neighborhood, 2006

as a police spokesperson, building, organizing, and breaking also require extensive cognitive ability and social skills. However, in strategic manipulation, there is clear responsibility for cognitive action. One has to strategize, make decisions, and take responsibility for decisions which the backstage of the squatters' scene will scrutinize and eventually criticize negatively when a house is evicted. Mistakes from such cognitive-based actions seem more intimate than errors in other areas, revealing an inner weakness or – even worse – stupidity on the part of the campaigners, which the backstage of the community judges harshly. It seems then that the pressure and intensity of scrutiny on campaigning decisions often intimidate a number of squatters, especially those who are less educated and/or originate from working-class backgrounds.

I have only heard critique about squatters' campaigns. Inevitably, all campaigns end with the evictions of the houses and so anyone can find reasons to criticize the strategy of a house's residents (see earlier story listing the critique of the Motorflex houses). Successful squatters campaigns (such as the long-term delay of an eviction by months and/or years, or in rare instances, legalization) are never openly recognized as the result of dedication and hard work on the part of those involved. Instead the acknowledgment of a successful campaign is made apparent in that the capital of the campaigners accumulates as a result of their work.

In *Distinction* (1984), Bourdieu discusses the connection between entitlement and political opinion. He examines large-scale political opinion surveys, focusing on how the content of the opinions relates to the class, gender, and professions of those who participated in the poll. He further analyzed the link between the abstentions and the class and gender of those who abstained. Finding that women and working-class people, by and large, often professed ignorance or answered questions in a way that did not serve the intentions of the polls, Bourdieu argues that with regards to politics, the capacity to articulate is intertwined with a sense of entitlement that is class based:

> To understand, reproduce, and even produce political discourse, which is guaranteed by educational qualification, one also has to consider the (socially authorized and encouraged) sense of being entitled to be concerned with politics, authorized to talk politics ... Technical competence is to social competence what the capacity to speak is to the right to speak, simultaneously a precondition and an effect ... Only those who ought to have it can really acquire it and only those who are authorized to have it feel called upon to acquire it. (Bourdieu 1984: 409–10)

Within this Bourdieuian framework, Shirin and Jenny's story highlights the invisible and naturalized assumptions for the types of skills required to enable the practice of campaigning. Shirin's marginality revealed the invisible logic of this practice because she failed to judge herself in this hierarchy of competencies and pull out of managing the campaign. Most squatters without an educated, middle-class habitus will *naturally* self-censor themselves and their participation in such campaigns. Either they opt out or they delegate the decision-making power to squatters who have an educated habitus or who already possess squatter capital attained through successful strategic manipulation. As Bourdieu writes, this process of delegation is common:

> The authorized speech of status-generated competence, a powerful speech which helps to create what it says, is answered by the silence of an equally status-linked incompetence, which is experienced as technical incapacity and leaves no choice but delegation – a misrecognized dispossession of the less competent by the more competent, of women by men, of the less educated, of those who do not know to speak by those who speak well. The propensity to delegate responsibilities for political matters to others recognized as technically competent varies in inverse ratio to the educational capital possessed, because the educational qualification (and the culture it is presumed to guarantee) is tacitly regarded – by its holders but also by others – as a legitimate title to the exercise of authority. (Bourdieu 1984: 414)

The story of Shirin is not an example of the types of social ruptures that occur when a working-class person finds themselves in a field where they do not belong. Instead, it reveals the invisible logic of campaigning practices, in which squatters, especially from working-class families, will exclude themselves from learning the skills required in strategic manipulation. This exclusion then reproduces a dynamic in which the same types of people possess prestigious skills based on cognitive abilities. Bourdieu refers to this process of natural censorship as a sense of one's place in which:

> Objective limits become a sense of limits, a practical anticipation of objective limits acquired by experience of objective limits, a "sense of one's place"; which leads one to exclude oneself from the goods, person, places, and so forth from which one is excluded. (Bourdieu 1984: 471)

By limiting his analysis of politics to opinion polls, Bourdieu neglects to understand the day-to-day practices of making politics, especially for activists. By examining practices, one sees that these social reproductions, although disturbing, have an underlying pragmatism. In a stressful and time limited situation such as defending the imminent eviction of a house, it is crucial that tasks are executed by the most skilled and productive people, as seen in the case of Jenny and Shirin.

Bourdieu's argument, furthermore, can be overly deterministic. In a paradoxical milieu where a classless ideal prevails although competencies and skills that derive mainly from class background result in the accumulation of capital, it is still possible for people to obtain skills if they are determined. A number of working-class squatters who were successfully socialized in the movement by learning a number of squatter skills and gaining capital, also learned how to excel at strategic manipulation. Furthermore, they strategically use their working-class habitus to their advantage in a radical left environment, where an unspoken and predominant assumption exists that most people are middle or upper class and ashamed of their background. Moreover, during interactions with the state and with the media, culturally central, white, Dutch, working-class squatters with squatter capital mobilize their working-class Dutchness to gain strategic advantages.

Tall, blond, blue-eyed, and broad-shouldered Fleur was raised on a houseboat in a sailing community in north Holland – a member of the, as she calls it, "respectable working class." Although at the time of writing, houseboats are fashionable in the Netherlands, when Fleur was a child, houseboats connoted "trailer trash" with its own community-based subculture. She grew up in a tight-knit, social democratic family in which both her parents worked as captains of tourist boats. Fleur disavows anarchism and proudly proclaims her membership in the social democratic party. Among anarchists, it's an insult to be called a social democrat.

Fleur moved to Amsterdam to study sociology and through various networks, became involved in squatting. She mastered squatter skills: building, breaking, organizational, non-instrumental acts of bravery, and strategic manipulation. At a certain point, she dropped out of university to pursue a commercial sailing and naval career where she excelled. During her brief periods in Amsterdam, she lives as a squatter and often serves as a media spokesperson. Her habitus exudes skills and capabilities but also an authentic working-class Dutchness that aids her role as a spokesperson. Once, she participated in a debate on a national news program regarding squatters and their use of violence in which her opponent was a right-wing politician in his mid-fifties. After the debate, he told Fleur how impressive he found her and that she reminded him of his daughter. In this case, despite their opposing political standpoints, Fleur's entire way of being moved this politician. Her blondness, her profession as a sailor with its cultural resonance in a country which defines itself as traders and fighting to survive above water, her working-class habitus, her intelligence, and her skills as a strategic interlocutor for the squatters movement impressed the politician to metaphorically embrace her in a show of nationalistic pride.

Tall, slim, and blond, Coen – another culturally central, working-class, white Dutch squatter with significant squatter capital who uniquely campaigned to defend his house from eviction – mobilized similar subconscious elements to his advantage both within the scene and in his strategic manipulation tactics with the Mainstream. In contrast to the other squatters who I have profiled, Coen is not university educated and works as a flexible manual laborer, in sanitation and in factories. He uses his working-class background to convincingly critique practices such as dumpster diving in the squatters movement. He told me, "I grew up with a single mother in a family of seven children. We were forced to find food from the garbage. I'm not going to do that as an adult when I have money. I like nice things and I like to buy new things, not just old, used crap." In Coen's case, his openness about his poverty as a child only served to increase his capital in a subculture where class background is not discussed, both to maintain the fiction of classlessness and since many assume the dominance of a middle-class banality. His ability to show pride in his poverty, shames the disavowed middle-class assumptions of those around him, and his rejection of the entire process of mastery and rejection that underlies such an act as dumpster diving, grant him authority.

When he campaigned to defend his squat, Coen mobilized similar subconscious elements. When he spoke in the neighborhood council to prevent the eviction of his house, he impressed the council members with his articulate working-class self, emotionally touching the disenchanted and bored former leftist activists who comprise the neighborhood council. Similarly, in one of the houses where I lived as a squatter, we deliberately worked with our working-class elderly neighbor to mobilize the blueprint of sympathies on the part of the Mayor's Office and the neighborhood council to publicly show solidarity for a member of the endangered species of white, working-class, and elderly Amsterdammers.[6]

These are examples of white, working-class Dutch people having successfully mobilized a historical solidarity between people of their class and more elite Dutch politicians, especially on the left. However, this unspoken solidarity is predicated on a background of racial and religious tension in Dutch urban life. The right-wing politician found Fleur impressive because of the contrast with the media's image of crusty, violent, and disrespectful foreign squatters. Fleur, Coen, and the elderly neighbor would never consciously participate in a racist act, but tacitly, subconsciously and ominously, they mobilized via an unspoken solidarity constructed on race and nationality.

The constitutive practice of gossip

Thus far, I have focused on the types of skills, competencies, habitus, and performances that lead to a squatter being recognized as an authority figure. These ethnographic examples focused on how, in the context of squatter campaigns, squatters achieve recognition as figures of authority through a combination of their skills and personal characteristics.

In this section, I portray two *kraakbonzen*, who are recognized as author-
ity figures on the scale of the entire squatters movement. Kraakbonzen is a
term that translates literally as squatter bosses. In the scene, the term is an
ambivalent joke that acknowledges the existence of "bosses" in a community
that defines itself as anti-authoritarian. This term must be expressed as a joke
because to transparently concede without irony that authority figures exist
in such a community produces excessive anxiety. Although the kraakbonzen
who I profile in this section are men, a number of women are also bonzen.[7]

In a subculture that fervently denies authority ideologically, authority is
then conferred on a micro-social level both in terms of the ability to produce
actions and via the circulation of gossip around particular figures. When
authority cannot be discussed openly, an ethnographer must observe and
listen to understand who has authority. In meetings, watching who proposes
a plan, who speaks, who is listened to, and which plans are actually enacted
and by whom reveals authority figures.

Accordingly, squatter skills that accumulate capital, and in particular,
skills related to strategic manipulation and the capacity to implement plans
and produce actions, lead people to receive silent recognition as authority
figures. I emphasize skills in particular because of the five authority figures
who I highlight (Jenny, Fleur, Coen, Dominic, and Damien), three origin-
ate from upper-class backgrounds and with the exception of Coen, all are
highly educated. If they lacked skills, then squatters would dismiss them as
rich kids playing revolutionaries or slumming. The capabilities that they
contribute to the movement form the basis of their authority.

The skills, and in part, the upper-class background of these figures, adds
to their habitus of emotional sovereignty. Richard Sennett, in *The Hidden
Injuries of Class*, describes such a habitus as an "inner, self-sufficing power,"
which highly educated and highly trained professionals possess. Sennett
elaborates:

> The power of professionals lies in their ability to give or withhold knowl-
> edge, they are in positions that by and large are not questioned by oth-
> ers; they are "authorities" themselves, "authorities" unto themselves. It is
> precisely the endowment of a professional with this inner, self-sufficing
> power that gives him a higher status than men with economic power. For
> the autonomy makes him seem "market proof," in that he can perform
> his functions no matter what is happening to others around him. His
> nurturing power appears as an ability that he brings *to* people; they need
> him in a way that he does not need them. It is in this sense that he is the
> only truly independent man in a class society – he is needed more than he
> needs. (Sennett 1977: 227)

For these authority figures, the combination of skills and a performance
of emotional sovereignty makes them elusive, attractive, respected, and the

subjects of abhorrent gossip and curiosity. Emotional sovereignty is a way of performing a totalizing emotional and structural independence. These figures project a sense of never requiring others emotionally, of not caring what others think, as well as an understanding that they have access to opportunities outside the movement that would welcome them and their skills. Their totalizing individualism and their ability to convey that they privilege the movement with their presence brings them respect in a community that paradoxically preaches communal living, solidarity, and interdependence as superior to an individualist mindset and lifestyle.

The writing of European new social movement scholar, Francesco Alberoni, on charismatic leaders in social movements, elucidates the complicated role of authority figures in social movement communities and the ensuing intense emotional reactions of group members, in this case through eviscerating gossip, to these authority figures (Alberoni 1984). Alberoni argues that the ephemeral magic of these leaders lies in their metaphorical function as priests who mediate between extremes on two levels.

First, on the level of the movement, in which he (and in Alberoni's text, it's always a he) mediates between the movement's "centrifugal forces." Such forces describe the continuum from those who are more willing to negotiate with the external world outside the movement and are somewhat compelled to reintegrate into the Mainstream to those who advocate for a radical break. The charismatic leader, who forms the ethical center of the group, provides a source of unanimity in a movement that is continually on the verge of breakdown due to the tensions and conflicts between these extremes (Alberoni 1984: 141–2).

The second level where charismatic leaders mediate is within the individual and their participation in the movement, which Alberoni frames as, "a dialectic between individual and group in which the necessity of unanimity must coincide with the need for authenticity" (Alberoni 1984: 139). On the level of the individual, Alberoni argues that a constant tension exists between an individual's desire to maintain a sense of authenticity versus the overwhelming and strategic pull to fuse with the group. This dilemma between remaining true to oneself, one's values, and one's ways of understanding the world through the prism of one's experiences versus conforming with the group in the context of a social movement is itself a betrayal, according to Alberoni. In order to resolve this sense of betrayal and guilt, the charismatic leader offers both an absolution and a sense of unity and unanimity:

The leader is he who has the power to absolve from guilt ... an ethical leader, a strategist of moral behavior. There is nothing magical or mysterious about his behavior ... He is able to ensure salvation and social cohesion among the group's members and to overcome danger from without. (Alberoni 1984: 143–4)

Figure 2.3 Pro-squatting graffiti in De Pijp neighborhood, 2006

Beyond the function of the mediating priest who provides a sense of coherence among the cacophony of tensions within social movements, Alberoni further points that the relationship between the charismatic leader and the group is based entirely on an asymmetrical love relationship, in which those in the group love the leader but the leader loves them only as the total group collectivity, not as single individuals. Thus, no reciprocity exists in the relationship between individuals in the group and the leader:

> There are … cases of asymmetrical, unilateral falling in love, in which the one who loves inevitably ends up by being entirely dominated by the other, who delights in being loved but does not respond in the same manner. This is the type of falling in love that takes place in the consolidation of charismatic leadership. What in the couple is a failure, a distortion of love and a source of unhappiness for the one who loves, is the basis of the stability of the leader's power. (Alberoni 1984: 148)

Returning to the squatters movement, with its fraught and contradictory relationship to authority figures in mind, gossip has two functions beyond verbal evisceration. First, it serves to recognize authority figures. Second, it serves as a means to transact contradictory and ambivalent feelings of love, dependency, and jealousy through aggression.

Alberoni argues that the power of charismatic leaders is their ability to mediate various tensions in the individual and on the larger movement level. This leads to members of the group to project a sense of power and charisma onto these figures, which then induces an asymmetrical and non-reciprocal relationship of love between the charismatic leader and the members of the group. In the squatters movement, where the dominant mode of daily performance is hostility and where the existence of authority figures can only be acknowledged circuitously, the ambivalent and contradictory feelings of love and dependency provoked by the presence of charismatic leaders is expressed aggressively via negative gossip, especially in the realm of sexuality and sexual practices.

There is an ideal of open and non-judgmental discussion of sex, sexuality, and sexual practices in the squatters' subculture in comparison with a relatively more conservative and repressed view of sexuality in the Mainstream. Samuel remarks, "In the community, everyone is very open about these things. You can say and do anything and no one cares." Although a value of sexual openness prevails, the practice of exorbitant gossip about sexuality indicates that people in the community do, in fact, care.

Lara, a veteran squatter with high squatter capital, told me about a squat party at which, late at night, she went to bed with one of the men who lived in the house. An acquaintance of Lara's searched through the house for her. Eventually, she entered the room where Lara was in bed with her lover, spent some time in the room without their noticing, and then left to report to the party what she had seen. Lara, having learned about this reporting afterwards through rumors, said to me, laughing, "This is the scene. Everyone is in the room with you and watching while you are fucking." To emphasize her point, she rocked her hips forward and backwards rhythmically. We both laughed. Lara's comment illustrates the pervasive practice of gossip in the subculture. However, I noticed that gossip reflects status and hierarchy in which only a relatively limited number of people are gossiped about: authority figures in the movement or people who are excessively charismatic and talented, or both, such as Lara. The sexuality of marginal figures like Shirin is not discussed.

The manner in which squatters discuss sexuality and sexual practices suits the process of mastery and rejection that prevails in every point of practice within the movement, from breaking open doors to the dominant mode of stylistic choices. An anti-romantic mode is predicated on a mastery and rejection of mainstream middle-class mores which promote heterosexual normativity and heterosexual marriage and restrict female sexuality. Hence, a mode of anti-romanticism that values sexuality and sexual practices without emotional bonds, with multiple partners, and that celebrates female sexual assertiveness dominates. Furthermore, anti-romanticism is displayed by openly discussing practices that may seem taboo in the Mainstream. In an unexpected twist, this style of sexual gossip then enables a misogynist, homosocial dynamic betraying the feminist ideals from which such anti-romanticism partially originates.

The ethnographic portraits of the kraakbonzen, Dominic and Damien, illustrate these dynamics specifically. First, I will relate their biographies, then describe their skills within the framework of squatter capital, followed by their habitus of emotional sovereignty. I then recount the gossip around figures and the misogynistic homosocial dynamic that reveals itself through the aggression targeted at the girlfriends of these figures.

Dominic

Dominic, tall, Dutch, handsome and articulate, is in his early 30s and has squatted for almost ten years. He grew up in an upper-middle-class family in a wealthy town in the Netherlands. I knew him for over a year before he told me the occupations of his parents, although I had heard from others that he was a "rich kid," which they had guessed based on his habitus and small clues. According to Germaine, a former housemate of Dominic, "He once told me the name of the town where he grew up and *no one* in that town is poor." He evades questions about his age, his name, and personal details. He moved to Amsterdam to attend university where he became involved in leftist politics. He lived for years in various configurations of housing, from student housing to illegal subletting. Through involvement in leftist activism, he slowly became a squatter. He resided in a number of squats and evolved into becoming a "professional squatter," mastering various skills such as building, breaking, organizing, strategic manipulation, attending confrontational actions, and consequently, accumulating squatter capital.

He continues his involvement in prestigious squatting institutions such as the kraakspreekuur, the squatters' research collective, and the press group. He is a well-known press spokesperson and skilled in how he manages the press. As a strategic manipulator, he formulates house defense strategies, adeptly negotiates with owners, smoothly lobbies politicians, and possesses ample knowledge about housing law, city policies, and administrative procedures, which can derail any eviction attempt. In addition to his activities in the backstage of the squatters' scene, he is a homebody who enjoys cooking and communal living. Given his embodiment of nearly all the ideal qualities for a squatter, I have heard endless gossip and critiques about him.

Dominic's squatter capital is based on his having lived in a number of well-known squats in the scene, either because they were vibrant and populated social centers or because they had well-formulated and extensive campaigns which were the fruits of Dominic's labor. One squat that helped build his reputation, known as the Looiersstraat, had exactly the elements of a campaign with high status in the scene. The owner was reputed to be a mafia figure who launders money through real estate speculation. At one point during this campaign, the squatters organized an action in front of the owner's house. The squatters drenched themselves in fake blood and laid across his front door with a banner proclaiming the owner to be a corrupt mafia figure who arranges contract killings.

This action and a number of others from this house campaign featured widely in the press with Dominic acting as the articulate, middle-class, Dutch press spokesperson on behalf of the squatting group. Dominic was quoted in newspapers, interviewed on local and national television, wrote a number of the press releases published on indymedia, developed much of the strategy, and lobbied politicians. The riot police evicted the house twice. After the first eviction, the squatters reoccupied the space with sixty others dressed in black, wearing balaclavas (black ski masks), and helmets. They had built barricading using bricks from the street and scaffolding from the building, and succeeded in blocking the entire area against the police. The media coverage featured photos of squatters in helmets, dressed in black, standing dramatically in rock star poses on the scaffolding of the building.

Maria is a young squatter woman in her early twenties, who some squatters dismiss as a baby punk while others extol as "a hero" due to her totalizing dedication to the movement. According to Maria, who worked on the campaign, Dominic enjoys the role of the authority figure and spokesperson but proves unreliable for less glamorous and nitty-gritty jobs, often carried out by women. At the eviction of the Looiersstraat, at the point when the squatters were going to barricade themselves inside the building to the extent that once inside, no one could exit until the police broke through and arrested everyone, Dominic disappeared after a television interview. They tried to reach him via his mobile phone but he did not answer. Anna, who had organized the barricading, said, "I was really angry. I did all this work organizing the barricading and making sure everything was ready for the ME [riot police]. He talks to the press and disappears. Why does he get all the credit? He abandoned us." This incident was not unique. In general, a number of squatters critique Dominic for acting unreliably by avoiding conflict in groups, withholding information, and suddenly leaving for a holiday without notifying anyone when others need him.

Ludwic, a squatter in his mid-forties, obsessively disdains Dominic, "He is arrogant. He thinks he's the boss of everyone. He thinks he knows so much." Maria, who had an affair with Dominic, also calls him, "an arrogant asshole," reiterating his reputation in the scene as "an authoritarian egomaniac." After their affair, Maria worked with Dominic on a campaign where they wrote text describing the ideals and goals of the movement together. Maria felt that Dominic mocked her ideas, silencing her to the point where she did not believe that she could propose ideas without being ridiculed.

During an eviction wave, Maria's boyfriend, an eighteen-year-old baby punk, newly arrived in Amsterdam, had locked himself into a building scheduled for eviction. Locking down is a tactic in which those resisting an eviction barricade themselves into a room and then attach themselves to the utilities, such as gas pipes, to prevent the police from reclaiming the building as cleared of squatters. During this eviction, the riot police accidentally broke the gas pipes and created a gas leak. The squatters who stood outside the building, listening to police radio, heard sudden orders for the riot police to evacuate because of imminent danger. Maria felt terrified as the squatters, including her new boyfriend, had locked themselves inside, making it impossible to escape a building with a gas leak. In the end, nothing dangerous occurred. When Maria spoke to Dominic about the incident, she was offended by Dominic's attitude. She felt that he mocked her and her friends as stupid, little, baby punks who had created a bigger problem than they could manage. Despite resenting Dominic's condescension, Maria still sought his approval of her political activity and found it frustrating that he responded by dismissing her squatting group as baby punks who were merely interested in violence and rebellion as a thrill but who, ultimately, were not "really committed."

Habitus of emotional sovereignty.

Dominic lives in a well-known activist squat where the living room serves as a popular social space. Among the buzz of various conversations, music, and ringing telephones, he often sits behind a computer, in his own aloof world of research and strategy. In social situations, he tends to have quiet demeanor that doesn't appear to result from shyness or social discomfort. Rather, his attitude is one of rejection of others that seems to come from boredom or even, a sense of deserving a more stimulating and profound level of conversation. If such content is unavailable, he removes himself from social interaction. During internal squatters' meetings and his interactions with the media and the state, he's confident, militant, and dogmatic. He speaks about squatting with a self-assuredness that others view as arrogant and patronizing.

He also carries an air of mystery. As I wrote earlier, he provides almost no information about himself including his age, where he grew up in the Netherlands, his parents' occupations, his name or even how to spell it. In the squatters' scene, such secrecy is typical due to leftist activists' concerns that the state surveils their activities. However, I suspect, that his level of discretion derives from a feeling of class shame. Only after a year of living in the same community and occasionally prodding him, did he reveal his parents' upper-class occupations to me. Dominic's guardedness reflects a shame of banal middle classness, or even worse, being upper or upper-middle class among the radical left, and how such a class background somehow de-legitimates someone from achieving the status of authentic squatter. This shame is ironic given that the fiction of classlessness exists simultaneously alongside both a dominant middle-class habitus and an assumption that most people are middle class in the squatters' scene.

As a well-known womanizer, inordinate gossip surrounds Dominic and his relationships with women. A friend of Dominic's asked me playfully, astonished, "How does he do it? How does he get all these gorgeous women in bed with him every night?" Often, it seems that he has slept with every woman in the room. The gossip concerns his past with women, the number of lovers that he juggles at the same time, how he openly cheats on his girl-friends, and the naivety of his current girlfriend to sincerely believe that he is monogamous. This is the more benign gossip.

The following is a compilation of gossip that I have heard about Dominic from a number of women. To be clear, I cannot confirm the veracity of this gossip and in my personal encounters with Dominic, he has always treated me kindly and with respect:

> **Fleur:** He has a big dick and he knows how to use it.
>
> **Germaine:** He is supposed to be really good in bed. Apparently, he knows how to fuck. He's got the skills. Lianne has slept with him and told me all about it.
>
> **Alexandra:** The first time, it was in his room at the Brouwersgracht, this huge seventeenth-century attic room. There I was having multiple orgasms in this incredible room. He's amazing in bed.
>
> **Maria:** He's an asshole. It's nice to have sex with him. He can be very sweet. But he's an asshole. I slept with him a few times and then, I was sitting next to him at a voku, and he was kissing another girl. That's an asshole thing to do, right?
>
> **Lucy:** He's slept with everyone. Be careful around him. There's a trail of abortions and Chlamydia[8] following this guy all over the world.

There is a magazine produced internally by and for the squatters' scene with a section called "Gossip." When I initially began fieldwork in this community, this section related how Dominic had actively tried to seduce me at a party but had failed. None of this was true and months later I learned that the writer had invented the story due to lack of material. I relate the details of this gossip to illustrate that in a community of a few hundred, a number of people enjoy talking about Dominic in particular as a figure: critiquing him and his role as a kraakbonz, discussing his sex life, his sexual skills, and his treatment of women.

Dominic holds a position of authority and respect regardless of such stories that might potentially de-legitimate him. He seems oblivious to gossip and derision. One aspect of the emotional sovereignty required of having authority in this community then, comes from the ability to disregard the gossip and continue in the movement with self-respect. It's this, "inner, self-sufficing power," which Sennett (1977) describes that enables individuals like Dominic to exist in a social minefield without ever feeling affected by the exploding mines.

This habitus of emotional sovereignty is a mode of performing a total lack of emotional investment in a community where everyone who participates is emotionally invested. The habitus of emotional sovereignty and the fraught relationship to authority figures as theorized by Alberoni (1984) then provokes reactions among other squatters, in this case by calling Dominic arrogant and obsessively fixating on his sexuality.

Furthermore, a disturbingly misogynistic homosocial dynamic is then transacted through this gossip around sexuality. I once sat with Janneke, one of Dominic's girlfriends, at the voku, when Willem, a well-known breaker and one of Dominic's friends, approached Janneke, inebriated. Willem said, "You know he's just fucking you. He doesn't give a shit about you. Once he's done fucking you, he'll find someone else to give him blow jobs." Shocked, I related this incident to Lara. She responded with irritation, "Willem is a fisherman's wife" (meaning a petty, mean gossip, intended to be especially insulting since Willem is a masculinist breaker). Later, I spoke with Janneke about Willem's outburst. She said, "I don't understand why he tells me this and not to Dominic. He should say this to him if that's how he feels about Dominic."

In a subculture where every daily practice is examined and critiqued, from drinking a beverage considered "corporate" (like Coca-Cola) or listening to Mainstream music, why is Willem, in this case, able to treat Janneke in such a blatantly misogynistic and disrespectful manner without social disapproval?

The anti-romantic style of discourse around sexuality assumes that no subject is off-limits and that women possess an equivalent sexual agency to men's. However, in a subculture that pays lip service to feminist ideals but has not integrated feminism into daily practice – and thus no mastery and rejection of feminist ideals actually takes place – the anti-romantic style backfires and reifies the subordination of women by viewing them literally as vessels and stand-ins for their male lovers.

Further, Willem's aggression towards Janneke indicated his jealousy of her receiving the love of an authority figure as an individual, not merely as a member of the group, as formulated by Alberoni. Dominic's promiscuity conformed with movement ideals that promote sexuality with multiple partners and without emotional bonds. Dominic's much gossiped about sexual practices abided by Alberoni's characterization of the charismatic leader: he is loved and needed, but only loves the total group collectivity without loving a single individual. His sexual voracity implied that by loving so many women indiscriminately, he loved no one in particular. His relationship with Janneke proved an exception to this and caused jealousy, leading to Willem degrading her and belittling Dominic's love for her as exploitation.

Eve Sedgwick, in *Between Men: English Literature and Male Homosocial Desire* (1985), examines the homosocial dynamic in several centuries of English Literature. Sedgwick uses the term "the homosocial" to reconsider the trope of the love triangle of two men and a woman, arguing instead that this love triangle often serves as a form of male bonding predicated on a hatred of homosexuality and the exchange of women to symbolize asymmetrical power relations between men. In these love triangles, although each man engages in an intimate relationship with one woman, they are much more invested in the other man than in the woman.

The context of the contemporary squatters movement is a far cry from the socio-political-historical context in which the texts that Sedgwick analyzes were written. First, there is no taboo on homosexual sexual practices and a fluid ideal of sexuality prevails. It's commonplace for men who identify mainly as straight to have sex with men and a number of women who identify as lesbian also often sleep with men. In addition, those who gossip are just as often women as men. However, the model of homosociality that Sedgwick provides is helpful in revealing how the creation of bonds between two people can more easily take place through the vehicle of a third person with less status and authority (and often a woman) who has more value as an object of exchange than in her own right.

These homosocial transactions provide insight into the triangle of: authority figures, those who gossip about them, and the lovers of the authority figures. When Willem spoke to Janneke so offensively, he exhibited his emotional investment in insulting Dominic and, in a roundabout manner, of bonding with him through his aggression against her. The asymmetrical power relationship between Dominic and Willem exists on a number of levels. On the level of the movement, Dominic is silently recognized as an authority for his numerous skills where Willem is recognized only as a breaker.

The asymmetry extends further to Alberoni's description of the non-reciprocal love relationship between a group and a charismatic leader. Willem loves and admires Dominic without reciprocity. Within the movement subculture, such feelings cannot be expressed nor can the reasons underlying the love be discussed. Willem then expresses his emotions within the aggressive mode sanctioned within the movement, yet he refrains from conveying these emotions to Dominic directly due to the power relations between them. Janneke, as the lover, becomes a stand-in for Dominic. Because she is a woman, defined in relation only to Dominic, and due to her lower status, she is an easier and safer target for aggression than Dominic. I suspect that Willem never speaks in such an offensive manner to Dominic to maintain a good relationship with him. However, even if he were to do so, Dominic would most likely dismiss him carelessly, as conforming to his habitus of emotional sovereignty.

Damien

Damien is another kraakbonz from an upper-class background who is wholly committed to the movement. In contrast to Dominic, who hides his class background, Damien openly admits his bourgeois origins. To the few who ask, he talks about his family, a long line of psychoanalysts, and growing up in an elite milieu in France. He left home as a teenager to experience the countercultural edge of Paris, a world of parties, drugs, and leftist politics. He was expelled from secondary school, not due to his inability to understand the material, but because, according to Damien, he refused to conform to "bourgeois" notions of "being on time" and "listening to the teacher." After a few years of traveling around the world, he completed his secondary school exams and began university. He succeeded in charming the university lecturers to allow him pass his classes without actually attending them or completing assignments. Eventually, Damien never finished his undergraduate degree, and instead focused on a technical career. In his mid-twenties, he moved to Amsterdam with his then-girlfriend attracted by its underground artistic, cultural, and political scene. After a series of precarious housing situations and the slow death of his relationship, Damien went squatting with a totalizing dedication.

Squatters jokingly refer to him as "el presidente," "el comandante," "the general," or even "the king." These names[9] mock his authoritative manner as well as the squatters who follow Damien's lead. By calling him these names, squatters identify themselves as non-conformists who refuse to uncritically follow his authority. Jenny, a resident of the Motorflex houses, remarked, "We are the only squatters in this part of Amsterdam who are not under the influence of the King. We are independent from Damien."

Damien has taken a leadership role in the squatters movement. He participated in the founding of the Anarchist Choir and Indymedia Netherlands, and actively expanded other groups, such as ASCII, the hackers group of Amsterdam. He attends every SOK (citywide squatters' meetings) and LOK (nationwide squatting meetings). He participates in all Amsterdam squatting actions as well as special nationwide action squats. He is a member of the squatters' research collective and a founder of one of the most well-organized and productive kraakspreekuren in the city because the actions are thoroughly researched and the houses often remain squatted for at least two years. This is relevant compared to kraakspreekuren that organize many squatting actions but the houses stay squatted only for a few months before being evicted. He developed his house into one of the centers of the squatters movement for political organizing and he has actively campaigned to prevent the eviction of his house for nearly a decade (in comparison to most houses, which exist for a few months to at most, two or three years).

Like Dominic, Damien has also mastered much of the skills that comprise squatter capital. He is mostly well known as a skilled political strategist in his dealings with the press and local politicians. He is French yet speaks Dutch fluently. As a member of the press group, he manipulates and charms journalists. He writes articles in newspapers and news websites under a variety of assumed names. He calls himself an extra parliamentary politician. He delivers speeches at the neighborhood council, lobbies politicians on behalf of the movement, and has ties to relevant politicians and civil servants in his neighborhood. Uniquely among squatters, he maintains relationships with his non-squatting neighbors.

He proudly considers himself an ideologue of the movement and sees himself as a member of its intellectual vanguard. His discourse varies widely, from superficial arguments about political philosophy to complicated, knowledgeable analysis of housing policy and world events. He enjoys debating with others in a competitive intellectual performance. I often find these debates shallow and a mere repetition of various political ideologies that avoid complexity. However, he can switch seamlessly from this superficial, simplistic discourse to one that is in-depth, complex, and insightful.

He is loud, dogmatic, authoritarian, and unapologetic about being this way. At various discussion events and meetings throughout the radical left, he is well known for preaching the violent overthrow of the bourgeoisie. He regularly announces, "I believe that every politician and civil servant's life should be made public, up to the names of their children and where they go to school." He vociferously proclaims the use of "we" in a community that scoffs at the "we," preferring instead to use the "I," to avoid making statements on behalf of others. He makes statements such as, "we believe in common property," "we are anarchists," "we provide our labor for free in exchange for a state-free space," "laws do not apply to us because they are only for subjects of the Queen, and we are not subjects of the Queen." During meetings, he is arrogant, impatient, dominating, silencing, and he often insults other squatters with viciousness. He treats many squatters with utter disrespect. He accuses them of being "hippies on holidays" who are "not committed to the revolution," and carelessly humiliates them and devalues their lifestyles.

Damien inspires a mix of contempt and fascination that seems at odds but exists part and parcel in how others perceive him. Squatters enjoy deriding him and mocking him. They ridicule his simplistic political rhetoric, his French accent, his walk, and his awful treatment of others. They enjoy reviewing his mistakes in various campaigns and charging his behavior as "hyper-individualist" and "egocentric." To be called "individualist" is an insult in this community, although people are fiercely individualistic while maintaining a communal ideal, and hence switching their standpoints when it suits them.

Some squatters seek his approval and a connection. "This guy gives me so much anxiety. It seems impossible to connect to him. I don't think he

Figure 2.4 Banner outside of squat that states: Housing shortage → Squat

likes me," admits Marie, who has worked with Damien on many cam-
paigns. "I've never had a conversation with him so I don't think he thinks
much of me," says Gunther, another member of the squatting group. Other
squatters invent connections with him when they don't exist. Once, I sat
with a squatter friend working at an anarchist bookstore. A few squatters
were gossiping about Damien, claiming that in his frequent visits to their
house, he annoyed them with his stomping and lecturing. I knew for a
fact that Damien had only visited their house once a year for their annual
parties out of politeness. Another squatter once informed me that she and
Damien had argued passionately at the kraakspreekuur and that he was
furious with her. Later, I asked Damien about the argument and he did not
recall the conversation.

Despite their mocking discourse, the behavior of a number of squatters
demonstrates respect and a deferral of authority. In highly tense situations,
such as alarms and actions, squatters approach him upon arrival to inform

him what has occurred and seek his advice. If they have complicated problems that require a strategic solution, they ask Damien for help. Earlier,
I quoted Jenny, who proclaimed that her squatting group was one of the few
who maintained independence from Damien. Months later, during a middle
of the night surprise eviction of a squat where Jenny and I resided, I called
her at 4 a.m., waking her to inform her that the police had surrounded
our house (she was sleeping elsewhere). Shocked, scared, and having just
awakened, she repeatedly asked, "Have you talked to Damien? What does
he think?"

Habitus of emotional sovereignty

When Damien walks into the room, he receives attention. Even when silent,
people stare at him. He talks to his few friends but otherwise, seems uninterested in forming relationships or socializing. He only speaks to people
for instrumental reasons: to neighbors about the campaign to defend his
squat from eviction, the housing shortage in Amsterdam, and the squatters movement. He talks to other squatters about political actions and their
houses. He preaches to non-squatters about their housing situations. If a
non-squatter lives in a precarious housing situation, he shames this person
unless he can successfully convince them to squat. He appears to have no
interest in forming emotional bonds with anyone and seems immune from
loneliness. Yet, the paradox of his life is that he lives in a tight-knit community and spouts a rhetoric of socialism, community values versus individualist ones, and rants vehemently against the "the private life."

In comparison to the other kraakbonzen, who are renowned womanizers,
such as Dominic, Damien lacks the string of girlfriends and casual affairs.
Despite his heterosexuality and the adoration he receives from a number of
women, he seems disinterested in intimate relationships. His rejection of a
number of young and beautiful women who have attempted to seduce him,
and thus, of sex in general, is a plentiful source for gossip. The few women
who have had affairs with him talk about their experiences with him in a
trophy-like manner.

Frida, who was a good squatter friend of mine, was a non-punk Canadian
activist from the alternative globalization movement who had an affair with
Damien. When the affair developed into a serious relationship, like the earlier story about Janneke and Dominic, I watched as she became the target
of a phenomenal amount of aggression and curiosity, reflecting squatters'
intense and multi-layered emotions provoked by the figure of Damien. In
the past, Frida had affairs with other squatters without ensuing gossip or
aggression, so she knew that Damian was the trigger point.

The following is a compilation of various statements to Frida from
squatters, mostly women. I witnessed most of these statements while others

I heard from Frida secondhand. She knew most of these individuals only superficially, having had at most one or two interactions with them:

Germaine: Is he good in bed? Is he rough? Is he eager? I heard from Alexandra that he is a good fuck but that he doesn't want to do it too often. Once every eight days, she said. Is that how it is with you? I heard he's really into periods. Does he only fuck when you have your period?

Dirk: So I heard that Damien spent last night with you. How was it? Was he good? Tell us about what he was like in bed. He told us all about you.

Lucy: I had an affair with him. It was wonderfully romantic. He was very happy. He gives great head. The best time with him involved blood and shit.

Ludwic: Alexandra said that he was terrible in bed. They only did it a few times. He abuses everyone. He must also abuse you.

Jennifer (who is obese): [10]You're sleeping with Damien! I heard from Michiel that he sleeps with women and literally throws them out of his bed. He was hitting on me relentlessly all of last year. I felt so unsafe with him. You just got out of a relationship. You have to be careful because you don't know what you are doing.

Lianne: You know, I was convinced for a while that he was in love with you. But now, I see that he isn't. I've known him for a long time and I can see that he doesn't love you.

Clara: You must be a masochist to be dating a guy like that.

Marlous: You're dating Damien? Does he know that?

Anna: They say that Damien has changed and is nicer because he's sleeping with you. People talk about you, you know. Well, I guess I shouldn't be saying that.

Else: So, you're the one who Damien is in love with. What does he see in you? Maybe it's your looks? I guess you are his type – physically.

Jenny (visiting Frida in Damien's room): So, this is the King's room? This is where the King sleeps?

Henk (to Frida): What is your name again?

Rick (friend of Henk): You just need to know that she's Damien's girlfriend.

Horst: They are being mean to you because they are jealous. When the revolution comes, and El Presidente (referring to Damien) is on the balcony before the masses, it's going to be you standing next to him waving the little handkerchief, not them.

Once, at a squatters' party with Frida, Willem the breaker, approached Frida drunk, and said, "Hey, you, where's your man? Where's El Presidente? What is he doing letting you come to this party all by yourself. If he's not around, does it mean I have a chance with you? Why isn't he here? Where is he?" To this, Frida responded (in Dutch):

> Look at my forehead. Is there a sign that says that I'm Damien's secretary? Now, if you want to talk to Damien, you can call him, email him, stop by and visit him, find him in the squatters chat room, or see him at the kraakspreekuur. These are the ways that you can talk to him. If you really want to, you can fuck him too. I'm sure that he would let you.

Willem was dumbstruck while his friends nodded drunkenly with approval. After this incident, Frida confided to me that it was time for her to find a normal rental apartment to take distance from the squatters movement.

Returning to the concept of the homosocial, these individuals were more interested in relating to Damien. They treated Frida as a third-party substitute against which to funnel their aggressions which masked their feelings of love and dependency in response to his status as an authority figure. As discussed earlier, Dominic was a well-known womanizer whose sexual voracity conformed to expectations of kraakbonzen and movement ideals regarding sexuality. His sexual practices exhibited that by indiscriminately loving everyone, he actually loved no one in particular. Damien's sexuality in the movement provided a contrasting model. His refusal to engage in the sexual economy of the subculture also conformed to Alberoni's framework. By Damien literally not loving anyone in particular, he committed himself wholly to the movement for political reasons which increased an elusive sphere of emotional sovereignty that he maintained around himself towards other squatters.

The many comments that Frida received as a result of the affair reflect similar emotional negotiations to those levied against Janneke. They revealed jealousy towards Frida for being a single individual who, exceptionally, receives individual love from the charismatic leader, where previously, he exhibited love only to the total group collectivity. The comments relentlessly attempt to dismiss this love by disparaging the affair as "physical," and hence, a form of loveless exploitation, as well as label Damien as a dangerous abuser of women (none of which Frida had experienced). Again, in terms of the homosocial, these individuals were more invested in connecting to Damien through Frida, as the woman with less status, but still too in awe of him to express such feelings to him directly.

Emotional dependence and the absence of authority

To further examine how the squatters' subculture constructs authority, it's helpful to consider the foil of Ludwic, a squatter who calls himself a kraakbonz but is not recognized by others as an authority figure. Ludwic's inability to achieve recognition as an authority figure stems partially from his position straddling the line between insider and outsider since his outsider status originates from his working-class taste and habitus. Ludwic conveys a habitus of emotional dependency rather than emotional sovereignty. Despite Ludwic's having excelled in a number of squatter skills, his habitus betrays an emotional dependency by misrepresenting himself as a kraakbonz, through his incessant gossiping, and his state of cultural marginality.

Ludwic is in his forties, with chin-length, dyed dark hair, big glasses, and missing front teeth. Ludwic is kind, though not charismatic and easily fades into a room. He never has a girlfriend and announces to his fellow squatters if he obtains a woman's telephone number, proudly displaying the piece of paper. Although born and raised in Holland, his dark hair and relative smallness lend him a vaguely "ethnic" appearance. Once, at a squatting action, Ludwic dropped a lighter in front of police officers. While bending to retrieve it, a police officer looked at Ludwic with disgust and asked him (in Dutch), "Do you even speak Dutch?" His fellow Dutchmen consider him a foreigner in his own country.

Ludwic spent most of his youth in detention centers for petty crimes. As an adult, he worked in a factory as a skilled laborer, was married, and raised a family. According to Ludwic, after his marriage ended, he decided to embrace an alternative, communal life style, by squatting in the east of Holland. He claimed that he left the squat because it was overtaken by drug users (a process that commonly occurs in big squats, see Chapter 4).[11] After this experience, Ludwic moved to Amsterdam and became involved in the squatters movement without having any connections. When Ludwic told me his story, he emphasized that he slept in a hotel during his first night in Amsterdam.

Ludwic has a number of squatter skills that earn him capital in the community. He adeptly researches houses to squat by disguising himself as a building inspector. Once he squats a house, he installs electricity, gas, and water, and constructs floors and walls. He was a member of a group that squatted an enormous house with an owner who had violently evicted squatters with hired thugs in the past and took responsibility for protecting the house from its owner. Ludwic also enjoys confrontational situations and rioting. He demonstrates commitment and sincerity in the movement by attending all squatting actions and potentially violent actions, such as alarms and resquattings.

Despite his dedication to the movement and his extensive squatter capital, Ludwic has an ambiguous status, straddling between insider and outsider. His working-class taste and habitus mark him as not quite belonging. Markos, a fellow squatter, described Ludwic as "just a working-class guy with working-class taste." "The guy drinks Heineken and loves chicken. What else is there to say," laughed Markos. Rather than engage in conversations about microbreweries, beer culture, and the minute differences among beers, Ludwic instead prefers Heineken (a symbol of low quality, flavorless, corporate mass consumption) and complains that the beer in the social center is too expensive rather than appreciating its high quality for its relatively low price. He sneers at "the hypocritical vegetarianism of the squatters movement," and at the, "vegan fascists."

Ludwic's disdain seems to derive from his status as an outsider rather than the insider perspective of having mastered and understood the aesthetic cultures of the squatters movement and then rejected them. The insider perspective reflects another level of oppositionality, in which someone who has mastered the conventions of the squatters' scene then rejects them out of critical perspective. However in Ludwic's case, his non-compliance with the squatters community's cultural practices did not originate from this convoluted process of mastering and rejecting, but from never mastering at all nor even wanting to do so. In contrast to Coen, however, who articulates his rejection of squatter cultural practices from a position of personal working-class critique, Ludwic frames his refusal defensively and within a practice of gossiping and expressing disdain for a community that he clearly depends on emotionally.

If one only spoke with Ludwic to describe the squatters movement, it would seem that he occupies the status of the main kraakbonz. According to Ludwic, "People come to me to talk about their squatting problems. They need me to help straighten out complicated issues." Talking from inside his squatted house – whose owner was notorious and with whom the squatters had many violent interactions, Ludwic said, "Do you want to know why I have this room?" (pointing to a small room in the front of the house). "It's at the front, and if anything happens, if any of those fuckers try to come by, I'm the first to know. I watch everything."

At squatting group meetings, in contrast to Shirin, Ludwic can focus on a topic and contribute insights. Instead, he often argues with other people at the meeting and challenges the authority of the kraakbonzen rather than engage in the topic at hand. When Ludwic talks about his work in the movement, he emphasizes his presence at confrontational and potentially violent situations as well as his efforts at strategic manipulation. He never speaks about his considerable building skills. Most of the time, though, Ludwic spends insulting the other kraakbonzen. He obsessively disdains both Dominic and Damien. Dominic is an "arrogant asshole who thinks he knows everything." He gossips about Dominic's treatment of women and informs Dominic's many girlfriends that Dominic cheats on them. He can soliloquize for hours about Damien and how he "abuses everyone and everyone puts up with it." He wants to "cut off Damien's head to save the squatters movement."

It's difficult to ascertain if Ludwic tells the truth. He claims to reject a paying job to protest the Iraq war, calling squatters like Damien who have a high paying job, "hypocrites." Yet, it remains unclear if he refuses to have a job or if he cannot manage to obtain and hold a job. He told me that he left his first squat in the east of Holland because it deteriorated into a drug users' space. His former housemate from this squat scoffed at this assertion, saying instead that the living group asked him to leave because he pit housemates against each other, causing conflict to splinter the group. I watched him repeat the same tactics in a squat in Amsterdam, arguing with his housemates, exasperating them, escalating small conflicts between people, to the extent that they also eventually asked him to leave. He claims, in contrast, that he left the group out of frustration because they lacked political ideals.

All of these behaviors lead others to withhold authority from him because his actions subvert his intentions and reveal a total lack of sovereignty through the demonstrations of self-doubt, emotional dependency, and cultural marginality. By advertising himself as a kraakbonz, he demonstrates the opposite: that he is not one. In a community that rejects authority, those who hold it must deny first off, that such hierarchies exist, and second, that they hold positions of authority. His constant gossiping about others and derision of the kraakbonzen subverts his intention. He intends to decrease their authority but, instead, by gossiping about them, reifies it. By perpetually insulting others, he reveals a self-doubt that requires the dismantling of others to bolster his own fragile sense of self. He defines himself continuously in relation to others and openly seeks recognition for his investment in the movement, and as a result, does not receive it. Such demonstrations signify an inability to occupy the types of central positions in the movement that he seeks.

Ludwic constantly derides and insults the community where he is a member, but in doing so, shows only its substantial importance to him. He once said to me in a moment of heartbreaking honesty: "What are you still doing here with us? You are a smart woman. You can do whatever you want. You know, I have no other choice. This is my only community. I have no other place to go."

Conclusion

At the beginning of this chapter, I wrote that the squatters' subculture and its unspoken but omnipresent expectations of authenticity and authority create a social world full of contradictions. In the face of such silenced paradoxes that comprise the daily existence of squatters who identify as political and active, it seems appropriate to question what squatters gain from such struggles and negotiations. In the desire to be recognized as a figure of authority, both failed and successful, there is a quest for a sense of belonging, acceptance, and love that can never be spoken out loud in a sphere that is dominated by a hostile pose.

Putting aside the issue of skills necessary to enable the machinations of the movement, the figures of failed authority, Shirin and Ludwic, could never occupy the positions of authority that they sought because their actions revealed a persistent emotional dependency and vulnerability that rendered it impossible for others to recognize them as authority figures. Serving as mediating priests, authority figures should exude emotional sovereignty. Shirin and Ludwic's transparent striving for love led them to never receive it, at least in the form for which they aimed.

In contrast, the successful authority figures, Jenny, Fleur, Coen, Dominic, and Damien, all possessed a habitus of emotional sovereignty and, as Bourdieu names it, "a sense of one's place," (1984: 471) which enables them to project an elusive emotional independence, using their class backgrounds strategically when necessary to enact this sovereignty. Regardless of their performance of aloofness, they are as emotionally invested as the rest of the squatters but have the skills and habitus to portray themselves otherwise. They also are able to find love and belonging in more abstract ways such as by receiving a round of applause at a neighborhood council meeting after a speech or by the non-reciprocal and asymmetrical relations of love that they maintain with the members of the group, as Alberoni contends.

In this dialectical quest for love, the culturally marginal and the culturally central need each other and the squatting subculture. For the culturally marginal, the squatting community and its subcultural capital offers them the possibility to achieve love, belonging, and acceptance in a way that is impossible in the discursive mainstream. For the culturally central, the squatters' subculture offers a community consisting of a number of marginalized people who will more readily project a sense of magic and authority onto them for possessing a number of basic middle-class capacities.

Notes

1 Action squats are spaces specifically squatted to make political statements in addition to providing housing. These differ from spaces that are squatted only to provide housing.
2 I write "according to Shirin" because it's unclear if she truthfully represented herself. I believe that as a designer, she was well trained and had impressive skills, but that she most likely was unable to succeed socially as a member of a team and interacting with clients.
3 Even this honor of being invited to be a member of the kraakspreekuur was dubious since during this time, this kraakspreekuur was dominated by Lianne, who was well-known for being hostile to capable women. This meant that Lianne actively recruited women to join the kraakspreekuur, but only women of whom she did not feel threatened. Thus, the choice of Shirin, who felt honored by the invitation but whose capabilities were questionable, and as a result occupied a low status in the informal hierarchy of this kraakspreekuur.

4   In fact, after Shirin was evicted from the Motorflex, she lived as a guest in different squats for nearly a year since she was unable to squat a house on her own or find a group to squat with her. Eventually, she returned to Germany because she was unable to find a job and an affordable housing situation in Amsterdam.

5   Again, I doubt the veracity of this claim. I do not think that Shirin actively searched for a job, despite perpetually talking about needing a job and lacking money.

6   At the time of my fieldwork, it was considered unacceptable for privileged people to take advantage of a white, elderly, working-class woman, who was considered to be in a more vulnerable position.

7   In fact, Jenny eventually became a kraakbonz.

8   While I was a squatter, there were various epidemics that rolled through the scene: tuberculosis, Chlamydia (several times), and scabies. I witnessed a disturbingly high number of young women, who identified as feminists and complained about machismo in the squatters movement, put their health at risk through unprotected sex with men who had reputations as promiscuous womanizers. In conversations with these women, I always said that if the man in particular was not using condoms with them, then he wasn't using condoms with anyone. This information did not impact their behavior. Some women shrugged their shoulders and conceded sheepishly, "I know, I know." Others teased me for being excessively concerned with hygiene. These women interpreted my concern as undue attention to hygiene rather than highlighting male dominant behavior.

9   The fact that the names are in Spanish is another ironic word play, referring to Latin American dictatorships.

10 I note Jennifer's obesity because despite the subculture's disavowal of mainstream beauty ideals, obesity is not widely considered attractive. Obesity in Amsterdam is relatively rare, and particularly so in the squatters' subculture. Kraakbonzen in particular tend to date women who are considered attractive both in the Mainstream and in the subculture. To be clear, there is a difference between being considered overweight, for which there is more acceptance in the subculture, and being obese.

11 Many of Ludwic's claims are questionable. As stated later in the text, Ludwic's claim that he left the squat because drug users had taken it over was denied by one of his former housemates, who stated that they had asked him to leave because he caused excessive conflict in the group.

3

"Showing commitment" and emotional management

Excerpt from interview:

> **Teun:** Eventually we found a fairly big squat that was on sale. We spent a month sorting it out; how long it had been empty, if there were options of buying. We were doubting if it was really empty because there was a lot of stuff in there. Eventually we decided to squat it. The squatting group told us to wait a week because they were having a party. We squatted it a week after and two days before we squatted it, it was sold. So we broke open the door and occupied it through the summer. The new owner was a dodgy Christianity group.
>
> **Nazima:** Why was it dodgy?
>
> **Teun:** It's a very … the house they owned it, they put, they make it for students to live in. For Christian students to live in and they make a package deal. They rent the rooms, including the food, including the obligation as well to spend their amount of time into Christianity … They are very strict in it as well. It's not … in my opinion, they put a lot of bindings … They've got this twenty page list of things you should live by if you want to rent a room from them. And in my opinion, that's … I don't find that very honest. Or giving people a bit of freedom. And I think that is a very wrong way to convince people of Christianity.

This chapter presents a cartography of internal power dynamics within the intimate space of squatted houses. Squatted houses are fundamental to the structure of the squatters movement in Amsterdam. Living groups within squatted households who identify as part of the squatters movement,[1] consequently both reflect and refract larger movement dynamics of hierarchy and authority. They reflect the standards of a larger movement in the sense that one's squatter capital contributes to one's status position within a squatted household. They refract in that within a household, the highest values are to maintain a lively and peaceful group dynamic, silently maintain the unspoken hierarchies within a group without challenging them, and thereby avoid tension and conflict. Whereas in both the front stage and the

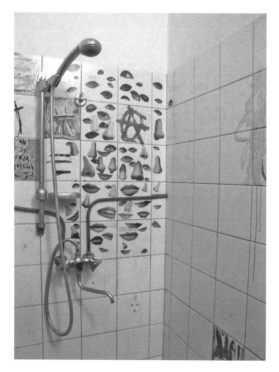

Figure 3.1 Shower inside of a squat, 2006

backstage of the movement, being an outspoken and argumentative persona
brings status and capital, such traits should be minimized within a living
group to promote a cohesive and peaceful home life.

In this chapter, I first argue that authority comprises a combination of
having organized and originally squatted a house, seniority, and consist-
ently "showing commitment." I highlight a range of squats: from the most
"active" in the movement to a squat that vigorously repudiates the move-
ment's ideals and social values. In these portraits of authority, one sees how
authority figures practice their dominance in a group, how they express
expectations of others, encompassed in the term, "showing commitment,"
and how housemates with lesser status negotiate this terrain of unstated
hierarchy. Moreover, I examine the term "showing commitment," using
Arlie Hochschild's concept of emotional management. The act of showing
commitment is deliberately a vague and ambiguous term because it depends
on the authority figures in the group to determine what it means to show
commitment while simultaneously denying that they possess this authority.
Further, authority figures are exempted from "showing the commitment"
that they desire of others.

I then discuss how people who were invited to move into a house after its squatting hold authority because of their skills and squatter capital. Following this, I describe the story of Karima, an undocumented East African woman who lived in a squatted house as a guest and unusually for an undocumented person, participated in the squatter community. Due to her personhood rupturing the normative "feeling rules" in this community, in which people felt pity for her rather than a fictitious sense of equality, the living group did not invite her to become a housemate, leading her to move out of the squatters' community. The final part of this chapter discusses the consequence of not taking authority in these liminal spaces and how in such cases squatted houses are often taken over by heroin users.

Squatting a house as the constitutive act of authority making

In the squatters movement, squatting one's own house is the first and most pivotal step in being recognized as a "real" or authentic squatter. Within a living group, those who squatted a house hold the position of the most authority. One Sunday, I attended two squatting actions held after one another. The first squatting action, of an empty eighteenth-century building in the center of Amsterdam by a group of four people, failed because after the group broke open the door, they found evidence of a resident, including freshly purchased food in the refrigerator and a warm and unmade bed. Everyone present fled to avoid arrest.

The second house was squatted by a different group of four people who had originally only intended to occupy one floor but unexpectedly found themselves with a three-story apartment building with a colossal ground floor space. At this second action, I asked Mario, a Romanian student from the first failed squatter group, who had been participating in the movement for less than a year, if his group could move into this second house. He said, "Well, I don't think so. Darius [a squatter from the second group who organized the action] is well, *Darius* [implying that Darius disliked him and that Darius is a difficult person]. And you know. Its property." Mario's statement indicated that despite the squatters movement's disavowal of property, because Darius had organized the action and had successfully squatted the house, the house became his property in the social dynamics of the movement. Mario's remark also demonstrates how quickly participants in this subculture learn its unstated rules.

In an anti-authoritarian and anti-hierarchical subcultural milieu, this hierarchical dynamic is rarely discussed openly. Instead, it's referred to obliquely by housemates with less status who moved in after the house was squatted while those who hold authority positions deny the existence of such dynamics. In one house I moved into a few months after it had been squatted, one housemate, Alicia, had been a member of the original group who squatted the house. After the first week of occupation, she never actually moved in to her room, instead staying with her boyfriend in a rented house. After four months of the squat's existence, her room remained empty, a fact that I found shocking amid the housing shortage.

Marie, a veteran squatter with ample squatter capital who lived in the movement for over ten years and had organized the squatting action, often complained to the housemates and the members of the squatters' community about Alicia's absence while never confronting her directly. Another housemate, Joris, groused incessantly about Alicia's empty room – again, in her absence – mainly because he wanted to live in the light-filled, spacious room with exceptional privacy. Arjen, a veteran squatter in his late forties who had also moved in months after the squatting of the house, once snapped at Joris in front of me, "There is no point in complaining to me about Alicia. If you want her out, you know that Marie is the one who has to make the decision." Despite a number of housemates feeling disgruntled about Alicia's empty room, the members of the group felt that Marie was the only person entitled to ask Alicia to move because she had organized the squatting action.

In a different house where I resided, Dana, a housemate with substantial squatter capital as a reliable and responsible person who efficiently organizes actions, announced suddenly that she had found another house to squat and that she planned to move the following week. In private discussions about why she had decided to leave (no one asked her directly) between myself, Roel (who had originally squatted the house), and Samuel, a veteran squatter who moved in afterwards, Samuel said, "Well, she moved in after the house was squatted and I guess she was tired of not getting her way with how the house runs." Roel, holding the position of most authority, responded by fervently denying the existence of such a hierarchy.

Living groups and "showing commitment"

Living groups are communal living structures in which people commit to living together cooperatively as an alternative to residing alone or in a family structure. There is an expectation that housemates eat meals together, contribute equally towards household expenses, spend time together, and somewhat share their lives with the people with whom they reside. There are different standards for living groups than for residing in a group or a student house, in which each individual's room is their private space, only sharing the kitchen and bathroom when necessary, and without expectation of emotional connection. In the United States, living groups are referred to as communes, with the connotation that such groups exist mainly in the countryside in contrast to squatter living groups in Amsterdam, which are urban. Living groups exist outside the squatters movement in the Netherlands, including in the social housing system and the private market.

Living groups are thorny structures because an expectation exists of cooperatively sharing household tasks and expenses while demonstrating and genuinely feeling an emotional commitment to the group and to one's housemates. In squats, communal living is further complicated because of the disjuncture between the ideal of a living group – mutual responsibility, cooperation, and emotional connection – and the lifestyle choices and interests of most people who choose to squat.

One essential component of communal living is the equal partaking of household tasks and finances. Yet the inherent contradiction is that a number of people choose to squat to avoid performing such tasks and financial accountability. Washing dishes, cooking, food shopping, cleaning, purchasing household supplies; such tasks are the daily, mundane, and necessary components of communal living. They seem too boring and repetitious for squatters who are only interested in the thrills of actions or lack the capacity to complete such tasks.

The same principle counts for financial accountability. A number of people squat to avoid financial responsibilities and paid employment. Many squatters who have paid jobs prefer not to spend their earnings on communal expenses. They are saving money for trips or simply use their wages on expenses such as vacations, partying, drinking, and drugs. Larissa, a veteran squatter commented, 'The other day, we had a dinner party and a friend of Jan said, "Oh, you guys must save a lot of money since you don't pay rent." We all just looked at each other and like, uh, hmmm. Then Joseph joked, "If I saved my money, how would I pay for my drugs?"'

The term "showing commitment" can only be understood in a context in which the majority of people do not want to commit. The fact that the behavior associated with showing commitment is highly valued means that it's uncommon among the majority of squatters. I have often heard this expression in two modes: first, as a critique in which someone is described as not showing commitment by never spending time in the squat, cooking, cleaning, etc. Second, as a way to explain someone's motivations, as in the following remark about Teun, who had docked his sailboat in a cavernous squat, "He goes there every weekend to help with the repairing of their dock to show commitment." In this case, in exchange for the housemates of this squat allowing Teun to dock his sailboat in their house, Teun had to "show commitment" by helping with the building project of repairing their dock. By spending time in the space and working on a communal project with this group, Teun demonstrated his gratitude, that he was communally minded, and possessed squatter skills.

Showing commitment is tricky because it's ambiguous, open to interpretation, depends on the person who purposely "shows commitment," and the recognition of the people to whom one endeavors to show commitment. In a living group, showing commitment often signifies investment symbolically in the house and emotionally to the group. It is made up of concrete deeds: regularly cooking, cleaning, shopping, repairing (thus, why a reliable and skilled builder is highly sought as a housemate), occupying, barricading, generally taking care of a house, and being financially reliable. Other ways of showing commitment is to manage the legal defense of a house: working with the lawyer, organizing the paperwork, campaigning, researching, arranging the court case, etc. Idealistically, the act of showing commitment is intended to be inherently altruistic and communal, benefiting the group versus solely serving one person – like cooking for oneself and eating alone in one's room.

The second part of showing commitment seems more complicated because it refers to an emotional connection that may or may not exist. As for household deeds, others have to recognize this emotional connection and define it as "showing commitment." Emotional connections are demonstrated via a general hanging around and an effort to spend time with, show interest in, and bond with one's housemates. This expectation lies at the heart of the living group ideal in its attempt to create an alternative to the perceived alienating models of the nuclear familiar or of living alone.

Between the obligations of squatter living groups, movement expectations, and the fact that one resides precariously in a house that could at any time be evicted, this type of lifestyle can easily become all encompassing. Such expectations allow little room for other activities, for example, being an artist or a student, two groups attracted to squatting and the freedom enabled through no rent housing.

Consequently, performing a genuine emotional connection becomes fraught due to the larger context. First, the housing shortage in Amsterdam signifies that a number of people – students and artists in particular – desperately seek low-cost housing. Therefore, when such people reside as guests in squats or are allowed to remain as housemates, a power dynamic exists between these people and the ones who squatted the house who granted them a residence. Thus, an unacknowledged dynamic of gratitude and dependency is masked behind a fiction of equality and radical left communal living. Since this power dynamic exists, but cannot be discussed, those who hold authority have expectations of people who they invite to live with them, but often express such desires circuitously rather than transparently. Furthermore, authority figures are exempt from the conditions they demand of others; unless those with less status challenge them, creating conflict which proves antithetical to having a peaceful home life.

The power dynamics of squatter living groups are inherently convoluted but well worth the difficulty of unpacking. Arlie Hochschild (1979), the pioneering feminist sociologist, coined the concept of emotional management, which encompasses the concepts of emotion work, emotional labor, and feeling rules. Hochschild argues that in service-oriented professions, particularly those associated with or dominated by women, an essential aspect of these jobs are to manage one's emotions and of one's co-workers and clients. This facet of the jobs tends not to be discussed but are intrinsic to these professions and are productive of stereotypical gender roles, such as emotional care in nursing, or the types of client interface required of airline flight attendants.

Emotion work describes the process of either masking one's emotions to give a different impression (surface acting) or actively internally changing how one feels to enable a symmetry between one's internal emotional state and the impression that one transmits to others (deep acting). Hochschild uses the metaphor of acting methods to describe these two approaches: the Stanislavski school for surface acting and the Method school for deep acting. Hochschild frames emotion work as a private act influenced by larger social and cultural norms (feeling rules) in which one matches what one internally feels to what is considered appropriate to feel and express.

Hochschild distinguishes emotional labor as the private process of emotion work being transferred to the public world of work (Wharton 2009). In describing the process of emotional labor required in paid labor situations, Hochschild argues that management disciplines workers to provide more than their physical labor, but this part of themselves that exists outside of a professional context ideally should be protected from being managed. These demands of masking one's "true" self in a labor context, either on a surface or deep level, is stressful and leads to consequences such as burnout.

Hochschild's work helps to further understand the internal dynamics in living groups in squatted houses because she describes expectations that are present but become invisible because they are not discussed. She also describes how in situations where emotion work is necessary, people adapt themselves to such demands, internalize them, and perform them without explicitly naming this process of management. Hochschild sheds light on the emotional gymnastics one undergoes in a space that is ideally intimate and safe, but because it both constitutes and is the product of a social movement with its own criteria for capital, subcultural performance expectations, and a housing crisis, such a space is infused with multi-layered power dynamics. The ethnographic portraits of hierarchical dynamics within three squatted houses illustrate these points.

Frank and Janny

Housemates who have squatter capital in the movement and who originally squatted a house have the capacity to hold notable authority over a living group if they desire to wield it. Frank and Janny, both veteran squatters, had organized the squatting of a three-story building, which featured eight

Figure 3.2 The "Leidsbezet," a squatted social center in the center of Amsterdam, 2006

bedrooms and an atelier. They refurbished it into a magnificent building, which exhibited better conditions than most rental property in Amsterdam. Over the years, the living group comprised a revolving door of house-mates. Given the housing shortage, I never understood why so many left an immense, beautiful, building with sizable rent-free bedrooms that could easily have been rented for hundreds of euros a month. After spending considerable time with this group helping them with their campaign, I learned that the hidden expectations for being a member of this living group could potentially cost more energy than the time and effort entailed in paying rent.

As the people who had originally squatted the house, Janny and Frank silently occupied the positions of most authority. Miles, a former housemate comments, "Janny and Frank are the heart of that house. They are the axis on which that house and the living group turns." After having squatted a number of houses and lived in squatted living groups throughout the Netherlands, Janny and Frank decided to carefully choose their housemates for this particular squat. They wanted housemates who participated in the political aspects of squatting, took responsibility for the house by reliably conducting maintenance and ensuring that the gas, electricity, and water functioned properly. They also sought housemates to create a "cozy" atmosphere (cozy translates into *gezellig*, a Dutch word that connotes a warm, sociable, comfortable, atmosphere) by cooking, cleaning, and acting sociably within the living group. Further, they looked for potentially interesting people, such as activists, students, or artists.

This is a tall order; so, unsurprisingly, conflicts arose when housemates failed to fulfill these expectations. If the housemates were artists or students, heavily involved in these activities and their own social networks, Janny and Frank criticized their lack of participation in the squatters' community and lack of commitment to the living group. According to Frank:

No one has to participate but it's nice if they do. There is so much that people can contribute to. The giveaway shop. Going to the voku. Working at the voku. The way I see it, without the movement, they wouldn't have a place to live. But no one has to do anything that they don't want to do. It's just nice if they do.

On the other hand, when "real squatters" moved into the house who were "active" in the squatters' community and often spent the entire day lounging in the house and socializing with the living group, Janny and Frank criticized them for acting "passively." The term passive encompasses a set of behaviors, from neglecting household tasks, repairs, and finances, to an attitude of general reluctance to take initiative in their lives in the discursive Mainstream as viewed by Janny and Frank. Janny habitually criticized the "real squatters," who often resided in their house as guests after being evicted, for not studying in higher education, being habitually unemployed, lacking financial responsibility, and for allowing the squatters' community and its repertoire of actions, parties, and social centers to function as their entire social world.

The housemates who succeeded in living with Janny and Frank for the longest amount of time were two young women who effectively negotiated these unstated expectations. Amalia and Janneke were both integrated into the Mainstream. Amalia, from Finland, studied in a Master's program in media studies and Janneke, from the south of the Netherlands, worked full time as an intern for a graphic design firm. Living in Janny and Frank's house was the first time either had experienced squatter living and neither possessed squatter capital. For them, squatting, its political activities, and social scene provided them with an easily available social network that they appreciated as newcomers to the city. They enthusiastically participated in the squatters community by working in various institutions: Janneke volunteered weekly in the giveaway shop and Amalia served as a member of the activists' samba band. They also took responsibility for the house by working on its defense campaign, cooking, cleaning, managing finances, and periodically maintaining repairs.

Most significantly, neither challenged the authority of Janny and Frank. With Frank in particular, they skillfully placated him. When he criticized them for neglecting to clean, they never challenged him for holding them to standards that he failed to fulfill. Janneke complained to me once, "Frank just goes around, making a big mess in the house, and the three of us don't say anything. We just let him do it." Amalia told me that during house meetings, when the three women planned how to implement the house's defense campaign and allocated tasks, Frank often became upset, arguing that he felt silenced and excluded. Both women learned to appease Frank by immediately apologizing, patiently listening to his ideas, and then continuing with their earlier discussion once he felt comfortable.

Frank is a Dutch squatter in his late twenties. Trained as a filmmaker, he works during the summer, filming music festivals around Europe, and lives off his summer salary during the rest of the year. Unusually for squatters, Frank grew up in Amsterdam, the son of an architect and a school nurse, both of whom professed leftist politics. He was raised to call them by their first names and dislikes describing his class background, refusing to, as he says, "put himself into a box." As a fifteen-year-old punk sporting a Mohawk, he became involved in the squatters movement when he read a newspaper article interviewing squatters who were preparing for the eviction of their mansion. Excited, he skipped school to help with the barricading. Having spent half his life in the movement and having squatted houses throughout the Netherlands, Frank comments in his current non-punk state, "I feel at home in the scene. I feel at ease. If I'm in Amsterdam, I'm going to go squatting. It's a natural choice. I get a house and I participate in the scene that moves around it."

Frank possesses sizable squatter capital for his skills. He can break doors, build effortlessly, serve as a police spokesperson during actions, has acted courageously during countless direct actions for a number of radical left causes – a connoisseur of "scene points," and has been jailed numerous times for non-instrumental acts of bravery. During actions in particular, he exhibits an unflinching confidence in the face of danger where others may show fear. He speaks his mind refreshingly, criticizing squatters who attend meetings high or drunk whereas others feel uncomfortable and remain silent. When I interviewed him, he articulated thoughtful opinions on his motivations to squat as a protest against the dismantling of social housing, on the effectiveness of squatters' barricading methods, and his reasoning for whether or not to campaign to defend the squats where he had lived. He has a reputation for being well organized, outspoken, articulate, and a strategic thinker.

Upon spending time with him and his housemates by helping them with their defense campaign, I learned that Frank's squatter capital for being well organized and strategic lacked any basis and were disguised by his verbal acuity and confident persona on the backstage of the squatters movement. Frank's partner, Janny, a capable and intelligent young women with considerable skills and squatter capital, had in fact organized most of the squats from which Frank's capital derived. Although Frank believed in campaigning to defend squats and often criticized other squatters for neglecting their court cases and the political issues that surrounded their houses, he lacked the organizational skills to campaign for his own houses.

Luckily for Frank, his partner and his two housemates unobtrusively produced campaign materials, met with the kraakspreekuur for advice, lobbied politicians, conducted extensive research, prepared the legal issues, and wrote press releases, all without involving him. However, in public forum, such as the neighborhood council and at actions to support their house, Frank served as the house's spokesperson. I once asked Janny how she managed this situation in which a team of three feigned being a team of four without the knowledge of the fourth member. She replied:

> During meetings, I give him space to talk for as long as possible. When it's time to divide the tasks, I make sure that he gets the tasks that are the least important and take up the most time because he has a lot of time on his hands and he is not efficient. The rest of us are working so we don't have as much time as he does. Like giving out flyers. That takes lots of time but it's not so important. The important stuff – talking to the lawyer, or dealing with the politician, things that have to be done quickly, either I do it or I ask one of the girls to get it done.

In this case, the three women were perfectly aware of their emotion work with Frank to maintain a sense of peace in the household. They self-consciously delegated public speaking opportunities to Frank to enable him to feel that he was more of an authority figure than he actually was. These women strategically acted to maintain a sense of harmony in their group and did not feel disempowered in their machinations. Janny participated in this surface acting of emotion work for the sake of her relationship. While for Janneke and Amalia, they understood that with a little emotion work to engineer Frank to feel that he was "the Big Man" (quote from Amalia), they lived contentedly in a uniquely beautiful house in excellent condition without having to organize and manage squatting their own spaces.

Frank's misrecognition in the squatters' community as having skills that he did not possess poses an interesting example to consider for a Bourdieuian framework. Frank had the privilege of two sources of socialization: his upper-middle-class background and the squatters movement. He disliked speaking about his class background, for example, understanding that his father's profession as an architect marked him as being upper-middle class, a classification that disrupted the overall fantasy of classlessness enforced within the squatters' subculture.

From his family background, he was inculcated into middle-class tastes and habits that enabled a subconscious recognition of affinity and competence in the hierarchy of skills and predispositions of the squatters movement. His cultural capital provided him with a sense of entitlement and confidence to speak and be heard in public settings, particularly the backstage of the squatters' scene, and to enact an oppositional self which gained him further capital since public speaking and oppositionality are highly esteemed in the squatters' subculture. Dana, a veteran squatter with significant squatter capital, unmasks Frank's confident posture whenever given the opportunity. She had once assisted him with installing gas and water pipes and found his confidence appalling. She remarked, "He's so arrogant about his abilities but he doesn't actually know what he is doing. With gas pipes, that's dangerous."

From the squatters movement, he was socialized into the movement's values, ideologies, and acquired respected skills such as building and breaking. Frank learned that campaigning to defend a house from eviction was highly prestigious on the squatters movement's backstage. To explain why he never campaigned in the past, he articulately informed me that after a careful analysis of the legal situation of the house, he realized that such campaigning was a waste of time and that as a result, he refused to conform to movement expectations. Thus, he presented himself as aware of the expectation, but having the critical awareness to evaluate it and rebuff it when it proved unnecessary. Frank refrained from admitting that he decided not to campaign because he preferred to spend his time by lying in bed in his room for days on end, watching television, and surfing the internet.

The case of Frank and Janny presents an example in which squatter capital fluidly transfers into household dynamics. Frank and Janny possessed tremendous capital in the movement and this reflected in their authority in the hierarchy within their squat. More intricate configurations of hierarchy and authority within living groups arise when a disjuncture exists between a person's squatter capital on the movement scale and one's "commitment" to a house.

Larissa, Fleur, and Barbara

Larissa is a Dutch squatter who has lived in her squat for over five years, a nineteenth-century building with four stories and an immense ground floor space. Her squat is unusual because it's considered "safe," meaning that it's not under impending threat of eviction because the owner fled Europe due to criminal charges of money laundering. The group who originally squatted the house intended to create a self-consciously apolitical space. According to Ludwic, one of the original squatters, "This house is for people who just want to have fun. No politics are allowed. Just fun." Ludwic's statement indicates a rejection of a rejection, that is, a repudiation of an overly political life that is an imagined norm in the squatter subculture, which in itself is a spurning of the image of an alienated Mainstream life. Ludwic and his housemates sought to create a living group where no one felt pressured to discuss politics and thereby refusing what they considered to be the hypocritical dogmas of the squatting scene. Further, this living group consumed without showing consideration to the taste habits of the squatters movement, renouncing vegetarianism and holding bacchanalistic meat barbecues in which they reveled in eating the industrial meat that they purchased from the supermarket – versus organic meat from the natural foods store as sanctioned by the squatters' subculture. Although this living group identified themselves as apolitical, they still participated in the squatters' scene by attending squatting actions, political actions, parties, and working at the social center.

The living group of six people comprises a mix of veteran squatters and people without experience in the squatters movement, and thus, no capital. Larissa, an assertive and outspoken Dutch woman who studies urban planning and writes poetry, is a senior member of the group despite not having squatted the house initially. She moved in six months after the original group had already extensively repaired the house (that is, built floors, walls, a kitchen, two toilets, a bathtub, a shower, installed gas, electricity, heating ducts, heaters, plumbing, and insulation), successfully defended it from the owner's thug friends who periodically broke their windows until the squatters confronted them, as well as won their court case. Compared to the veteran squatters in her living group and because she missed the confrontational and labor-intensive aspects of squatting her house, Larissa possesses limited squatter capital.

Unusually in the squatters' community for someone in a position of authority, Larissa speaks openly about the hierarchy in her living group:

> The house is mine and Solomon's [the person who originally squatted the house, organized the action, repaired the building, and won the court case]. Fleur is never here and yeah, she's good about squatting stuff, but otherwise, she's never here. She's so lazy in so many ways about the house. She never cleans. And the others are, you know, the others. The perfect housemate though is Barbara.

Fleur, Larissa's housemate, is a young Dutch woman who possesses all the components of squatter capital (see Chapter 2 describing Fleur as a spokesperson): she's a breaker, she can build, she is well organized, she is an articulate spokesperson, she's strategic, and she has participated in violent actions in which she performed non-instrumental acts of bravery. Because she has a career as a commercial ship's officer, she spends less than half of the year in Amsterdam. As a result, Fleur is well known in the squatters' community and retains capital for her skills and past deeds but, within her living group, she is less valued because she does not "show commitment" due to lack of emotional investment and by neglecting household chores. Fleur still has more authority than her housemates without seniority and capital, as illustrated by Larissa's quote, "and the others are, you know, the others." But in the delicate power relations within a squatters' living group, she has less authority than Larissa and Solomon due to her frequent absence and general lack of "showing commitment" to the living group and the house itself. Larissa's dismissal of Fleur ("She's so lazy") also points to Fleur's extensive capital in the movement in that only authority figures on the level of the movement are actively disparaged (see Chapter 2). Furthermore, Larissa's description of the house as "mine and Solomon's" is both refreshing in its openness as well as another indicator of the hierarchy. It shows that she holds a position below Solomon, who is the person with the most authority in that house but would never openly admit this fact.

Lastly, Larissa's mention of Barbara in this quote significantly demonstrates the meanings of "showing commitment." Barbara is a young Dutch woman in her early twenties who came to Amsterdam to train as an elementary school music teacher. Through her network, she first lived as a guest in Larissa's house and eventually the living group invited her to stay as a housemate. Barbara has no squatter capital and although my interactions with her were brief, she entirely lacks an oppositional habitus. Instead, her overall attitude is of someone who seeks to please others. Despite her lack of squatter capital, Larissa and her housemates valued Barbara because she did household chores without complaint, was socially available and pleasant, participated in the group without challenging authority, and avoided creating conflicts. Thus, Barbara's qualities as a perfect housemate in which she treated people kindly, was socially warm, avoided conflict, and effortlessly did household chores were antithetical to being a "real squatter" where the performance of a constant hostile oppositionality symbolizes sincere political conviction.

Gerard and Allen

Gerard, a German man in his mid-twenties, came to Amsterdam to study in the Dutch university system. Through informal contacts, he met a group of people who were preparing to squat ten houses located in a housing complex on the outskirts of Amsterdam built in the 1970s for the workers of the nearby municipal jail. Because most of the workers did not want to live in these houses, half of the houses were empty for over five years before they were squatted.[2]

For Amsterdam, these houses were unique. They were spacious, with four bedrooms, a living room, two bathrooms, storage space, an open kitchen, a balcony, and an enormous garden. Squatters found them especially appealing because the owner, the municipal jail authority, had not destroyed the structures and utilities as is the common practice of owners to deter squatting. As a result, the houses were ready to live in without a need for refurbishment.

The squatting action of the ten houses was ambitious and immense. Although different groups had organized themselves to live in the various houses, the whole action – that is, the research, the organization, the breaking of the doors, the consultation with the kraakspreekuur – were all coordinated by a Dutch organizational management student, Deanna.[3] Deanna carefully selected the residents, avoiding "people with dogs," a.k.a. crusty punks. Instead, she sought squatters who were students, musicians, dancers, theater people, and visual artists.

The physical location of the houses on the outer rim of Amsterdam and the lack of activist squatters alienated most of the residents from the more entrenched activist squatters' subculture. When this complex of houses is mentioned, squatters who identify as activists scoff that the residents are lazy, artistic, hippies who squat only for free housing. They criticize them for failing to politically campaign, legalize the houses, or create a more vibrant squatters' community. The complex's residents claim to refuse the ideological and behavioral norms of activist squatters by retaining a low profile in the eyes of the state so that they can, in fact, live in these houses for free and dedicate themselves to their art and studies. When pressed to participate more in the political areas of squatting, the residents reply that they avoid politics because they believe that the city housing authority has forgotten the houses and fear that the publicity resulting from political or social activities will lead to eviction.

Gerard was one of the students who Deanna allowed in the group. He initially lived for one year with a random living group. Having no squatter capital, he felt uncomfortable, disliked the authority figures in his living group, and general movement culture. Compelled by his dissatisfaction, Gerard decided to squat an empty house on the complex with Paul, another man who sought his own space. Because Gerard had organized the squatting of this house, he felt more comfortable and more ownership of his new house. He and Paul invited Allen, a Spanish photography student, to become a housemate. Within a year, Gerard and Allen were the only housemates left since Paul spent most of the year traveling around the world to organize performance art pieces. Gerard used his authority as the only person who originally squatted the house in a way that the Dutch classify as "anti-social." In addition to his own room, he took over the living room as his private study, often borrowed money from Allen without paying him back, stole bikes from his non-squatter neighbors, and stole from the private rooms of his housemates, understanding that no one dared to confront him.

Gerard holds a more extreme opinion from his fellow squatters because he actively disavows the movement and does not justify his lack of participation in radical left politics. He states, "The only thing that I have in common with squatters is that we all use the same loophole in the law." Coming from a lower-middle-class family, Gerard describes himself ironically as aspiring "to be a capitalist." When discussing his career plans, he continues semi-ironically, stating, "This is how I plan to conduct world domination." By calling himself a capitalist and using such language, Gerard demonstrates that he understands that openly discussing the desire to accumulate wealth is unacceptable among the European radical left. Thus, he shows that he understands and spurns the conventions of the squatters movement but in a different modality than what is acceptable in the squatters' subculture. In the squatters' subculture, the path to sovereignty and authority lies in dismissals of dogmas while still maintaining a general anti-capitalist perspective. Furthermore, he squats because it benefits his lifestyle in that he receives a uniquely spacious house rent-free, but he hides his living in a squat from his friends because he dislikes the radical left and feels ashamed of being a squatter.

Gerard's refusal of the unspoken assumptions of the squatters movement nearly cost him his home. One summer, he arranged to rent his room to a student while he was in Germany. His housemates learned of this arrangement and forbade it. If he had rented out the room and news of this rental had reached the activist squatters, the activist squatters would have evicted him immediately with or without the permission of his housemates. Twenty squatters would have shown up at his house, moved out all of his belongings, and changed the locks. They would have told him that he had broken a sacred rule and then exiled him from the scene. They would have enjoyed evicting him.

I know all of this information from Gerard and from Gerard's housemate, Allen, the photography student from Spain who, contrary to Gerard, embraces the squatters' subculture. Although Alan lacks the skills that comprise most forms of squatter capital (breaking, building, organizing, and strategic manipulation), he frequently participates by cooking in the voku, working at the bar, helping others build, consistently attending weekly squatting actions, helping occupy squats during their first two weeks when it's still possible for the police to evict, and assisting with barricading. His squatter capital consists of his enthusiastic though unreliable participation versus capital based on skills that derive from long-term commitment, or from taking initiative and responsibility.

Frustrated with living with Gerard and too afraid to confront him, Allen complained incessantly about Gerard and his attitude towards the squatters movement to his friends in the social center. Allen's friends, including myself, after listening for months to his complaints, encouraged him to kick Gerard out of the house. Allen, vacillated, stating that he did not feel entitled to make such a decision since he was not a "real squatter," having moved into the house after it had been squatted. Allen asked the kraakspreekuur for advice. Jeremy, a member of the kraakspreekuur with over fifteen years in the movement and ample squatter capital, responded:

> The guy is an asshole but he hasn't done anything wrong. Yeah, he wanted to rent out his room but you guys did not let him. Other than that, there is no reason for us to interfere. If you want him out, let us know and we'll help you, but without that decision, no one is going to punish this guy for being an asshole. He squatted the house and he has the right to be a prick about it if you guys let him be this way.

In the case of Gerard's house, despite his dismissal of the movement and its norms, the value prevailed that the person who had organized the squatting action holds the most authority and only in extreme cases – such as renting out a squatted space – can this person be kicked out. To be clear, although no one interfered with Gerard, his behavior has social consequences. Most likely, because he wanted to rent his room but was stopped by others and thus not showing a consciousness of the lack of ethics of such an act, he will not be able to squat again with the help of any kraakspreekuur in the city, putting him on the equivalent of a squatters' blacklist. Also, if and when the complex of squatted houses where he lives gets evicted, finding a group to live with or squat with him will pose a challenge due to his reputation.

Cherries

People with squatter skills are often invited by established living groups to their houses, which demonstrates the material rewards of squatter capital. Squatters who possess abundant skills on the scale of the movement transfer their capital into their status in the hierarchy of a living group. According to Solomon, "If you are well organized, responsible, and active in the community, you always have a place to live." David, a veteran squatter in his early fifties, remarked, "It's like cherry picking. You have to choose carefully to get the best of the batch." The "cherries" are people who participate in the movement with ample capital, usually as builders, campaigners, and/or are well organized and have reputations for being good housemates in a living group in the sense of showing commitment, possessing social skills, and adeptly doing emotion work to minimize conflict. Such squatters have more status than housemates who have no squatter capital, especially those who entered a house as guests and simply remained, relying on the fact that most people are too conflict averse to specifically ask guests to leave. In terms of their squatter skills, "cherries" are invited to become housemates with the unstated assumption that they will use their skills in exchange for a room and authority in the group. If they fail to fulfill expectations, the housemates will feel disappointed but most likely not confront openly, choosing instead to complain behind the person's back.

Guests and housemates

In squatted living groups that identify as part of the squatters movement (versus wild squatting), it is common practice to host guests for months at a time, especially if a guest is a recently evicted squatter. Such a convention reflects movement practicality and ideology. Practicality because the cycle of squatting and evictions requires a network of mutual aid in which squats within the network house each other. After evictions, squatters require space to recover from the eviction, search for a new house to squat, and have a backup space during the initial few weeks of a new squat when it's still possible for the police to evict. The ideology of this practice reflects a diffuse sense of solidarity in that squatted houses are not solely private, but communal movement spaces that ultimately belong abstractly to all squatters.

The practice of such a convention is that a hard line of distinction exists between housemates and guests. First and foremost, guests are expected to eventually leave. A housemate takes responsibility for the house and is accountable to the living group while a guest merely resides there. Different houses vary in their rules for whether guests pay for utilities or the amount of household responsibility expected. In such a situation, a guest feels less entitled than a housemate and shows consideration to the living group since guests depend on their generosity. Such careful considerations are common for long-term guests in private homes. However, in squatted houses, its further complicated because they are symbolically movement spaces and not exclusively private. Accordingly, a different set of rules exists that result in negotiations, which conform to both movement ideologies and living group dynamics.

The status of guests can create difficulties for living groups and for guests. After the successful squatting of a house that appears safe from immediate eviction, a living group is often deluged with requests from squatters and friends of friends searching for a room "temporarily." Given the amount of responsibility and work entailed in the squatting of a house, including refurbishment, repairs, legal management, household duties, social obligations, combined with the unfortunate fact that the majority of people who seek to reside in a squatted house endeavor to avoid such responsibilities, the whole situation is potentially problematic. If a living group permits guests to reside in a house without articulating expectations or a departure date, living groups find themselves doing all the work to enable the house's existence while guests live off their labor parasitically. It is also common for guests to simply never leave unless the living group forces them out, which proves uncomfortable for everyone involved.

These reflections arise from my personal experience and observations. In the last squatted house where I was invited as a housemate, I remember spending several hours cleaning the filthy kitchen one afternoon. While I cleaned, a seventeen-year old Finnish hacker who was hanging out in the squatters' scene after having run away from his parents, sat in the kitchen and silently watched me, never once offering to help. He had been living in this house for two months as a guest before I moved in as a housemate. After I finished cleaning, I explained that perhaps, as a young man, he had not been taught the value of helping someone doing domestic chores. I had just been evicted dramatically with another fifty people, so I also explained that if he lacked interest in household tasks, any one of the fifty squatters who had recently been evicted would feel thrilled to move into his room and gracefully assist with chores. In response to this request – which was the first time anyone had articulated such expectations during the eight months that he resided in squats – the Finnish teenager left the next day.

With the understanding that most people are not interested in "showing commitment," a guest can then acquire value in a living group and eventually be invited to stay as a housemate simply by acting responsibly and showing consideration, as illustrated in the case of Barbara, the "perfect" housemate of Larissa. In situations where guests exert themselves to "show commitment," living groups and guests conduct emotion work in which everyone is conscious of, without acknowledging openly, that guests seek to ingratiate themselves with the goal to be invited to stay long term.

To successfully show commitment entails the enactment of a series of increasingly altruistic and communal acts, from helping occupy, build, repair, cook, and clean to more risky gestures. At one large, multi-story squat, Marcus, a Dutch squatter, had been living as a guest for months while he saved money for a year-long trip to South America. He helpfully occupied, cleaned, and cooked, but the living group considered him "a loser." After three months, he asked if he could stay as a housemate and the living group denied his request. However, his status changed months later when he gave his name for the court case to evict the house. Most members of this living group refused to provide their names because doing so causes the name giver to be personally financially liable. Such an act is especially risky since squatters rarely win their court cases. Despite the general consensus that Marcus was a "loser," by taking personal risk for a communal case, he showed a level of commitment that when he asked again if he could become as a housemate, the living group was forced to accept him.

With these dynamics in mind of authority, hierarchy, "showing commitment," the differences between guests and housemates, and the necessity and assumption of emotion work for everyone involved as a method to negotiate such dynamics, the story of Karima, an undocumented African woman living as a guest in a squatted living group, presents an interesting case to further examine the feeling rules in these spaces.

Karima and the squatters

Karima was born in East Africa and moved to the Gulf with her family as a child. Her mother fell ill early on and Karima quit primary school to take

Figure 3.3 A squat alongside the Amstel River in the center of Amsterdam, 2006

care of her family. When she became older, she worked as a domestic servant for an Arab family, residing with her employers during the week and visiting her family on her day off. She felt desperately unhappy and caged within her family and her job as a domestic servant. She did everything possible to leave her life in the Gulf with the options available to her, such as dating foreign men in the hope of marrying.

Eventually, she saved the exorbitant broker fee for transport and a tourist visa to Europe. As is the case for undocumented migrants and refugees, Karima's migration journey is mix of legal and illicit. She illegally purchased a tourist visa that enabled her to legally enter Europe as a tourist, in which she illegally intended to live and work. Border officers often treat people from the Global South suspiciously, assuming that they plan to overstay their tourist visas. With these challenges in mind, Karima arrived in France and successfully charmed immigration authorities to allow her to enter.

As Karima walked through Paris, she thought, triumphantly, "I am finally free. I have found freedom. I am in the West." Afterwards, she took a bus to the Netherlands, where she declared herself a refugee. She managed to manipulate the refugee process in the Netherlands, negotiate contacts and networks among the East African community in Amsterdam to obtain a job as well as procure a room in Larissa's living group. Her actions and behavior, although a typical story for a refugee/undocumented migrant, are extraordinary considering the constraints on her emotionally, physically, and the discrimination she faced as an illiterate, black, African woman in Europe from a low social class. Karima showed independence, initiative, and cleverness in her ability to smuggle herself from the Gulf to Amsterdam.

In the activist community in Amsterdam, it is fairly common for undocumented people to live in rooms in legalized and regular squats. However, most of the time, undocumented people only reside in squats and do not participate in the scene or in the living group, nor is there an expectation that they "show commitment." Karima acted uniquely by participating in her living group and the squatting community. She was welcomed whole-heartedly both as an individual and a symbol of the squatting community's solidarity with undocumented people, and the movement's general anti-racism and inclusivity. When Karima arrived, she told her refugee story to the living group in a gesture of honesty and supplication. She explained that she had become pregnant in the Gulf. Expecting to get married to escape her mother and her life as a servant, she found herself abandoned by her lover, an Arab migrant technician. Her mother then forced her to have an abortion, the final straw that pushed her to leave. In response to this story, the living group accepted her as a guest.

Karima contributed to her living group and in the squatters' community by diligently cooking and cleaning in her house and at the voku. In comparison to the overall attitude of reserve and hostility exhibited by squatters, she smiled, was friendly, sweet, and flirtatious. This attitude, along with her beauty, her tiny stature in comparison to tall and broad European squatter women, and her silence arising from her lack of fluency in Dutch and English, led many squatter men to find her attractive.

Furthermore, as a Muslim woman, Karima was a novelty. In the Gulf, she wore a burqa[4] in public spaces and was chaperoned by a man at all times. In Amsterdam, she went swimming with squatters where the men swam proudly naked and her housemates teased her for refusing to wear a bikini out of modesty. Karima's novelty as a Muslim derives from the tension in Amsterdam surrounding the so-called lack of integration of working-class immigrants from Turkey and Morocco. Squatters often live in predominantly immigrant neighborhoods where women wearing headscarves and niqabs abound. Although living side by side in a relatively small physical space, a chasm exists between squatters and immigrants, especially Muslim women, who are seen as off-limits and entirely Other. Karima symbolized a world, which the squatters saw daily but could not connect to due to gulfs of culture, race, and class.

Karima, then, had a good chance of successfully living in the squatters' community and benefiting from the available support through its networks. Why then did the squatters in her living group ask her to leave despite her diligent participation and contributions to both the squatters community and to her living group? I asked Solomon, who is the unstated authority figure in this living group. He explained that despite the care and responsibility towards the house that Karima displayed by vigilantly cleaning and cooking, instead of viewing it as "showing commitment," Solomon and his housemates interpreted her housework as a result of her training to be first, a "slave" to her mother, and then, as a "slave" to her Gulf employees.

Ultimately, the housemates asked Karima to leave because they thought that she never showed interest in "an autonomous life." To prove that she was autonomous, she had to demonstrate some level of DIY qualities such as improving her English language skills, by learning Dutch, or by learning how to ride a bike. Despite the many times people offered to teach her these skills, Karima missed the opportunities and caused frustration among her living group. This living group generally permits guests for a maximum of three months but, to concede to her cultural and undocumented status, they allowed Karima to stay for six without becoming a housemate, an exception that they would never have made for a white European. Finally, the living group never felt intimate with her. Solomon and his housemates perceived her permanent smile as fake. They believed that Karima felt deeply exhausted and depressed from having fled her country and her family. Hence, Karima's positive facade disturbed her housemates, creating distance rather than intimacy.

Karima's story and the dissonance with her squatter living group reveal the consequences of the disruption of feeling rules. From Arlie Hochschild's overall framework of emotion management, feeling rules are societal norms about the appropriate type and demonstration of feeling in a particular situation, for example, sadness at a funeral or happiness at a wedding (Wharton, 2009). Hochschild focuses on the emotion work that people undergo to superficially project particular emotions, change their inner feelings to match the feelings rules of a situation, or how people enforce feeling rules on each other

Solomon stated that the reasons for not allowing Karima to stay were due to her insincerity and dependence (the smile masking depression and the repetition of "slave" behavior). Yet, in my description of the internal dynamics of squatted living groups, the surface acting of emotion work and the relationship of dependency between authority figures and their housemates who have less status, dominate the modes of performance within these squatted living groups. How then did Karima excessively leave the impression of insincerity and dependency in a milieu where such dynamics are rampant?

The underlying ideal of this subculture promotes communal living consisting of self-possessed, independent, and oppositionally minded individuals who treat each other as equals. The sacred feeling rule is then, that people within the movement should be able to interact as equals in which no one should feel more or less privileged. Such feelings of equality that guide relationships should, ideally, lead to people being able to speak openly and honestly to each other.

Karima's manner of presenting herself to the group clashed with this feeling rule of equality. Her openness about being undocumented, and in particular, the story of her abusive mother and the forced abortion that motivated her migration, disrupted this feeling rule of equality. Karima portrayed herself as someone who should be pitied and who depended structurally on the living group. The transparency and the necessity of the dependency, I imagine, made the Dutch squatters who made up the living group, highly uncomfortable. With this open dependency as well as her habitus and aspirations diverging sharply from the taste cultures of the squatters movement, the living group could not trust her because her dependency, vulnerability, and lack of openness tainted her actions.

Even if Karima had not presented herself as pitiable, the same problems with Karima as a housemate would have persisted. This is because the very body of Karima, her undocumented status, her vulnerability as an underclass, black, East African woman, and her lack of education, disrupted the feeling rules of equality between the housemates and their visions of anti-capitalist bohemian communal living. Her presence inserted into this household the disturbing world of undocumented migration into Europe resulting from the inequalities between the Global North and South. She impeded the fiction of classlessness and the invisible normativity of the comforts of the welfare state, in which European squatters partake without acknowledging the privileges and the overall sense of security that they receive from their entitlement to it.

Figure 3.4 Building on the Damrak, where ground floor space was in use commercially while upper floors were squatted, 2006

As a symbol of these global political realities and their intrusion on the fantasy of the anti-capitalist bohemian squatter life, Karima paradoxically worsened her situation because she veered from the usual behavior of undocumented people in the squatters movement as shadow figures who use its resources but do not participate in the community. Because Karima sought to create emotional bonds with other squatters, interacting with her only increased the awareness of the inequality, vulnerability, and dependency rather than relieve it.

This was particularly the case because she had a number of squatter lovers. A diversity of lovers is common in a community that values multiple partners but the style with which she had the lovers, again, reflected her structural vulnerability. It was clear to everyone in this community, including myself, that she sought to marry for citizenship. Again, failing to understand the cultural and political norms of this community, she conducted her search in a way that counteracted her goal instead of helping to achieve it. Rather than stating openly that she sought a marriage partner for citizenship, for which she could have then found someone willing to participate (marriage/partnership for European residency is commonplace in the left activist community), she dated various men hoping that they would fall in love with her and then want to marry her. Such a plan in a radical left squatters community was destined to fail. First, marriage is seen negatively as a bourgeois, Mainstream, and oppressive institution. Second, a number of young men in this community are not interested in commitment, structural responsibilities, paid employment, nor do they want nor have the capacity to manage the bureaucracy required to enact such an operation. Karima's general impression of insincerity reflected an unawareness of the multiple and unstated rules of this community that someone in her position could not understand, leading to her being asked to leave.

The consequences of no authority

With this context of silenced hierarchy and authority, it is helpful to explore the consequences of no one taking positions of authority or leadership in squatted households. I will first use my personal experience with such a household as an example to consider this question, an experience from which I do not pretend to have any objective distance.

To situate myself in the schema that I present in this chapter, I occupied different positions along the hierarchy. Over a period of two years, I lived in four squatted living groups. In the first house, I moved in initially as a guest and the living group eventually invited me to remain as a housemate. At the time that I moved into this squat, the little squatter capital I possessed came from having worked as a cook in the voku for six months prior in which I showed that I was reliable, responsible, and a good cook. In collective projects like vokus, it is difficult to find people who commit to a project by consistently arriving every week, on time, to enable its occurrence. During the year and a half that I resided in this first house, I accumulated further squatter capital with the acquiring of organizing and strategic manipulation skills. I formed an integral part of the team that developed and implemented the house's campaign against eviction. I also often cooked for actions, participated in squatting actions weekly, and regularly attended radical left political actions every few months.

After this house was evicted, I resided as a guest in a squatted house but left after several weeks due to the oppressive atmosphere created by a sadistic emotional relationship between two of its inhabitants. At that point, I had been planning to squat my own house but lacked the time and energy to prepare an action because I felt desperate to leave the second house. I was then offered my own flat in a block of squatted houses where I lived for two months. Although I shared a kitchen with another person, I did not feel that we formed a living group since we each had tremendous personal space. This block of houses was subsequently evicted in the most violent and unexpected eviction of squatters in nearly thirty years, in which I was present and left scarred and shaken

Prior to that eviction, another living group had already invited me to live with them. I knew the two authority figures in this group, Roel and Marie. Marie was a veteran squatter whose capital was based on having lived in a number of high profile social centers in the past ten years and was known as highly organized and intelligent. Roel was an exceptionally skilled builder. He was an amateur plumber, heating engineer, electrician, and carpenter. They lived in a sprawling squat of four stories with multiple bedrooms. Bored and frustrated with living alone, Marie had squatted this space to live communally. Unfortunately, with the exception of Roel, she had assembled a group of housemates who squatted to avoid rent, paid employment, household responsibilities, financial accountability, and whose priorities were to party, use drugs, and travel. After the squatting action, Marie and Roel found themselves responsible for the tasks necessary to enable the house to exist: from managing the legal aspects, negotiating with the mafia owner, to constructing floors.

Four months after they had squatted the house, Roel and Marie invited me to move in as a housemate. Although they never openly stated this, I understood that they needed someone who was organized, reliable, had campaign skills, and would not feel intimidated by the aggressive owner. They offered me one of the most spacious and loveliest rooms in the house (displacing one of the deadbeat housemates to a smaller room) and since the house was not under eviction threat, I took their offer. I lived in this group in a position of high status although with less authority than Roel and Marie.

During the first two months, I cleaned the house physically and metaphorically. I cleared out rotting old furniture, replaced it with cleaner and more attractive furniture that I had found on the street, threw out unused items that cluttered the space, and put down rugs to cover the stained and ancient carpet. I removed the decrepit wallpaper and decorated the common areas with plants. I converted an unused space into a dining room and cleaned out closet spaces throughout the house that were filled with items from years before the house had been squatted. I painted the bathroom walls and replaced the rotten linoleum in the toilet, which stank of years of urine (we wore face masks while removing it, during which Roel yelled, "It stinks of the pee of a hundred old men!"). Before I moved in, the electricity and the gas originated from a hacked source. I arranged for the group to pay for the utilities instead of stealing it. I set up an internet connection. I also contributed to the group's cohesion because I cooked almost every night leading to the group habitually eating together.

Metaphorically, I cleaned the house of the many who viewed it as a crash pad to hang out, party, and use drugs. This cost more energy than the physical cleaning. Despite Roel and Marie's extensive experience and skills, both avoided conflict. Consequently, the house was filled with random guests who considered the space their private lounge area in Amsterdam.

After having lived in and spent time in squats that were more structured and selective regarding who they permitted inside their houses, I found these strangers unbearable. Leaving for work in the morning to encounter someone passed out in front of my bedroom door, coming home from my university job to find random French hippies in a multi-drug stupor in the living room who had eaten all the food that I had purchased the day before, or waking up screaming at 4 a.m. to discover a stranger in my bedroom who was walking through the house playing a portable radio at full blast – I found this situation intolerable. Marie's solution was to never spend time at home, sleep elsewhere, and complain to members of the squatters' community. Roel was also never home, being an avid drug user in which he passed the days at party squats. Even if they had been present, both were unwilling to confront these people and set limits. Instead, they hid in their rooms.

I strove to get rid of these people without explicitly kicking them out. As per the earlier story, the Finnish teenager left once I asked him to help with household chores. There was a common space that had been empty except for a mattress where people slept after partying and using drugs. I cleared out the mattress, installed a dining table and bureau, and transformed the space into a dining room. Throwing out the filthy furniture also removed further "crash" areas. Having connected the utilities and the internet to the house, I introduced the idea of housemates and guests contributing financially, which led to more people leaving. I continually set limits until the only people left were those who were responsible, reliable, and considerate. Afterward, I changed the locks.

Despite the effectiveness with which I enacted these changes, the experience was horrible. I had moved into this house in a traumatized state from having been evicted in the middle of the night by the police, dealing with the hysterical behavior of the squatters during the siege, the claustrophobia of being in jail, as well as having to re-obtain my impounded belongings. Instead of resting from the exhausting shock of this experience, I found myself in a situation in which I had to bully out random people without support from the authority figures in this squat. Although both Marie and Roel told me in private that they felt pleased with the changes that I had made, they hid behind my straightforward character to maintain friendly relationships with the people who I was pushing out and therefore, hated me.

My personal experience with having to perform the taxing role of setting limits and managing the space made apparent the necessity for leadership within a squat. I also understood clearly that for many people within this movement, the challenge of transgressing the feeling rule of equality, and settling limits and boundaries proves so difficult that the squat itself becomes vulnerable. Moreover, for many in this movement, this feeling rule of equality and the corresponding rejection of any form of authority within a squat, is so sacred that a squat becoming chaotic and unsustainable is preferable than taking a leadership role.

After this experience, I understood the process behind a term that I have occasionally heard, "when squats go wrong." I had heard comments such as, "Everything is fine in the Motorflex. It hasn't gone wrong." This expression is a euphemism for squats that have transformed into locations for using heroin. I realized that this transformation results from an internal dynamic in which no one takes a position of authority within a squat, thereby allowing a wide variety of people to use the space, leading to a space becoming a "junkie house."

Among activist squatters, heroin is taboo and becoming known as a heroin addict means losing one's capital entirely. One of my first interviewees, Jacob, who had been an active squatter as a teenager and then left the movement after five years, mentioned his involvement with a squatted orphanage with beautiful gardens that housed 120 people, which he euphemistically described as "disorganized." When the group who had organized the space were bought out with replacement housing and cash, a small group of ten activist squatters remained. According to Jacob, this group was "invaded" by "disorganized people," whose main interest was to avoid paying rent and who refused to contribute financially to the house. Many had serious drug problems so that the house developed into "a problematic area," where Jacob saw disturbing things, such as "junkies half dead in the hallway" and people "putting baskets full of shit in their fridge." After the house was evicted, the police discovered a dead body in the basement.

I had heard other stories of "squats that go wrong." Carlos, a Slovenian squatter, said to me once, "I've seen it so many times. One guy or girl in the house starts doing heroin. Then this person gets a boyfriend or girlfriend and they do it together in the house. Next thing, everyone in the house is doing it. It becomes a junkie house." I asked two veteran Spanish squatter friends about their experience with "squats that go wrong." Miguel, a Spanish squatter, initially replied, "If someone does heroin in a squat, the group kicks him out." I pressed, not accepting this answer. Marta then added, "That's not true. What happens is that for junkies, it's hard to find places to do it with other people. So once they find a place, more and more go to that place and do it there. Before you know it, you are the only one left and the house is filled with junkies. You have to leave, not them."

Conclusion

Mapping the cartography of power dynamics within living groups who identify as part of the squatters movement in Amsterdam is fraught because of the incompatibilities between imagined ideals and silent practices. The ideology of the movement rejects property as "theft." Meanwhile, the silent practice is that those who squatted a house have the most authority and "own" the house in the social logic of the movement. Furthermore, the behavior and skills that contribute to one's status in a household are related to but not necessarily the same as those that add to one's capital in the movement. With some skills, such as building and campaigning, one's capital in the movement transfers fluidly into one's status in a living group. However, the oppositional, argumentative, persona that holds merit in the movement's public spaces should be suspended in the private sphere to avoid conflict and maintain a peaceful and "cozy" group living environment.

Squatted houses present a convergence of the public and private in a dramatic way. On one level, these houses are private spaces, where ideally a resident should feel comfortable in a convivial and warm living group, which provides a safe haven from urban alienation via an alternative to the nuclear family. However, they are also public spaces in that they both constitute and are produced by a social movement. Hence, movement capital of individual residents impacts the micro-social dynamics of the group. Further, these houses are spaces for socialization, skill acquisition, and are in fact, organizations in which the participants must cooperate and take responsibility for tasks to enable the houses to exist and run effectively.

Returning to Hochschild's emotional management, she distinguishes between emotion work and emotional labor, stating that the first is primarily a private act influenced by broader social and cultural norms that define feeling rules while the second is a process directed by management in a paid labor context (Hoschschild 1979). Squatted houses complicate this distinction. The ambiguity between private and public in these squatted houses, the expectations around "showing commitment," the denial of hierarchy and authority in these spaces while silently maintaining these power dynamics, combined with the housing shortage; all of these simultaneous factors make it difficult to distinguish between emotion work and emotional labor.

With such contradictions in mind, does this social movement community offer emancipation on any level beyond a discursive one? Do the feeling rules of equality that dominate the emotional landscape offer liberation from the shackles of Mainstream life from which many of this movement's participants seek to flee? The case of Karima and the examples of squats where people refuse to enact authority leading to their transforming into "junkie houses," present cases when the feeling rule of equality, so sacred to a non-hierarchical, anti-authoritarian social movement community, are explicitly challenged. For Karima, she framed herself as someone to pity and care for rather than as a self-possessed, oppositional activist. This led her squatter housemates to feel that she overly depended on them. Despite the numerous cases of dependency and unequal power relations that prevail in a squatted living group, her inability to perform "autonomy" led the housemates to feel uncomfortable to the point where they asked her to leave.

In houses where no one enforces authority, such as the last squatted house where I resided and houses that eventually become overwhelmed by heroin users, the requirement that one or more people, usually those who originally squatted a space, claim their authority by openly setting limits and standards on the behavior of others, confront conflict, and position themselves as figures of potential dislike, the prospect of refuting this revered feeling rule of equality proves overwhelming. Rather than dispense even temporarily with the feeling rule of equality and the paragon of a warm, "cozy" atmosphere, squatters would rather abandon the space in search of new opportunities to be "autonomous."

Notes

1 I distinguish between living groups in squatted households that identify with the movement versus squatted houses which make no claim to being part of the movement, including wild squatting (see Chapter 1 for definition of wild squatting).
2 These houses further complicate the definition of "squat" since most of the tenants who were employed at the jail had stopped paying their rent for years before the squatting action.
3 Deanna was the de facto queen of this squatters' village, to the extent that approximately two years after the squatting of these houses, she moved to Finland permanently. However, she left her belongings throughout the house and retained her room – and demanded that no one else live in it – so that she could stay in her room during her vacations to Amsterdam. Her housemates never challenged these demands but complained about them to others in this community.
4 I learned this detail from Karima's Dutch housemates. However, it's unclear what type of head covering Karima factually wore in the Gulf because in the Netherlands, people colloquially refer to all head coverings as burqas. This term is inaccurate since burqas are predominantly worn by women in Afghanistan. In general, Dutch discourse does not distinguish between various head coverings worn by Muslim women around the world and their symbolic connotations.

4

Liminal adolescence or entrapping marginality?

In his memoir, *Another Bullshit Night in Suck City*, the poet Nick Flynn wrote:

> I worked with the homeless from 1984 until 1990. In 1987 my father became homeless, and remained homeless for nearly five years ... Sometimes I'd see my father, walking past my building on his way to another nowhere. I could have given him a key, offered a piece of my floor. A futon. A bed. But I never did. If I let him inside I would become him, the line between us would blur, my own slow-motion car wreck would speed up ... If I went to the drowning man the drowning man would pull me under. I couldn't be his life raft (Flynn 2004: 10–11).

I begin this chapter with this quote because it captures the fluidity between marginality and centrality in an activist's biography and how social movement subcultures serve as a space for liminal adolescence. Flynn, a renowned American poet, first met his father while working at a homeless shelter. The memoir features two parallel stories. One is the story of Flynn's father, which Flynn imagines through bits and pieces that he learns from friends and family since his mother committed suicide when he was an adolescent. The second is Flynn narrating his own biography. Their lives run parallel: both men envision themselves as poets and both struggle with alcoholism. Flynn's father, both as the charming, young poet and the abusive, homeless alcoholic, haunts Flynn as a ghost and a warning. Flynn's memoir serves to highlight the themes of narrative, self-representation, the construction of "youth" and biography that I repeatedly revisit in this chapter.

Returning to social movement studies, an ambiguity exists around the predominant participation of youth in "new social movements". Melucci, in particular, attempts to consider the appeal and the function of social movement subcultures for young people and further interrogates the meaning of youth as a biological category in "post-industrial societies" (Melucci 1989, 1996). However, due to the lack of an ethnographically informed perspective, his analysis tends to be abstract and often myopic.

In this chapter, I consider a number of questions around why social movement subcultures often serve as a form of youth culture. A number of activists construct their involvements in social movements as a liminal, youthful stage in their lives before they transitioning to a so-called adult lifestyle which requires long-term commitment and responsibility, such as dedication to a career and/or a family. For many activists, social movement subcultures serve as a space of extended adolescence. Moreover, someone who has already transitioned into an adult lifestyle can, by entering a movement subculture, revert to a youth culture way of living defined by change-ability, temporariness, and lack of responsibility.

This construction of movement participation as a form of liminal adolescence sheds further light on issues of cultural centrality and marginality. As discussed in Chapter 2, cultural centrality is comprised of the demonstration of a number of skills, competencies, and a particular habitus both within the movement and in the Mainstream. Cultural marginality is defined directly in relation to cultural centrality. It is marked often by a squatter's long-term addiction to drugs and/or alcohol as well as excess aggression, emotional and material dependence on the squatters' subculture, and displaying a lack of emotional control. I argue that since culturally central people assume that the movement is a space of liminal adolescence in one's biography, activists who are unable to exit the subculture are constructed as marginal. Furthermore, the very presence of culturally marginal people and their perpetual existence in social movement subcultures dissuade culturally central people from dedicating themselves to the movement on a long-term basis.

Ethnographies that chart the careers of participants in subcultures demonstrate that the period of time a culturally central activist spends within a social movement subculture comprises a career with stages that eventually and ideally lead to retirement. Using a career framework, I contend that the unstated end goals of having surpassed the accumulated stages of an ideal squatter's career is a sense of self-realization demonstrated through the acquisition of squatter skills, the inculcation of an oppositional habitus in which one has mastered and rejected both Mainstream and social movement subcultural lifestyle and taste norms, and finally, a display of increasing conviction in movement ideals. Again, the self-realization resulting from a successful career in the movement exists in a community which also consists of culturally marginal people who have either never progressed through such stages due to lack of capacity or who have moved through a number of stages but failed to exit the movement. Hence, despite the unstated assumption that self-realization is the inevitable and ultimate goal, such a self-realization is not assured but an achievement.

Finally, by interrogating the assumptions regarding finite time in the movement and the existence of careers, I assert that the path to the autonomous life is highly scripted and fairly exclusive. The cultural specificity required to be recognized as autonomous is exhibited in relation to the entrance and exit of Karima, an undocumented black East African woman in the squatters' subculture first introduced in Chapter 3.

The movement as a period of adolescence and the "militant for life" as a marginal old man

Culturally central, activist squatters articulate the assumption that their time in the movement is a finite period of their lives. They associate their time as activists with studying in university and emphasize that upon finishing their studies, they expect to progress to another phase of their lives. In this sub-section, I only use quotes from interviews with female squatters who are culturally central and identify as movement activists. These women narrate their experiences in the subculture differently from male squatters. They readily admit that their time in the movement is determinate and often associate having a family with leaving the movement. Their statements contrast sharply with those of male squatters. None of the men who viewed themselves as active in the movement describe their involvement as limited nor did any of the male squatters interviewed, including those who considered themselves retired, associate having a family as a reason for leaving. Furthermore, female squatters' narratives tended to be more expressive and emphasized their feelings about their experiences as squatters. This sharply differed from those of male squatters who tended to narrate their experiences according to plots which centered events that revealed squatter capital, such as their participation in a violent eviction, their managing of a campaign, or their involvement in a social center.

Svenke is a punk Swedish squatter with long blond dreadlocks in her late twenties who came to the Netherlands to study in the university. Her entire wardrobe consists of black clothing with strategically cut holes and she has piercings around her body. She has worked in the kraakspreekuur in a neighborhood in Amsterdam for nearly ten years. When I asked her about her future goals, she replied:

> I want to finish my studies. I've been studying long enough and I want my degree. I want to have a normal life and a nice job. Maybe I can work for an organization. Right now, I live in two rooms and a kitchen, and it's fine for now, but I eventually want to live in a bigger house and have a child.

Juliette, a Dutch activist squatter, answered that in the future, after she finished her Bachelor's degree, she planned to learn Chinese in China, and then return to Holland to study in a Master's program in Asian Studies.

Speaking more specifically about her housing plans, she expected to eventu-
ally receive an apartment from the social housing list, explaining:

> In the end, I don't want to squat forever; but maybe in twenty years the
> house (her squat) is still here and so maybe we don't need to do that
> (move into social housing). I don't want to have kids and I don't want to
> get married ... I've always said that. My family says, I guess it's not your
> thing. But other people say, you wait until you are thirty and then you
> will want kids because everyone wants kids. People do expect it but I just
> don't want it ... I'm not into doing "the normal thing."

When I asked Maria, a Dutch activist squatter in her early twenties,
about her future goals, she related her current squatters' life with a point
in the future when she imagined that she would desire a different lifestyle,
specifically at the age of twenty-eight. At the time of her interview, she had
been temporarily renting a room in a friend's social housing apartment after
having been evicted five times in the previous three months. Renting the
room enabled her to rest and focus on her studies rather than spend all her
time and energy organizing political actions, getting evicted, and moving.

Although Maria appreciated the stability of living in a rental house, she
preferred a squatters living group and "to squat out of principle." Maria
envisioned living in social housing as a choice for a twenty-eight year old,

Figure 4.1 The squatting of Drawing School, part of the Rijksmuseum, 2008

which she clearly deemed as the age for adulthood. To explain why she planned to continue squatting, Maria listed what she appreciated about the squatters' subculture:

> I like this world really very much because almost everybody. People are really active. People are really, like, having ideals where they want to fight for, very they stand for. It's not like, some students from my school are like they don't give a shit as long as they have shopping hours and nice shoes, and they are so unaware of politics and stuff. That's really nice about it and people are really nice, it's non-commercial and that's the things I really like.

Following this praise, Maria criticizes the isolation, hierarchy, and prevailing gossip in the scene:

> But it's also, sometimes I think it's a really closed world where everybody only sees each other and nobody else outside this little world. And also everybody talks about everybody. It's also like a sorta world on its own. Some people who have, like, think they are, something like not really a hierarchy, but some people think they have more to say than other people. It's just like actually like a normal society where everybody is dressed in black.

Immediately after she lists her criticisms, Maria corrects herself to reaffirm her view of the squatters movement as full of politically convinced people who actively fight injustice:

> No, that's not really true. I really like to be part of this, I think there are really good people who are active and who are really aware about what is happening in the world and stuff.

She then reiterates her earlier criticisms, specifically its isolation from the rest of Amsterdam, the gossip, and the hierarchy, and states that she is happy that she continues towards finishing her higher education degree:

> But sometimes it's also like you are no better than anyone else. You know it's also like I said, there is a lot of gossip going around about everybody. That is, sometimes it makes me a little bit tired and then I am glad that I am still in school and I can also meet people outside this little world.

In this last statement, Maria indicates that she expects to become disillusioned with the movement for failing to provide a positive alternative to the Mainstream ("you are no better than anyone else … it make me a bit tired"). For Maria, finishing her studies has a number of symbolic and material advantages. Education enables two types of mobility: one in the Mainstream, allowing for more employment and cultural opportunities, and another that enables the freedom to leave the movement if she chooses. It symbolizes cultural centrality and the ability to make choices and have opportunities in a context with a preponderance of cultural marginal people who are partially defined by their inability to function without the subculture.

To further explore what demarcates her life currently from the one that she envisioned for herself in the future, she replied that she imagined that she would grow tired of the lack of privacy of group living and the amount of energy required to maintain a squatter's life:

> Maybe when I'm twenty-eight, I still want to squat. Maybe, because it's like, it's quite intensive to live in a living group or to have to move all the time. You don't have so much privacy … you are living with four or five people. There are always people in your house, and there are always stuff going on in your house. It can be really nice but sometimes when you want to be by yourself and you want some peace or quietness, sometimes it's difficult. And also because squatting takes a lot of time. Most of the time, you have to build your own house because a lot of time the electricity is not working and stuff like this and it costs a lot of time to search out all the permits, and to get a lawyer, and blah blah blah, yeah, I think it's almost a day job if you want to search it really good.

She then hesitated, uncertain if, in fact, at age twenty-eight, she would become weary of the squatter's life. She quickly concluded by comparing herself with Peter, the oldest squatter in the Netherlands:

> Maybe when I'm twenty-eight, I feel like, okay now I want some more quiet and a more stable environment but maybe on the other hand I think, no I want to still keep squatting, I don't know. I can imagine, at a certain point, that you feel like maybe then I would like to have a social renting house and still be part of the action world but not like moving stuff all the time.
>
> You know Peter? He did a lot of stuff. But I think if I will be like this on his age … I don't want to be like him on that age.

Maria refrains from talking about Peter more in-depth, stopping after emphasizing that she does not want to be like him at his age.

For a number of culturally central, activist squatters, they encountered figures such as Peter very quickly upon their initial involvement with the squatters movement. Most middle-class, culturally central squatters avoid elucidating in-depth what precisely disturbs them about these figures and echo Maria's sentiment, merely encapsulating their hesitancy by stating that they do not want to, "be like him at his age."

Margit, a Dutch activist squatter, deftly articulates what seems too difficult or uncomfortable. She compares the outlook that she acquired from her middle-class upbringing with attitudes of poor and culturally marginal squatters in her first living group:

> The first squat was really some kind of awakening for me ... I was bought up in a family that was really nice and well-educated, we were never really poor ... it was never really bad. I met some people there who were really, like ... with less opportunities, they didn't have the opportunities to study, they were working in building construction work. Some other people were working as a cleaner ... I found it a social structure that I never knew. It was like, woah, I never knew about this side of society. But it also hard because some people used drugs ... it was kind of an aggressive atmosphere.
>
> I was always ... I think I was brought up with the idea that there were so many opportunities in life. And these people who had another kind of philosophy, like life is hard. They were not so hopeful or not so enthusiastic about living.

Margit then describes both how she considers a state of uncertainty and lack of ambition to form a part of adolescence. She proceeds to describe how a number of squatters in her first living group existed in an extended period of adolescence that she found inappropriate. By focusing on squatters who she considers marginal and problematic, Margit articulates an ideal biographical timeline as well as her expectations of "normal" professional and lifestyle choices:

> Most of them were older and I was used to the idea, I am maybe still a bit used to the idea, that you have an adolescent period until, like, maybe until you are twenty-five and then you really know what to do with your life. You have a perfect job, you have ambition, you get a house, you get a car, you get a child, etc. etc. And these people were like thirty-five and still doing construction work and still not happy with their lives and still not knowing exactly what to do and still I would say, like, messing around a bit. I would say a negative word. Of course they have their ... ideas and dreams. But for me, it was like, you are pretty old already, how come these dreams never already came true? Or something like that. Yeah and most of them were smoking marijuana which I do not disapprove of but my idea is that you do it when you are an adolescent like you want to try out everything. You have a period smoking marijuana.[1] But when you're thirty-five, I'm like, ok, get over it now. I mean, it's a kind of phase that you should have left behind. When you're thirty-five or something and they were still doing that. It was, for me, it's a kind of sign, it's like, for me, this kind of behavior is for people who don't take really take their life serious.

So far, I've provided examples of young (early twenties), culturally central, women who identify as activists in the movement and envision their time in the subculture as a finite period in a linear timeline of stages that constitute their biographies. In contrast, Adam and Ludwic are two older male Dutch squatters in their early forties. Adam initially squatted when he was in his late twenties and then left the movement for ten years before returning to a squatter's life, while Ludwic became a squatter after he had raised children and divorced.[2]

When Adam describes his first period as a squatter in Nijmegen, he emphasizes the pleasure and excitement. He enjoyed the community living, the feeling of belonging to a group, and the satisfaction of fighting against injustice by working at the kraakspreekuur. He appreciated collaborating in communal projects with his fellow squatters, such as by building wooden bike racks to solve the problem of lack of bike parking rather than rely on the municipality to construct them. Adam elaborates:

> The moment that I was not squatting, when I was living in a rental house or something, that I noticed that I didn't feel so connected with the squatters' community, let's say compared to when I was living in a squat. The moment I am living in a squat, I had this feeling that I was connected to some kind of struggle and that is nice to be feeling, I think.

When I asked him why he stopped squatting, he answered vaguely, saying he could not remember his reasons but that he had "had enough" and that he had wanted "to concentrate on other things and do something new." It was difficult for me to ascertain if he sincerely could not remember his reasons or felt uncomfortable discussing them with me. He then explained that he moved from Nijmegen to participate in New Age therapy training in a small village in the south of the Netherlands. Adam did not finish the training and shortly afterward found himself homeless in Nijmegen, sleeping in shelters. He eventually obtained a rental house on account of his homelessness. Years later, after a number of housing situations, he returned to living in a squatters' community in Amsterdam.

Ludwic similarly emphasizes the community lifestyle as one of the main reasons he squats and that squatting allows him "to be free." He proclaims that he never became an adult, which he defines as "fitting into society, to have a house, to have a life, and a car and a tree in the backyard." When I questioned him, mentioning that earlier, he had been married with foster children, he replied:

> When I was married, of course, I had to provide for my family and I couldn't do the stupid things that I do now, like squatting, like drinking, maybe do some drugs, go to a festival for one week, sometimes I don't come home, I sleep in other places, you know. I parked my car in front of

my door here in Amsterdam for two years, I got a ticket every day, and I didn't pay it. So totally irresponsible.

Most people think that squatting is a political thing. For me it's a social thing, even if I could rent a place for free, just stay legally in a place, and don't pay any rent like a caretaker, I wouldn't do it. What's the excitement of living like this? I like the excitement, I like to take risk. I like to try new things. I don't want to be a slave of my own habits or society. I want to live free. I want to leave whenever I want. For me, it's like five minutes, I take my hard disk out and I'm gone.

These narratives complicate the discussion of youth and the functions of movements as liminal adolescent periods in the biographies of activists in social movement studies. New social movements scholar, Alberto Melucci (1989), devotes considerable analysis to the appeal of social movement participation for youth as well as the quality and the character of such involvement. According to Melucci, "youth" participate in social movements for a limited period of time and for particular issues, and that after their period of mobilization, eventually activists are drawn into other channels, such as the market or other institutions.

Melucci contrasts this form of limited participation with the image of the "militant for life figure," which he argues "was tied to an objective condition and a specific class culture" (Melucci 1989: 78). He elaborates that for new social movement activists, "Involvement in public-political action is perceived as only a temporary necessity. One does not live to be a militant. Instead, one lives, and that is why from time to time one can be a public militant" (Melucci 1989: 206). He further states that the different processes, tensions, and conflicts within movements:

Makes individuals commitment to them risky and uncertain ... the experience of being involved in a movement is both temporary and highly fragile. The quality and length of individuals' commitment depends very much on the resources available to them. (Melucci 1989: 215)

Melucci's writing on youth cultures and social movements proves, at turns, to be both problematic and illuminating. His analysis is based on a myopic vision of a uniform, homogenous, undifferentiated group called "youth" which does not exist. It assumes middle classness, whiteness, cultural centrality, a background of higher education, and European welfare state entitlement on the part of the social movement activist youth who seeks thrills and rites of passage to prove themselves. As a result, his analysis falls short for any social movement participant who does not possess these privileges and/or has already faced a number of challenges that are outside the types offered by social movement communities, such as violent confrontation with the police.

However, Melucci's problematic myopic assumptions are identical to those within the squatters movement itself. Consequently, his analysis elucidates the motivations of the participation of activists with such backgrounds as well as adding insight into why these social movement subcultures can become spaces of retreat from the challenges of the Mainstream.

Melucci's characterization that social movement actors view their participation as a temporary necessity before they progress onto other stages of their lives conforms to how the four women activist squatters (Svenke, Juliette, Maria, and Margit) represent their period of mobilization within an imagined timeline of their lives. These women assume their involvement in the squatters movement is provisional and that by studying in higher education, they acquire the skills and resources necessary to live and work in the Mainstream as middle-class professionals. Their dedication to complete their higher education is one of the resources to which Melucci refers when he notes that individuals' commitments to social movements depend on available resources.

Melucci's analysis does not consider how activists imagine the duration of their participation is formed and negotiated within a context of a social movement community. In the case of the squatters movement, the relatively short-term involvement of culturally central squatters and the permanence of culturally marginal squatters impact how participants envision the length of their involvements. Nancy Whittier, in *Feminist Generations* (1995), a study of activists in a radical women's community in the United States, found that activists' participation and their construction of their identities as feminists were formed in relation to both the larger political generation of which they were members and the micro-cohorts of activists with whom they worked. Hence, the quotidian interactions with other people within a social movement community tremendously impact how activists imagine the quality and duration of their participation.

Whittier, however, depending on her interviews with highly educated, reflective, and articulate women with pasts in the radical women's movement, reproduces a narrative assuming the cultural centrality of all participants. It is likely that the radical women's movement during the period that Whittier examined was diverse and composed of more that highly educated, assertive and articulate women. However, with an approach that relies on narratives without observation, the impact and perspectives of the inarticulate and ineloquent, whether or not such individuals are culturally marginal, are often rendered invisible.

In the case of the squatters movement, the existence of culturally marginal, older men – often addicted to drugs and alcohol, dependent on the movement both socially and materially, and consequently, lacking the capacity for independence, much less "success" in the Mainstream – serves to deter long-term commitment for those who are culturally central. The militant for life to whom Melucci refers is not merely the product of a particular class culture, and thus a hero to be admired. In this subculture, the activist for life is a ghost figure to be avoided into becoming at all costs. Such figures are not discussed nor gossiped about (see Chapter 2 for the relationship between authority and gossip). Rather, they serve as warning tales, referred to only by a first name, such as, "I don't want to be like Peter."

Moreover, Melucci's writing on youth in social movement communities resonates with the self-representations of Adam and Ludwic; two examples of marginal, older men. According to Melucci, youth as a category and stage of life reflects a symbolic and cultural definition more than a biological condition:

> People are not young simply because of their particular age, but because they assume culturally the youthful characteristics of changeability and temporariness. By means of models of juvenile existence, a more general cultural appeal is issued: the right to turn back the clock of life, to question professional and personal decisions, and to measure time in ways that are not governed solely by instrumental rationality. (Melucci 1989: 62)

Adam, by returning to the squatter's subculture ten years after he had decided to leave that stage of his life, shows the ability to "turn back the clock of life," by returning to the pleasures of community living that he so fondly remembered from his experience squatting in Nijmegen. He could erase his failed studies, his years of homelessness, and the vagueness that surrounds the reasons for his initial departure from the squatters movement, by re-entering the squatting world in a new city and committing himself to it. Meanwhile Ludwic's self-narrative exuberantly celebrates temporariness and non-instrumental rationality. He squats to act irresponsibly and for the fun that derives from the risk, refusing to espouse political rhetoric to justify his actions. His statements are particularly striking because he is a man in his forties, who claims to have had a wife and raised several foster children, behavior which demands responsibility and commitment.

The womb

These sets of statements can be divided into several different categories of oppositional pairs: women versus men; youth versus middle age; culturally central versus culturally marginal. Rather than reify various poles of comparison, I'd rather focus on how these categories (with the exception of gender) exist on a continuum that define each other. The lines between youth, middle age, culturally central, and culturally marginal are fuzzy and indeterminate.

A twenty-two-year-old squatter, occasionally employed as a dishwasher in a restaurant, who grocery shops by dumpster diving, resides in a squatted living group, works at the kraakspreekuur, breaks doors every Sunday, and spends the entire day smoking marijuana, drinking all night, and sleeping until 4 p.m. to recover from the hangover and the partying from the night before, is a youthful, subcultural, and social movement activist. The same squatter, living the identical lifestyle twenty years later, is culturally marginal.

There is a repetition, circularity, and inertia to the social movement subcultural life that is simultaneously comforting, marginalizing, and entrapping. The fear of this inertia is implicit in the narratives of the young women and encapsulated by their invocation of marginal older male figures. On one level, social movement communities offer opportunities for skill acquisition, identities, and roles for people who are marginalized in the Mainstream. On the other hand, the predictable circularity of the squatter's life in which one can accumulate squatter capital ultimately fails to provide challenges once one has mastered all the tropes. As per Maria's remark ("You know Peter? He did a lot of stuff."), it's possible to progress through the different stages of a career in the movement but still be "stuck" in the subculture without having acquired the skills to function in the Mainstream.

Melucci provides insights into why social movement communities can paradoxically serve as both spaces for personal growth and inertia:

> Participation in collective action is seen to have no value for the individual unless it provides a direct response to personal needs … a group might simply become a site of self-centered, defensive solidarity, protecting individuals from their insecurity and allowing them to express their needs in a convivial environment … the difference between an orientation towards collective goals and a purely defensive enjoyment of the security offered by the group is nebulous.
>
> Today's social movements contain marginal countercultures and small sects whose goal is the development of the expressive solidarity of the group, but there is also a deeper commitment to the recognition that personal needs are the path to changing the world and to seeking meaningful alternatives. (Melucci 1989: 49)

In connection to this point about the appeal of social movement communities to youth, Melucci also claims that complex, post-industrial societies fail to provide opportunities for "youth" (again, without any differentiation for class, gender, race, ethnicity, and the types of skills that comprise centrality versus marginality) to undergo a formal rite of passage which enables a transition from youth to adulthood. This lack of ritual detrimentally "prolongs the youthful condition even when the biological conditions for it no longer exist" (Melucci 1996: 126). Furthermore, the absence of ritual impedes "youth" from challenging themselves and learning their capabilities:

Today it is difficult in youthful experience to take one's measure against such obligatory passages; that is, to gauge one's own capabilities, what one is, what one is worth; for this means measuring oneself against the limit, and ultimately against the fundamental experience of being mortal. Initiation awakens the person from the juvenile dream of omnipotence and confronts him/her with the powerful experience of pain and suffering, even the possibility of death. Today's wide range of symbolic possibilities is not matched by concrete experiences that test individuals to their limits. The indeterminateness of choice and the attempt in any case to postpone it as much as possible, keep young people in the amorphous, comfortable, and infantile situation of the maternal womb, where they can feel at ease with everything seemingly possible. (Melucci 1996: 126)

Melucci suggests that the appeal of collective action for "youth" is that it allows a type of rite of passage that is not available in "complex, post-industrial societies." However, since the youth themselves choose collective action as a form of rites of passage and since the value of participating in collective action is that it provides a direct response to personal needs, Melucci characterizes this challenge as being an inauthentic:

fake challenge which does nothing to modify the deep weakness of the personality and leaves intact the condition of indeterminateness – that is, the position of standing before the threshold of the test without entering into the world of the limits and risks of the adult life. (Melucci, 1996: 127).

This fake rite of passage offered by the movement indicates why the narratives of the more culturally central women all featured the role of education and family in their lives because they represent stages and rites of passage outside of the movement. With higher education, supposedly impartial authorities evaluate one's academic abilities. While with regards to committing oneself to a family, the responsibilities and the skills necessary are not the types for which the movement offers for training. For example, living in a squatted living group, if one dislikes one's housemates, one can move out and squat another house or merely wait until the eviction. Peter, the veteran squatter referred to by many as the symbol of the marginal old man, once said to me, "Eviction has more than one purpose" With this statement, Peter obliquely explained that he no longer desired to continue residing with his living group and that eviction would eventually solve this problem for him rather than his having to move out or resolve the conflict. Such an attitude reveals a highly contextual and fleeting attitude about relationships, one that contrasts with the types of commitment and responsibilities needed for emotional configurations such as a long-term partnership, interdependence with a family, or where one is depended upon by a child.

Activist careers in the movement

With the ambiguous role of the movement subculture as either a space of training and self-realization or a space of entrapping marginality, it's helpful to examine what exactly it means to have a career within a social movement. David Graeber, in his ethnography of the alternative globalization movement, paints a portrait of the career of the "typical direct actionist," from one's entrance to the state of semi-retirement (Graeber 2009: 251). According to Graeber, initially activists become "politicized" in high school through the punk scene or in college via campus organizations. After leaving college, they then intensively live and work as activists from one to ten years. Supporting themselves in part-time or casual jobs and residing in group houses or squats, they are members of political groups and attend meetings several times a week, with that number exponentially increasing before large-scale mobilizations. Graeber characterizes this first phase as impossible to sustain for an extended period due to its overwhelming intensity. Hence, activists often take long-term breaks in other countries, by partaking in solidarity projects in Latin America, hanging out with the radical left in Europe in squats, participating in radical environmental groups who conduct tree-sits, or working on an organic farm. Graeber's career description applies to the international activists who make up a part of the squatters movement in Amsterdam (see description of hippies in Chapter 1).

The activist subculture that Graeber describes comprises "active" participants and self-proclaimed semi-retired ones. Careers, families, and partners often provide reasons for retirement. A number of people attend graduate school, where they remain involved until they drop out of activism when they commit to their careers. He concludes that from their late thirties and onwards, activists usually burn out and withdraw except for occasionally attending actions or parties, from which Graeber deduces that semi-retirement is inevitable.

A few ethnographies of subcultures offer insight by charting the careers of subcultural participants. Fox (1987), in her ethnographic research on punks in the American Midwest in the 1970s and 1980s, found that punks hierarchically organized themselves into subgroups according to the intensity of individual commitment to the punk counterculture and their performance of a punk fashion and lifestyle. With more intense commitment, the more exclusive the subgroup becomes. Hardcore punks consist of participants who demonstrated the strongest devotion to the punk lifestyle and value system and who possessed the highest status. Softcore punks were less devoted than the hardcores to the oppositional punk lifestyle and had relatively less status than hardcore punks. However, the hardcore punks considered the softcore's involvement as sufficient and generally viewed them as transitioning towards hardcores. The preppie punks, who Fox characterizes as minimally committed, viewed their punk personas as a costume, and comprised the largest portion of members of the punk scene. The softcores and hardcores disdained the preppies due to their lack of conviction and interest in participating fully in the scene. The fourth group, the spectators, were outsiders interested in the punk scene who attended punk nights at clubs and who literally watched the other three groups.

Fox's work demonstrates an interesting relationship of fluidity and mutual dependency between the four groups. She argues that participants in this subculture gradually transition from one group to another as their commitment to punkness increases. The "core punks" – which included the hardcores and the softcores – often began their careers as spectators to the punk scene, in which they experienced the core punks ignoring or ridiculing them. Spectators then progressed into softcore punks, meaning that they espoused a provisional conviction for punkness. This transitory dedication coincided with their use of marijuana, alcohol, and amphetamines. Their consumption contrasted with the hardcore punks, who demonstrated a totalizing commitment to punkness and who sniffed glue for recreational drug use, which Fox notes has a more damaging and long-term impact than the drugs used by the softcores. Lastly, a symbiotic relationship existed between the core punks and the preppies in which the latter, who were often middle class, supported core punks financially as well as serving as an Other against which the core punks created an identity.

Marsh, Rosser, and Harre (Gelder and Thornton 1997), in a study of football supporters in the UK, use a career framework to analyze the social structure of football supporters. This study illustrates a linear hierarchy of increasing commitment in which supporters begin as "novices," sitting in one section of a football stadium filled with young boys. They eventually join the section of the stadium for the "rowdies," where they have opportunities to establish their reputations for fighting, behaving like a "hooligan," or manifesting their ability to drink heavily. Eventually, the rowdies who had established themselves with the most formidable reputations according to the value system of football supporters, sat in the section of the "town boys." After completing advancement through these three different stages of being a football fan, a supporter will eventually retire to attending games by sitting in sections of the stadium with "older" fans (older than twenty-two), accompanied by their wives or girlfriends.

The squatters' subculture offers its own set of structures from which one can establish a career and accumulate capital within the movement. The different stages reflect increasing capital, the seeking of and obtaining more responsibility, gaining higher prestige and status within the movement for having demonstrated a number of skills, having mastered and rejected both Mainstream and movement style tropes, and displaying a mounting sense of conviction. These various stages offer squatters a sense of self-realization that conforms to an ideal activist self who is the product of a specific historical, social, and political context.

The three biographies that follow illustrate these ideals and their failed by- products. The first individual, Jacob, who eventually retired into the life of a middle-class professional with leftist politics, serves as an example of a movement success story. The next story features Dirk, who entered the movement in a comparable way and similarly advanced through the stages of an ideal career, but remained in a state of inertia and fails to exit. The third biography tells the story of the famous Peter, the oldest squatter in the Netherlands, and the most referred symbol of failure in the movement.

As a result of methodological coincidence/convenience all three of these biographies are of male squatters, and their communications reflect a highly gendered narrative style. I was introduced to Jacob as someone who had been active in the squatters movement as a young person, so Jacob's story was from the viewpoint of someone reflecting on his past. Dirk's identification as a retired squatter was unexpected since I had met him while working as a cook at a voku and had assumed that he considered himself an active squatter because he lived in a squat and worked at a squatted social center. Consequently, his narration of himself as retired provided a helpful example of someone who straddles exit and participation. As for Peter, his story is based on a combination of the negative gossip about him by other squatters and my own personal experiences with him.

Regarding the impact of gender on narrative style, as I wrote earlier, men tend to narrate their stories according to a plot in which they construct a number of linear events that correspond to squatter capital; a trajectory that demonstrates an increasing sense of conviction and skills which ultimately lead to self-realization. In contrast, women often represent themselves more modestly, not emphasizing their actions and movement successes, and discussing instead their feelings. To be clear, women squatters are as involved in high profile movement activities that build squatter capital as male squatters but they refrain from representing themselves in this manner and avoid discussing their accomplishments in squatter capital terms.

Jacob

Jacob's story is the ideal movement narrative. Originating from a disadvantaged background, he entered the movement without class-inherited privileges and skills, and thus, was wholly self-realized through the movement. His socialization in the movement could be traced by his progressing through various stages in a squatter's career, accumulating capital, until he mastered all the skills possible within the subculture. He then felt bored and frustrated and left the squatter subculture to concentrate on his education in the Mainstream, eventually completing a PhD abroad, and returning to Amsterdam to work as a researcher and purchase a house with his partner, transitioning into a middle-class life.

When I interviewed Jacob, he claimed that he was "old" at age thirty-two. He describes his youth as "disturbing." The state removed him from his family when he was five and placed him in foster care. At fourteen, he moved back to live with his mother but that "went wrong" and so the state sent him to a different foster family, who, after a period of time, suddenly asked him to leave. Having no place to go, Jacob moved in with some friends and then "went squatting" as a young punk at the age of fifteen.[3] Jacob remarks, "I took control in my own hands so I started squatting. At that time I was a punk and a part of the subculture. Squatting was part of the subculture and a solution for my housing problem." Jacob views his decision to squat as a way to take control over his life, a feeling that the state, his biological family, and his foster families had denied him throughout his childhood.

Jacob immediately accumulated capital within the movement by squatting his own house. After a year and a half of living in his first squat, a small apartment that he shared with another person, he arranged to legalize it with a rental contract, which increased his squatter capital. During his first two years in the squatters movement, he developed, "from being a sorta party punk to a more political person. I joined the squatters movement more and basically became an activist." He describes his life in the movement:

> There was always something going on, full time. You could always go somewhere and help someone build a house, there was always a problem with the owners, so you could always do actions around that, there were always evictions that were going to happen, there were always small things that were always going on within the movement. People would make radio, cafes, restaurants, there were all kinds of things you could get involved into ... I also started doing the squatting hour.

In addition to the plethora of activities that structured his life, the squatters movement provided Jacob with opportunity to create projects and to develop into a persona that he was denied in the Mainstream:

> When you are sixteen or seventeen, you have nothing, and squatting a place was like a big playing ground. You have nothing but ... when you break the doorway, and then you open the door, and there are buildings like this, just for you. You could just do everything. So on the one hand, you are just absolutely no one and everyone thinks that you will end up somewhere bad, but at the same time you have all the opportunities in the world, and that was the nice thing; ... You could just start a cafe, you could just start organizing concerts.

While the Mainstream was a place which refused him possibilities ("you have nothing ... you are ... no one"), the movement enabled opportunities and creativity.

During his teenage years, Jacob radicalized, stating that nothing in particular occurred that spurned this radical shift. Instead, he relates his radicalization more to his youth in which he easily conformed to peer pressure and the expectations of the movement as well as the lack of responsibility and material pressure. Jacob comments:

> It's partially because there is a movement that is radical and you are young and you want to belong to the movement so you start taking over opinions. And, of course, that is partially peer pressure, you know that. And you start to read about things and you start getting involved in violent confrontations with the police, and that helps to radicalize you. I don't know. There is some way of canalizing your own anger and disappointment in things, these are more personal reasons ... You start romanticizing the revolutionary action or these kinds of things. It becomes part of your daily environment and when you are with other people who are also radical, you easily take it up ... It became a daily activity ... You had no real material worries to find a job or anything. I could just hang out all day and do actions and these kind of things.

During this period, while living in his first squat, he was involved in an enormous squat with beautiful gardens, which housed 120 people that had once existed as an orphanage. Jacob describes this squat as "disorganized," because the group that had been managing it was either "bought out" – meaning that they had accepted money to leave or had received replacement housing, and moved out of the building. Of the original group who had organized the building, ten people refused to leave. However, the house was then "invaded" by "disorganized people," who Jacob describes as people who lived in the squat to avoid paying rent, refusing to contribute financially to the house, and many of whom had serious drug problems. Consequently, they overwhelmed the group who was managing the house and it developed into "a problematic area," where Jacob saw "disturbing" things, such as "junkies half dead in the hallway" and people "putting baskets full of shit in their fridge."

Jacob found himself bored with living with one other person in his small, legalized squat and moved out to squat with four people. The group squatted an immense building that had survived a fire in Old South, one of the wealthiest neighborhoods in Amsterdam. The squatters extensively repaired the building for months and opened a cafe. This squat existed for seven years before being evicted. Jacob left this space after two years to squat two monumental buildings next to each other that had been empty for five years in the Canal District, another exclusive area in the center of Amsterdam.

For Jacob, these houses were, "a political kind of squat, really organized with militants." At the time that they squatted it, the houses had just been sold. The owners immediately took the squatters to court. In this case, the squatters had a legal advantage in that the owners had to deliver the houses empty to the new owners by the Friday after the court case but the city would evict no earlier than the following Monday. The new owners refused to purchase the house with the squatters inside, so the Amsterdam owner offered the squatters 10 percent of the price of the house to leave. The squatters refused. The new owners, from Sweden, then offered the squatters 30,000 guilders, which represented a colossal amount of money when considering that the squatters lived on approximately 500 guilders a month. Despite the financial appeal, the squatters rejected the offer for political reasons. The sale was declared void and the city evicted the squatters on the Monday morning. By the Monday evening, the group decided to re-squat it. The re-squat featured 150 people, dressed in black with ski masks and helmets. They broke away the barricading and reoccupied the house. The squatters remained living in this house for an additional two years since the reason for the original eviction no longer applied. Jacob lived in this last house for a year and half and then left because, "I had enough of the squatters movement at that time. So after five years I had my burnout." When asked why he burned out, Jacob explains:

> It was more that I felt that I had been squatting for five years. You see the same faces, you see the same discussions, you see the same, the same amateurism, you see the same, you know? At a certain point you get fed up, you know? One year in the squatters movement and you learn how to print, you learn to make radios, you learn to break doors, you learn how to fix things, but after a year, you start repeating them. Like in the squatting hour. You get fed up with the alcoholics ... You squat houses, people who really make a mess of it and you almost want to evict them ... Even the police at that time ... sent people who could not find any house to us. We were some kind of social workers.

Jacob then moved to a living group in a legalized squat, where he lived for five years. He started and finished university and then went on to study in a PhD program abroad. At the time I interviewed him, he had just completed his PhD, was employed by a leftist lobbying initiative, and had recently purchased an apartment with his partner.

Jacob's narrative reflects the successful progression through a number of stages of an ideal squatter career in which he ultimately became self-realized through the movement. He began as a "party punk," meaning that he lived as a punk squatter without political ideals. Through involvement in the movement and mentorship by older squatters, he then developed into an activist, living his life with a sense of conviction. He learned all the skills available to him such as breaking, building, strategic manipulation, organization, and non-instrumental acts of bravery, as well as espoused the political rhetoric that he learned during his socialization. Furthermore, he gained tremendous capital because his houses were all movement successes; by being legalized, by developing into long-term social centers with cafes and restaurants, and by being high profile, prestigious actions that embodied movement values, especially the last house where the squatters group rejected substantial financial offers from the owners for the sake of anti-capitalist political ideals, bringing Jacob to the height of squatter capital at the age of nineteen. After having mastered the skills, consumption, and lifestyle tropes of the subculture, he then became bored, rejected it, arranged to move into affordable housing (a living group within a legalized squat), and finished his higher education. In a movement subculture where one achieves self-realization through a series of steps that prove mastery and rejection, the ideal career requires a rejection of the movement after having mastered all its tropes.

On the discursive level of movement biographical narratives in which Jacob's story is one of successful self-realization, it's helpful to further explore the aspects of his achievements that are not recognized. Although he frames his autobiography in the subculture along points of squatter capital such as by squatting his own house, legalizing it, squatting, building, and maintaining long-term successful social centers, and organizing actions around houses that held important political symbolism in the movement, the points of his biography that he neglects to highlight seem more impressive. First off, on the level of class, Jacob is especially striking on the backstage of the squatters' scene because he entered the movement and became an authority figure. His story is exceptional, since a number of authority figures have middle and upper-class backgrounds. Jacob's open articulation of his background further increases his capital in an environment that asserts a classlessness while assuming the norm of middle-class backgrounds.

Jacob's story further complicates Melucci's argument that collective action provides an inauthentic means to test oneself and one's capabilities in societies that do not provide opportunities for such rites of passage. For someone like Jacob, alone in the world at a young age, his life consisted of a constant test of his abilities. Homeless at fifteen, he impressively arranged for his housing when his biological family and the state had failed him.

Furthermore, Jacob avoided becoming a drug addict and/or an alcoholic. In this environment, people who have histories of abuse and with working-class backgrounds such as Jacob's, tend to be inarticulate or silent, addicted to drugs and alcohol, and materially and emotionally dependent on the squatters' subculture. As a young punk, more experienced squatters ensured that hard drug use was never in Jacob's immediate environment. Jacob found the behavior that he witnessed in the squatted orphanage disturbing rather than being drawn into it.

Rather than allowing his background to determine the conditions of his life, Jacob constantly sought challenges and new opportunities. If he only desired security, he could have remained in his first squatted house that he legalized with a social housing rental contract and received government benefits to assist him for the rest of his life. Instead, he moved out and continued to squat, seeking more challenging and politically relevant projects. Despite his disadvantages and his understanding as a teenager that in the Mainstream, "you are just absolutely no one and everyone thinks that you will end up somewhere bad," Jacob is a success story on the level of the movement and in the Mainstream.

Dirk

Dirk is another example of a young man, socialized in the movement, who successfully progressed through a career in the squatter subculture and accumulated capital. However, despite proclaiming himself "retired," he continues to live in a squat, and exists in an ambivalent relation to the subculture, in which he claims to want to exit but is factually unable to leave. Dirk grew up in a small town in the south of the Netherlands in an orthodox, Catholic family. Due to a difficult situation at home, he ran away twice, succeeding the second time. As a pre-teen, he was compelled by Do-It-Yourself and progressive politics, squatting, anarchism, communism, and left-wing radicalism, ideas that clashed with his family's conservative values.

Dirk initially went to the Hague because he knew someone from his small town who had run away and joined its squatter subculture. When he arrived, his friend advised him to move to Amsterdam where the scene was larger than in the Hague, since Dirk couldn't expect to join a living group without knowing anyone or having proven himself. He arrived at the Vrankrijk, a famous squatter bar in the center of Amsterdam. There, people advised him to go to an enormous squatted warehouse called the *Calenderpanden* because it was a large enough space that the residents would allow him to stay temporarily. He slept in this complex for a week before anyone noticed him. Suddenly, he joined a group organized by the kraakspreekuur to squat a house that had been empty for sixteen years. It was an unusual situation because it was a direct project of the kraakspreekuur rather than one initiated by a group to squat a house. The group comprised a random mix of "apolitical people" who lacked knowledge about squatting, including Dirk. The house was also a tremendous amount of work and the people who squatted it were not interested or capable of making the space habitable nor handling its legal challenges.

During this period, Dirk felt lonely, unhappy, and spent most of his time stoned. Eventually, he met some teenage squatter punks his age and they formed a group of the three youngest people of the Amsterdam squatters

Figure 4.2 Interior of a newly squatted apartment that requires rebuilding floors, Amsterdam, 2009

movement. He developed into "a professional squatter." He learned how to break doors and became the main door-breaker for a kraakspreekuur in a neighborhood in Amsterdam. Dirk squatted a number of empty houses, viewing them as projects to transform into homes, not just habitable spaces. After renovating a house, he and his friends spent their days talking about politics. They did not need to work because they didn't have housing costs as squatters and they ate by "skipping" food. In his squats, he often created social centers such as a late night, cheap punk bars, or restaurants. His squatter capital comprised of his being a breaker, the number of houses that he squatted and renovated, which showed building skills, and his having organized a number of social centers.

He also demonstrated skills in strategic manipulation and organized prestigious actions that gave him "scene points." He was evicted from one house located in Old South, the most elite neighborhood in Amsterdam, because the owner claimed that he had to urgently renovate. When six months had passed and the owner still had not begun renovation, Dirk organized a re-squatting of the space by sixty people, which he defined as "an action squat." An action squat is when one squats a house not necessarily to inhabit it but to make a principled public statement on behalf of the squatters movement. Often, these action squats are short term, are squatted despite the high probability of eviction, and hence, impractical for long-term housing.

Dirk and his group "action squatted" this house to protest how the Old South neighborhood council avoided the enforcement of a law that a third of all housing should be social housing available to low and middle-income people. Instead, Old South is a posh neighborhood with a heavy concentration of expensive real estate where only wealthy people can afford to reside. By squatting a group of houses in this neighborhood and by robbing a nearby construction site every night, the squatters felt that they protested against the neighborhood council's housing policy and the bourgeois ambiance of the neighborhood.

Although these houses were only squatted for two months before they were re-evicted and during which the squatters spent the entire two months barricading it, Dirk describes this summer as the best time of his life. When I asked him why, he responded:

> Because we felt strong, because it was fun, because it was summer and it was a great place. Because we had nothing else to do and we were young and we didn't have jobs. It was our kingdom. It was a big vacation. Even though it was about having a place to live, it wasn't so much about politics but it was social. It was like, "Hey, I live here so piss off."

The group consisted of Portuguese, Dutch, Brazilian, Polish, New Zealand, Czech and German squatters. The Portuguese squatters proved particularly useful because they somehow managed to steal everything required for the house. Every morning, Dirk handed them a list of what the house needed and by the evening, the Portuguese delivered the goods. For the eviction of this house, the squatters group decided to comply with the tradition of the squatters movement to confront the police with the posture of, "we are never leaving," and throw paint bombs. At the eviction itself, the squatters got carried away and despite their earlier agreement, threw everything at the police.

After squatting for a few years, Dirk then moved into a legalized squat and continued intensively participating in the squatters' subculture. At a certain point, he stopped working at the kraakspreekuur and withdrew from the movement to focus on his career as a musician. Ironically, at the point in which he claimed to retire from the squatters movement, he moved back into a squat because he could no longer pay the rent at the legalized squat. He moved into a well-known activist squat with a notorious mafia owner and a campaign to defend the house and ruin the reputations of the owners. Dirk had already established himself with ample squatter capital, by being a door-breaker, working at the kraakspreekuur, having squatted a number of houses, and having successfully organized an action squat with an infamous riot at its eviction which earned him "scene points."

According to Dirk, moving into this house began his "retirement" from the movement. Despite his retirement, he then became involved into the drama of living in an activist squat, with criminal owners, thugs, and undocumented people residing in the house. In the non-squatted floors of this house, the owner placed people with whom he had vague relationships, mostly undocumented people whom he employed as well as people the owner called, "his friends." For a while, these "friends" of the owner, who Dirk calls thugs, caused problems with their constantly barking dogs and by fighting in the street. Since the stereotype of squatters is that they own dogs and create nuisances in the neighborhood, the neighbors blamed the squatters for the problems. In reaction, the squatters developed relationships with the neighbors to build support.

This squatted house featured tremendous conflict, harassment, and acts of violence between the owners and the squatters. As Dirk articulates it, the squatters slowly "conquered" the entire house since it took years to squat each floor and sometimes they had a matter of hours to strategize and takeover the floors. When the owner emptied the attic of the house of its tenants, the squatters sneaked in and "conquered it." In reaction, a tobacco store next door to Dirk's house, which never actually sold cigarettes, informed the squatters, "starting tonight, you will have problems."

The owner then hired people to go to the second floor (which was still not squatted) and terrorize the squatters below them on the first floor. The squatters conjectured that the owner hired a number of street thugs, provided them with cocaine, and advised them to wreak havoc in the building. The thugs then pissed onto the floor until their urine went through the ceiling and into the squatters' kitchen below. The thugs made a tremendous amount of noise and threw furniture out the window. Dirk found it an odd situation since the squatters expected a more direct form of attack, in which the thugs would kick in the door and try to beat everyone up. Instead, they succeeded in terrorizing the squatters since the squatters had no idea what was going on and what to expect because the thugs were acting outside the norms for *knokploeg* (hired thugs) behavior.

Eventually, the neighbors called the police resulting in the riot police arriving. This proved even stranger since squatters are accustomed to the riot police arriving to evict them from their houses, not defend them. Plus, squatters abhor the idea of calling the police for assistance and cooperation. After this incident, the squatters occupied the remaining non-squatted floors less dramatically such as when one of the undocumented residents, a quiet, left-wing, Iranian man, gave the group the key to his flat when he moved out.

At the time that I interviewed him, Dirk reaffirmed that he was "retired." He reiterated how bored he was by the squatters' subculture and its repertoire of squatting and anti-fascist actions. When he reflects on his time as a professional squatter, he describes himself as, "drowning in squatting and escaping from life. Squatting can become all-consuming. One can spend twenty-four hours helping others out in the name of the cause and because it's a good thing to do." According to Dirk, his focus on squatting prevented him from having a personal life, from developing himself, his own interests, and a sense of who he was. Instead, he focused his energy on learning how to effectively pick a lock or on legal strategies for winning a court case.

Dirk values his current ability to integrate into "society." No longer a punk, he works as a manager of an organic produce cooperative and emphasizes that his position demands a substantial level of expertise in comparison to the low skills required for working at a supermarket. He has a permanent contract and is considered *netjes*, a decent person rather than a dirty, marginalized squatter that society holds in contempt. Dirk identifies primarily as an artist and musician. He emphasizes how busy he is with his music and participating in the cultural life of the city. Everything that Dirk accentuates about his current lifestyle contrasts with his teenage, punk, squatter self, who lacked employment, "skipped" food, hung out aimlessly, scorned the Mainstream, and drowned himself in the subculture.

Despite Dirk's emphasis on having retired from the squatters movement, his behavior manifests ambivalence about both participating in the squatters" subculture and leaving it. Dirk claims to have surrendered his feelings of responsibility towards the squatters movement. His involvement in the campaign to defend his squatted house is minimal: running paperwork errands and being physically present during the array of legal and municipal proceedings to harass its owners. Yet, he continues to live in the squatters community and dedicate himself to the running of the social space.

Dirk's contradictory feelings about the squatters' subculture in which he declares himself retired but continues to participate actively reflects how this community can become so safe, that it's crippling, and so insular, that it's suffocating. To retire from the movement signifies surrendering many of the benefits this community offers in a highly alienating urban environment. The scene offers a plethora of parties, social spaces that provide cheap food and drinks, and a general sense of belonging through the relative ease of socializing once one has been accepted in this community. But the same ease can prove crippling since one can drown in the subculture and stop functioning in mainstream society. For someone like Dirk, who has lived his entire adult life in the movement, the subculture feels both safe and boring. Melucci sheds light on Dirk's ambivalent feelings about the appeals and inertia of the movement:

> A group might simply become a site of self-centered, defensive solidarity, protecting individuals from their insecurity and allowing them to express their needs in a convivial environment ... the difference between an orientation towards collective goals and a purely defensive enjoyment of the security offered by the group is nebulous. (Melucci 1989: 49)

To remain in the scene is to continue in a safe and boring vein, sheltering oneself from the stresses of Mainstream life, which often have stricter demands and more transparent hierarchical structures than the squatters' subculture. Yet, hiding in the scene in order to evade such standards in the Mainstream also signifies avoiding challenges which, as Melucci argues, serve to, "gauge one's own capabilities, what one is, what one is worth; for this means measuring oneself against the limit" (1996: 126).

In the linear biographical ideal of the movement, Dirk's story presents a case of inertia. He progressed through the stages of the subculture, accumulated skills and capital as much as possible, and then moved on to rent a room in a legalized squat. Despite the formal transition into becoming a renter which often coincides with retirement from the movement, Dirk continued his life in the subculture. Moreover, the financial obligation of monthly rent proved too demanding for him, so that he returned to reside in a squat, demonstrating a regression in a movement biography rather than progression. I imagine that Dirk, having mastered the tropes of the movement, understands that to fulfill the movement's ideal of autonomy and self-realization, he must demonstrate mastery and rejection. Thus, he verbally rejects the movement but factually continues to live and work in it. Meanwhile, he remains in this suspended state and refuses to enter the Mainstream.

As stated earlier, there are a number of marginal old men who depend materially and emotionally on the community and lack the capacity to exit. These shadow figures haunt squatters such as Dirk, who persist in a state of inertia, and motivate them to leave the subculture in order to avoid similar fates. Their squatter cohorts have progressed and integrated into the Mainstream, while they remain in the subculture, in their forties, fifties, and sixties, appearing ten to twenty years older than they are, their faces ravaged by alcohol and drug use, drinking at squatted social centers where everyone else is half their age.

These figures, who I characterize as the culturally marginal, in addition to being housed by the movement, have structured their lives around the subculture. If it weren't for the squatters movement, some may have become homeless, embedded in a program of semi-independent living, or dependent on their families since it may be impossible for them to function independently in the Mainstream world. Having a job, paying rent, connecting electricity and gas services, and other such tasks that one must manage on a daily basis in a highly bureaucratized welfare state do not seem possible for such individuals. Yet, paradoxically, they are able to manage the complex hierarchies and expectations of the squatter social world and arrange for others to take care of them in ways that they cannot take care of themselves. Furthermore, despite their social dysfunction, some are still able to manipulate the social scene to their advantage.

Peter

To reflect on this paradox more in-depth, it's helpful to consider Peter, a squatter in his mid-fifties who is notorious among all the squatters' communities in the Netherlands as the oldest active squatter. Peter appears at least fifteen years older than his biological age due to alcoholism and being chronically stoned on marijuana. He has been involved in the squatters movement since the late 1970s, when he initially moved to Amsterdam. He originates from a working-class background and speaks with a heavy working-class accent. He is one of the few Dutch people in the Amsterdam squatters' scene who refuses to speak English. His life is the movement. He attends all squatting actions in Amsterdam and, if possible, squatting actions in other parts of the Netherlands. He presents himself at all meetings regarding squatting, takes part in every info-evening, attends every party, eats at every voku every night of the week. To earn money, he receives benefits from the government and he works random jobs for extra cash. He has lived in almost fifty squats over the past thirty years and thirty-eight of them have been evicted. He extols this fact to others.

In the squatters' subculture, squatters exist more through their reputations and squatter capital than as individuals. Peter has negative capital. Rather than accumulating capital for his deeds and his acquisition of skills, his reputation progressively becomes worse. Various rumors circulate about him. Some squatters claim that despite having participated in the squatters' scene for over thirty years, he has never squatted his own house – a devastating accusation since squatting one's own house is fundamental to building one's capital in the movement. Instead, Peter manages to move into a house as a guest and then succeeds in staying in that squat until the eviction. Due to this fact, he also has a reputation as being an albatross, the bearer of bad luck: when he arrives, eviction will soon follow.

He has a terrible reputation as a housemate in living groups as well. He fails to do household chores or to build. He is known for creating and escalating conflict in living groups by choosing one person in the group on whom he focuses, talking negatively about this person with others, disparaging the others in the group with this person, playing on already existing tensions, and creating strife. He is interested in the prestigious strategic manipulation tasks of squatting and yet is seen by others as not skilled enough to handle the intricacies of legal procedures as well as the strategic elements of a campaign. Ninke, a Dutch squatter who lived with Peter, comments:

> With Peter, you first think, okay, at least he's interested in defending a house and the court case. But soon you realize that he only messes everything up. In the beginning, it's like, no harm done. But then you spend all your energy trying to keep him out of things otherwise he screws everything up.

Peter has participated in the kraakspreekuur of one of the neighborhoods in Amsterdam for over twenty years. The other members of this kraakspreekuur have tried to kick him out for decades, but have failed. These

groups have rotating membership since most people spend anytime from
a few months to a few years maximum participating in a collective of the
squatters movement. He succeeds in waiting out the membership until the
group forms again. I do not know if he uses this tactic intentionally.

The ethos of the movement is that projects and collectives are open to
anyone willing to participate. How this factually functions is that men join
groups without being asked, while women often participate when they are
formally recruited. If women are not explicitly asked, they tend not to enter
collective projects. This model of group membership renders it impossible to
remove someone from a collective project. If group members want someone
to leave, it requires a concerted effort of social ostracism to cause someone
to feel sufficiently unwelcome and disregarded so that they withdraw out of
their own sense of self-respect rather than succumb to a hostile group envir-
onment. It proves impossible to expel Peter formally because he is pitiful
and poses no threat. As for the informal method of social ostracism, Peter
either fails to notice the blatant disrespect of his squatter colleagues who try
to push him out in this manner or he perceives it but perseveres regardless.

There are various ways to analyze the position of Peter. One way is to
see him as someone full of idealistic conviction – the militant for life figure
who Melucci romanticizes. In a movement where the majority of people
are in their early to mid-twenties, he remains out of dedication to the ideals
despite his age. He is permanent where they are temporary. In a community
that mocks him, Peter persists to participate actively out of the strength of
his beliefs rather than withdrawing out of protest.

Many squatters see Peter's continued dedication to the movement not as
a choice that he makes out of conviction but a decision that he makes out of
a lack of choice. They believe that he stays in the movement because he can-
not function in the Mainstream rather than from a higher idealistic calling.
Thomas, a squatter who lived with Peter, remarked, "If Peter wasn't in the
squatting scene, he would be homeless." In his thirty years in the movement,
Peter has learned how to make a life in the subculture without assimilat-
ing its internal behavioral norms nor by accumulating any squatter capital,
much less achieving a state of self-realization and autonomy. He manages to
infuriate people so that he has negative squatter capital. At the same time,
many squatters feel enough pity for him that they do not reject him with
outward aggression. They lack respect for him but they do not blame him
for his incompetence.

Having lived as a squatter for two years, I had the good and bad luck of
residing with Peter in one of my squats. Every squatter I knew had, at some
point, lived with Peter, so this was one of my rites of passage. I lived with
him in a colossal squat that featured a sunny garden in the morning, which
meant that I often sat with him in the sun, drinking coffee before I went to
work, while my other housemates slept until the afternoon to recover from
their late night drinking and drug use. Peter also spent his days and nights

drunk and stoned but managed to wake up earlier than the rest. He triggered a mix of feelings in me during our interactions. Sometimes I felt pity, other times, fury, and just as randomly, he charmed me. I never understood whether he was genuinely incompetent of if he feigned it in order to avoid a task.

Once, Peter was lamenting that his girlfriend had left him. Broken hearted, he wondered if he would find another woman. I tried to cheer him up. I told him that he had nice legs and that he could more easily find a new girlfriend if he fixed his teeth and bathed more often. Peter's mouth was a cavern of decay, a testament to the accumulated neglect from decades of drug and alcohol abuse. He then informed me that he had to wait another three months before he could visit the dentist because he had a psychiatric evaluation scheduled in this period to determine if he should continue to receive public assistance. Consequently, he needed his teeth to be in a horrendous state to prove to the evaluators that he was psychologically unfit for employment. Six months later, he had yet to visit the dentist.

Although in the squatters movement, Peter is universally recognized as the symbol of the marginal old man who activists do not want to become, he presents such an extreme case that his example fails to illustrate the fluidity between marginality, oppositionality, and centrality. Peter's marginality and dependence is clear cut, an internal Other against which squatters in the movement can create an identity. However, the rest of the marginal old men actually produce more anxiety because they have progressed through the movement, acquiring skills, and accumulating capital. Often they can adeptly build, are exceptional breakers, and have a dedicated presence at political actions and alarms. Despite their successful socialization and their skills, they failed to exit, living in the extended adolescence of the movement, and posing as examples for young squatters as either a possible future or a path to avoid.

The anxiety around the fluidity seems only possible to describe ethnographically. I lived with another old man named Hans in two of my squats, a painfully shy alcoholic in his late forties. Hans had been in the squatters movement for at least twenty years. An excellent builder and breaker, Hans attended all squatting actions in Amsterdam and potentially violent actions, and had gained substantial squatter capital (breaking, building, and instrumental acts of bravery). As a housemate, he was considerate, did his share of chores, and worked hard on renovating the houses where he lived. Despite sharing a toilet, a shower, and having seen each other in various states of undress, I lived with him for almost four months before he spoke to me directly.

In the last squat that I lived in, I found Hans's presence more enervating than Peter. Although Peter was unbearable to live with, I could imagine that Peter had always behaved this way and would continue to do so, twenty years in the past, twenty years in the future. Hans, on the other hand, was a

Figure 4.3 The painted exterior of a squat, 2008

capable person whose abilities I respected. He was highly skilled in building and construction, he could manage the financial aspects of his life, he was sensitive, and during the few occasions when he did speak, he was articulate and thoughtful. He loved the music of Kate Bush. He was even handsome, with large eyes and finely chiseled features. He had lived in a legalized squat for a few years and left. To supplement his income as an occasional handyman, he sold drugs, but just enough to support himself, not to earn significant amounts of money. He did not receive public assistance and had erased himself from the welfare state for legal reasons.

In the mornings when I had breakfast before going to work, I used to sit with Hans at the dining table and would often observe him absorbed in his world, quietly eating his breakfast of boiled eggs and buttered toast and recovering from the solitary stupor he drank himself into every night. What was it that had led him to reside in squats for decades in this perpetual state? His childhood? A woman in his past? A chemical imbalance? Or was it the accumulation of small decisions that he made every day that pushed him further into marginality?

I found the combination of his impressive skills and his marginality incredibly disturbing and it provoked fears about my own life. I was unhappy during this period. I had been evicted twice that year already, had moved three times, and been jailed; all of which was obstructing my research to the point of incompletion. I no longer wanted to squat but was having trouble obtaining affordable housing in Amsterdam. I felt frustrated in my part-time job in the university and I was unsure if I wanted to continue with my boy-friend at the time. It seemed that my life was also suspended and I developed a dread that despite my education and my skills, this state of inertia and confusion could persist unabated unless I made a drastic change. The line between centrality and marginality appeared very thin and I had the impression that if I continued in this environment, I could easily slip to the side of marginality and get lost.

The scripted path to autonomy and self-realization

The self-realization resulting from the ideal career of an activist in the squatters movement exhibits a number of characteristics. First, an activist should display an increasing commitment to the movement's ideals and a growing conviction. Second, an activist should ideally acquire and master a number of skills through the practice of squatting. Third, an activist should possess an oppositional habitus in which one demonstrates a constant mastery and rejection, initially of the Mainstream, and ultimately, of the movement life-style and consumption norms.

All of these characteristics are encapsulated by the term, "autonomous," within movement discourse. In his discussion on the ideal of authenticity and self-realization, Charles Taylor describes the assumptions of originality and self-discovery that are synonymous with the meaning of the squatters' use of the term "autonomous":

> There is a certain way of being human that is my way. I am called upon to live my life in this way, and not in imitation of anyone else's life ... Each of our voices has something unique to say. Not only should I not mold my life to the demands of external conformity; I can't even find the model by which to live outside myself. I can only find it within. Being true to myself means being true to my own originality, which is something only I can articulate and discover. In articulating it, I am also defining myself. I am realizing a potentiality that is properly my own. (Taylor 1994: 30–1)

Discursively, originality is essential to this ideal of autonomy and self-realization that results from a squatter's career. In practice, however, becoming autonomous is highly scripted and culturally specific and requires a constant dialectic between performance and recognition.

The biographies that I have highlighted so far are part of a repertoire of personhood that are easily recognizable to squatters who are successfully socialized by the movement. The accomplished movement activist who moves onto a middle-class professional life, the retired squatter in a state of suspension, and the marginal old man. All of these figures are classic types understood within the framework of the movement. Only by looking at examples of biographies outside the movement's repertoire of person-hood, can one understand that the path to an autonomous, oppositional, self-realization is highly inflexible and the result of a specific social, his-torical, and political context which renders it nearly impossible for those socialized outside of such a context to be recognized as autonomous.

In the scripted path to self-realization, the ideal biography has a number of different models. The models of Dirk and Jacob, in which they began as teenage runaways, interested in partying, slowing developing into activists as their convictions grew, trying more challenging projects which both dem-onstrated their skills and further accrued capital. After having mastered all the skills possible, they retired from the movement. The middle-class student presents another model in which she or he is introduced into the squatter subculture through squatting a house or leftist politics and also becomes more convinced by the politics of squatting with a sense of irony and dismis-sal, moving through various projects with different levels of responsibility, and finally, after having mastered the skills, retiring from the movement. The details of these biographies vary; such as the types of skills learned, cam-paigning versus building, organizing versus non-instrumental acts of brav-ery. Further variety exists in the constitutive moments of a squatter's career; whether it's a well-known squatted house, a particularly violent action, a dramatic eviction, or involvement in a successful social center.

As a result, the steps of a career, the contents of the biography, and the trajectory contain a number of finite and established tropes. Understanding that the tropes are defined and the moments of self-realization are well-rehearsed, to be autonomous then is not a form of original, opposi-tional self-realization and self-discovery. Instead, to be autonomous signifies conforming to a certain type of homogenization. Melucci comments further on how social movement subcultures, while seeming to offer opportunities for self-realization actually create spaces for homogenization where social movement participants can escape from insecurity:

> The more we are exposed to the risks associated with personal responsi-bility for our actions, the more we require security. We actively search for supports against insecurity. This is why the desire for self-realization can easily turn into the regressive utopia of a safe and transparent environ-ment which enables individuals to be themselves by becoming identical with others. (Melucci 1989: 210)

Ultimately, the terms autonomy, oppositionality, self-realization, and origin-ality, mask a process of conformity to a specific ideal in a community that cannot tolerate diversity.

To further examine this point, it's best to return to the story of Karima, the undocumented black African woman of a low social class and her inability to integrate into the squatters' subculture. By understanding her failure, the exclusivity and the assumptions for an ideal path to autonomy are rendered visible. When I asked Solomon, the unofficial authority figure in the group, he told me that they asked her to leave because she was not interested in "an autonomous life." He added to illustrate his point, "Come on, she liked the Backstreet Boys." Karima's story reveals the inflexibility of the script towards self-realization in the squatters movement in which the style by which someone lives their life and thus, exhibits one's conviction hugely impacts whether someone can accumulate capital and is recognized for having conviction. On the one hand, Karima's resourcefulness and cleverness are admirable. On the other, her skills and the challenges that she faced and surmounted were illegible in this movement subculture.

Karima demonstrated oppositionality by refusing to remain a domestic servant and being ruled by her mother and her employers. But this oppositionality did not lead to her accumulating squatter capital because being oppressed within a family context is not considered political nor is it recognized as a revolt. In general, squatters tend not to discuss their family backgrounds in order to maintain a fiction of classlessness. Even for those with abusive family backgrounds who may have empathized with Karima, they ultimately relied on the welfare state to care for them, as in the case of Jacob, whether or not they acknowledge the psychological security offered by this safety net.

Karima's dating men as a means to exit her material circumstances is taboo in a community that promotes a discourse of women living their lives independent of men. The squatters in her milieu originate from countries where abortion is free, legal, and accessible. They could not understand the shame and guilt around extra-marital sexuality and the trauma of the forced abortion by her mother in the Gulf, where abortion is illegal. The months or years that Karima spent saving money to pay the brokers for her visa to Europe, in which she had to surrender a significant portion to her mother, is similarly unrecognizable in a subculture where a number of squatters live this lifestyle to save funds for pleasure trips abroad. Lastly, her negotiations at the border into Europe were similarly incomprehensible in that they fundamentally could not understand the challenges for an undocumented, black East African woman to face European immigration authorities and successfully deceive them. The gulf of experience was too wide and led to a total lack of comprehension on both parts.

Moreover, Karima's presentation of her accomplishments worked against her. She told her biography to the living group and the squatters in the community, but in a style intended to enlist pity rather than respect. To fit in this community, she had to demonstrate mastery and rejection. Hence, a successful display would have been to narrate her deeds as acts of convictions committed with a sense of anger and oppositionality. By portraying herself as a victim and survivor, rather than an outraged, empowered activist, her actions conveyed an underlying motivation for material gain and a hint of possible emotional manipulation, both of which the squatters viewed as crass and lacking conviction. If she had understood the hidden logic of this community, she would have known that to be accepted, she had to participate in the narrative of rejecting material advantages in favor of anti-capitalist conviction. Unfortunately for Karima, such acts that prove anti-capitalist conviction and which accrue squatter capital were fundamentally impossible for her to both understand and commit. After having saved for years for the trip from the Gulf to Europe, why would she risk arrest at a squatters' political action and subsequent deportation for the sake of scene points?

In addition to the failure in strategically performing oppositionality, to be accepted as autonomous, Karima would have to display a rejection of her culture to assimilate in the culture of the radical left. This rejection would have entailed erasing herself and the culture that she was expected to deny. When she refused to wear a bathing suit out of modesty when she went swimming with her squatters' community, at a time when the men in the group swam naked, the squatters interpreted this as her exhibiting shame about her body that they found quaint on one level but discomforting on another. She also was unable to repudiate the aspirations that drove her to Europe, of living a middle-class, suburban lifestyle, exhibited by her taste in music (Backstreet Boys), and her clothing style, a dream that squatters found banal and disappointing. All of these differences, of culture, of global political realities, of class, proved too uncomfortable for her squatters' community. While they pitied her, they lacked respect for her aspirations and her habitus. Unable to address these issues with her due to the pity, the squatters were left with a deep sense of discomfort. In a subculture where the dominant performance is an articulated hostility, the uncomfortable silence is dismantling. They consequently asked her to leave.

Conclusion

With this presentation of squatter biographies, it appears that to live "an autonomous life," signifies the ability to seamlessly perform a life motivated entirely by conviction. Squatters who are addicted to drugs and alcohol in an environment where drug and alcohol use and abuse are rampant are not autonomous because despite their sincere political convictions, they leave the impression of being more committed to their addictions than to the movement. Thus, the use of heroin is a strict taboo in the squatters' subculture due to the perception that few people can withstand becoming addicted. The taboo of heroin contrasts with the status of other drugs, such as alcohol, marijuana, speed, and ecstasy, where the borders around who becomes labeled as addicted are more complicated to define since their use is rampant in the subculture. Thus, the moments when someone is publicly labeled an addict reveals a power relation between the classifier and the classified due to the implication that addiction reveals deep personal weakness and hence, a lack of conviction.

As in the case of Karima, or anyone who does not fit into the two extremes of squatter personhood – the culturally central activist versus the culturally marginal participant – the need for material and bodily security renders a squatter unable to reach a state of autonomy. Examples include the single mother juggling a low-income job, benefits, and raising her children, while illegally subletting an apartment that costs more than her total income; or the undocumented refugee who fled a war zone, has been rejected by the Dutch refugee machinery, and lives in the margins of Amsterdam. They can be tolerated within the community but not treated as equals within the framework of squatter capital and standards for being recognized as autonomous. If one is afraid of the police, lacks interest in participating in violent actions and going to jail, finds barricading and occupying time-consuming and stressful, or feels intimidated by the barrage of paperwork, owners, and lawyers, then the constitutive challenges of the squatters movement serve to disempower rather than be thrilling rites of passages. The inability to handle such stresses causes someone to be non-autonomous because it demonstrates a lack of faith in the movement's ability to support its members to withstand such challenges. Consequently, the desire for security on a bodily and material level decreases one's convictions within the strict framework of self-realization that depicts illegible the challenges outside of the *bildungsroman* of the left activist self-celebrated by the movement.

The myopia of a privileged viewpoint, whether it's through whiteness, education, European welfare state entitlements, gender, or class, is beautiful in its naivety and sincerity and disturbing in its exclusionary fantasies. In Amsterdam, I attended a talk by an American anarchist activist about the state of anarchism in the United States. The audience, consisting of mainly punk squatters of the Amsterdam left activist subculture, seemed shocked by the speaker's tales of decade-long prison sentences for the direct action projects of radical left environmentalists, such as burning cars and breaking windows. I asked him why he was so surprised since if these same acts had been committed by any despised minority in the United States, their prison sentences would have probably been longer. The speaker did not know how to respond to my questions and the audience seemed highly uncomfortable and defensive. Afterward, we spoke privately and I asked the speaker if by dressing like a punk, did he honestly feel that he was resisting capitalism? He responded that his fashion style of black clothing with carefully placed holes, piercings, tattoos, and dreadlocks (he was white), reflected his internal convictions. He then said that in the past, he wore a skirt as a form of resistance but that it proved too inconvenient due to the harassment that he received.

Afterwards, reflecting on his statement, I realized that to be autonomous signifies constantly being able to choose. Choosing whether or not to be in the movement versus the Mainstream, which reflects a measure of cultural centrality and the possession of skills to negotiate contemporary urban life within and outside the movement. On the level of daily life, being autonomous is based on the assumption that one has a safe and secure existence and that to express one's autonomy is to temporarily choose to be the object of willful precarity and unpredictable violence, whether it's at the hands of the police or thugs contracted by owners. For anyone whose bodily integrity has been violated or has lived in a constant state of danger and risk, from the visibly queer to the quotidian experience of women managing street harassment throughout the world, it seems a profound contradiction that the autonomous life can only be inhabited by those entitled enough to heroically revel in the temporary suspension of their privileges.

Notes

1   To clarify, when Margit says "smoking marijuana," she does not mean smoking occasionally, or even once a day. She means people who smoke marijuana from when they wake up until they go to bed and are constantly inebriated.
2   Although I am using this example of Ludwic and information from the interview that I conducted with him, I doubt that he provided accurate details about his life.
3   Jacob was not a baby punk since the term emerged to describe a group of punks in their late teens and early twenties who joined the squatters movement at the same time in the early and mid-2000s. The next generation of punks who followed this group were called embryo punks, playing on the term baby punk.

Conclusion: the economy of unromantic solidarity

In 2010, a law that criminalized squatting,[1] went into effect. Having been classified as an "expert" in squatting, I found that I was repeatedly asked the same question by journalists and in housing forums: will squatting continue after it is officially deemed illegal?[2]

I typically responded by challenging the definition of squatting. Specifically, squatting as a practice in which people reside in spaces where they lack legal entitlement, hidden from the public eye, which I'm sure has continued especially as it receives little attention in the Netherlands. As for squatting as a movement, which is defined by public overtaking of properties, squatting has continued but in a different form. I never expected it to "die" because as long as the squatters movement has been visible and prominent in Amsterdam, the pronouncement that the movement is dead is as much a part of discourse about and within the movement as evictions and riots.

Rather than focusing on whether the squatters movement will persevere, it's more relevant to ask, who squats publicly and have they continued squatting? Without legal permission, has this "autonomous" selfextolled in the movement subculture persisted? To answer this question, it's helpful to consider the general profiles of who comprises this movement, as I have already contended in this book.

The contemporary squatters movement consists of people who can be broadly classified as the culturally marginal and the culturally central. The culturally central, or as Melucci characterizes, "the new elites" (1989), have the benefits of their backgrounds, education, and skills to help them navigate the labyrinthine housing market in Amsterdam. I imagine that such people have continued squatting either for their own housing needs or by setting up radical left anarchist social centers. The practice of squatting social centers in European countries (e.g. Italy and Spain, where squatting is illegal) is known as the Social Centers movement. Thus, illegality provides the opportunity for culturally central activists to articulate themselves against the state.[3]

Figure 5.1 A utility bicycle built by squatters and used collectively, 2008

When considering the consequences of the squatting ban, I am concerned about the culturally marginal. Living the autonomous life has become increasingly demanding. Being able to reside for a significant amount of time in a squat requires more skills, energy, investment, and capacities. The squatting ban has only heightened the pressure and level of skills necessary to negotiate this terrain of existence. Such demands may prove impossible for people who lack the capacity to handle them. Further, I do not know how many culturally marginal people will function without the extensive support of the backstage of the squatters community. Melucci describes this abstractly as "subterranean networks" (1989) a term which describes informal institutions but fails to elucidate the affective bonds of solidarity and quotidian practices that form the backbone of this movement culture. It is this backstage where people invest in unromantic bonds of solidarity that is at risk of disappearing with the squatting ban.

I think of how culturally marginal squatters profiled in this book generate income outside of the movement. Peter receives state benefits of approximately 700 euros a month. Adam earns an equivalent salary from a position funded by a state program for the long-term unemployed. Hans sells drugs. Shirin works odd jobs and receives financial support from ex-boyfriends and her parents. Ludwic has occasional handyman jobs. Their relatively low incomes combined with residing in squats and eating communally leads to a fairly decent standard of living. They all live in a manner in which they feel independent, while highly dependent on the mutual aid and free housing offered through the squatters movement. For culturally marginal people, the community provides an informal safety net without the disciplinary apparatus of the welfare state.

In describing these two general social profiles, the question arises, what kinds of selves does this movement attract, produce, and reproduce? The ideal autonomous self who becomes socialized in the movement and then, ultimately, leaves it, is easily visible in the professional sector of Dutch life and provides crucial human resources to the production economy. They are members of parliament, representing the Socialist party, the Social Democrats, and the Green Left, from the national to the neighborhood level. They are architects, attorneys, designers, artists, poets, writers, contractors, urban planners, university professors, teachers, civil servants, social workers, researchers, computer programmers, system administrators, ship builders, carpenters, nurses, small business owners, management consultants, engineers, and policymakers. The squatter movement's function as a space of training for this class is simultaneously accepted as banal and tacitly displayed as an achievement of the left activist self. But what about the culturally marginal, who exist as the inverse of the autonomous ideal?

Morris, a culturally marginal person, illustrates this form of personhood, complicating the myopic narrative of the autonomous self in the squatters movement. The first time I saw Morris was in a documentary; one of hundreds that I viewed at the International Institute for Social History. This documentary profiled a squatted social center in the Staatsliedebuurt in the early 1980s and featured interviews with squatters. The background of Amsterdam looked like a post-war, apocalyptic nightmare. Dilapidated buildings and trash dominated the scenery and starkly contrasted the neat streets, shiny renovated architecture, and cute cafes that abound in Amsterdam of the 2000s. The filmmakers interviewed Morris at age eighteen, wearing a punk leather jacket, handsome, earnest, and articulately explaining his political motivations to squat with enthusiasm and sincerity. The next time I viewed the same documentary was in 2007, with a group of squatter friends. When Morris appeared on the screen, the squatters who recognized him reacted with shock, "That's Morris." "Wow, look at Morris." His youth, beauty, and lucidity flabbergasted them.

I heard random tidbits about Morris before eventually meeting him. Larissa, a squatter neighbor, mentioned that Morris had been banned for stealing from a squat where she lived. I noticed that Morris was a regular of the Motorflex bar (see Chapter 2) and a constant fixture in the living room of the punks. Thirty years after the film, Morris was bald, had gained 20 kg, wore the same leather jacket from the film, eyes bright and sincere, but unable to speak more than few words at a time which he enunciated slowly and carefully. He often ran errands for my squatter neighbors, picking up beer and tobacco. Having heard that he was a thief, I worried about finding him in my environment. Others reassured me that Morris would never steal from a squat out of principle. I had a hard time distinguishing the line between stealing professionally to stealing from a squat, so I kept my eye on him when he was in my presence.

My subsequent encounter with Morris was fairly dramatic. It was during the middle of the night eviction where I had been arrested (see methodology section of introduction). Hundreds of police had surrounded our block of houses. There were water cannons in front of the squat, violently spraying water against the windows. I was sitting in a bedroom with Solomon, another squatter neighbor, strategizing on what to do next. We wanted to leave the section of the house we were in because the partygoers on the floor below, after hours of alcohol, speed, and cocaine, were untrustworthy and we wondered whether they would start a fire in their resistance of the police. I knew that I was going to get arrested soon and felt afraid. I explained to Solomon, "I wish I didn't have these feelings." Unexpectedly, I heard, in the room, a male voice saying, "It's good to have feelings." Solomon and I turned to find Morris sitting in the corner of the room with us, waiting quietly for the police to arrest him. He repeated himself, "Don't feel bad. It's good to have feelings. Feelings are healthy."

In the last squat I resided, Morris was a frequent visitor. Despite our moment of connection during the drama of the night raid, I felt concerned about having Morris spend time in my house where my possessions lay unlocked in my room. I asked my housemate, Marie, who had been in the scene for over ten years, about Morris. She explained that Morris's adult life encompassed cycles of heroin addiction and recovery. Once, during a period in prison, he weaned himself off of his addiction on his own. In prison, he was given pills to assuage his withdrawal symptoms; since he kicked his addiction without the pills, he saved them and sold them to other prisoners. Another squatter, Darrel, described how once, squatters had found Morris half dead after several days of lying in his own vomit and filth. They took him to a hospital where he was revived.

Morris was incredibly kind to me during the period in which he regularly spent time in my last squatted house, but I was always a little wary about what would happen if he stopped taking his prescription medication. At this time, I had a number of priorities, such as my dissertation, my job at the university, and finding a non-squatted housing solution. However, in the corner of my mind's eye, I wondered what Morris's presence meant for the housemate with whom he spent time. Were they shooting heroin during those hours that they locked themselves in my housemate's room? Was my housemate also an addict?

Within a couple of months after deciding to find a rental at any cost, I found myself in a beautiful rental apartment. Morris, to show his support, and Marie, were the first squatters to visit me. I served them tea. I joked that I finally had white neighbors after residing for years in squats in multicultural areas with "bad" reputations. Morris responded, "Nazima, you know, I don't like white people either." I then said, "Well, Morris, that must be very inconvenient for you since you are a white person." He answered, "I'm not white. I'm black. My father is from Suriname." I was completely dumbstruck as Morris to all appearances was the personification of the white, punk squatter. He elaborated, "That is why I like you so much. Because you are brown and dark."

After this exchange, the three of us continued chatting. At one point, Morris asked if he could inhale speed in our presence. I felt uncomfortable with his use of hard drugs but it seemed rude to deny him since he had visited me to show solidarity. I nodded yes. As I watched him prepare the powder, I gently asked, "Why do you need to do it?" As far as I could tell, the three of us were drinking tea and talking. It didn't seem like an anxiety provoking situation that required the consumption of speed. He answered, "I do it because it quiets the voices in my head."

After this, I no longer saw my former squatter housemates as I had made a concerted effort to distance myself from the movement. I did, however, run into Morris, occasionally. I noted how much weight he had lost and the desperate intensity in his eyes. During this period, I had a conversation with a squatter who mentioned that, "Morris is not doing well," which obliquely meant that Morris had returned to using heroin. She also noted that she saw him furtively walking around the city center. We knew that Morris stole bikes expertly as a means of income. We joked that we wanted to approach Morris, show him our bikes, and say, "Please don't steal my bike and sell it to buy a hit. Go steal someone else's bike. Remember, Morris, I'm a comrade. I'm in the community."

Morris is a person whose life was and is embedded with this movement, an example of this alternative self that is the polar opposite of the community's autonomous ideal. Having lived his entire adult life in the squatters' scene, the movement provides him with structure and meaning. Horst, who has known Morris for nearly twenty years, joked, "Morris is what you call a Monday to Sunday user." This community has literally saved his life when he has overdosed, finding and hospitalizing him. When his plumbing breaks, a builder from the movement fixes it. Another activist has arranged to receive Morris's public assistance benefits to pay his rent, health insurance, and utilities, before handing Morris weekly allotments of cash. From the perspective of welfare state efficiency, the collective care of Morris and individuals like him by the squatters' community provides an affordable and manageable solution. The state does not have to employ social workers for the services that the squatters provide out of an unromantic and sober sense of solidarity.

It's this unromantic and sober sense of solidarity that is one of the ties that binds the backstage of social movement communities. The people who assist Morris do not necessarily like him or feel that by helping him, they earn "scene points" or increased squatter capital. They support Morris simply because he is a member of their community to whom they feel responsible.

As I have argued in this book, by ignoring both the backstage and culturally marginal figures like Morris, social movement studies has failed to understand a whole set of dynamics within social movement communities as well as this particular manifestation of solidarity. In classical social movement studies, solidarity as a motivating factor is absent entirely. While in the case of more recent studies of the alterglobalization movement, scholars represent solidarity romantically and abstractly rather than analyzing it as an unspoken ideal with a functional set of quotidian practices. Furthermore, the scholarly neglect is unsurprising since social movements themselves do not acknowledge both the importance of the backstage and the practice of quotidian solidarity.

Returning to this book, I have interrogated the ideal of the autonomous life from a sober and perhaps, cynical academic perspective. I have explored how this community simultaneously disavows and maintains hierarchy and authority and how the contradiction structures the social world of this movement subculture.

In Chapter 1, I argued that through examining squatter skills and negative classifications, one can see how unspoken status hierarchies function in this community. In Chapter 2, I contended that authority figures should display a certain performance of "autonomous" squatter selfhood, comprising assertiveness, the capacity for highly prestigious squatter skills, such as public speaking, campaigning, and presswork, and a habitus of emotional sovereignty. Moreover, I demonstrated how their authority is reified through negative gossip around the sexuality of these figures. In Chapter 3, I explored how hierarchy and authority manifest within internal dynamics of living groups within squatted houses. In this case, movement capital transfers into one's status within a group. However, for the sake of cohesion and a peaceful "home" atmosphere, it is necessary to suspend the argumentative, assertive self held up as part of the autonomous ideal. Finally, in Chapter 4, I examined the notion of activist careers in the movement, the movement subculture as a space of training and liminal adolescence, and how the autonomous self is based on a myopic construction of privileges held by entitled citizens of liberal democratic welfare states. To conclude, however, I would like to suspend this interrogative cynicism and celebrate the unspoken and sober practice of solidarity of this social movement community as illustrated by the Morris story.

I personally have benefited from countless acts of unromantic and sober solidarity. When I was unexpectedly evicted and had my belongings impounded by the police, a group of squatters who I did not know personally, transported my boxes from one end of the city to the other. One of these squatters was one of the perpetrators who was jailed for injuring Yoghurt (see introduction). When I had left my ex-partner and months later, he was being difficult about returning my personal items, a few squatter women presented themselves with me at his house, barged in, grabbed some suitcases, and filled them with my possessions, while I watched in a state of paralysis. I even benefited from this solidarity after I moved out of the community. Hans, my former housemate who never spoke and, I suspected, feared women, once fixed a broken stove burner in my house and then left as quickly as possible to avoid having to either speak or be alone with me. Despite his discomfort, he worked on my stove as a gesture of solidarity.

I laud these moments of unromantic solidarity because they are altruistic without the condescension of charity and reveal the best of this community's values of mutual responsibility, cooperation, and the pooling of resources. In this book, I have argued that the autonomous life is a fiction, a narrative on the movement's front and back stages that masks a deeper collective yearning for belonging and love through the performance of a non-conformist, anti-capitalist, individualist self. This fraught ideal is impossible to achieve and requires a constant disavowal and double-speak.

I believe that the economy of non-romantic solidarity that tacitly operates in this movement community presents a more accessible model through which to find love and belonging, especially in a highly alienating urban environment. It's a pity that in the squatters movement, this economy of unsentimental solidarity is taken for granted, that it's absent from the movement's rhetoric and its value system from which it confers status and, finally, that it operates at its best when no one else is watching.

The last time I saw Morris was at a massive demonstration protesting the squatting ban – an event which eventually turned into a bloody and violent riot. The black bloc had organized themselves at the head of the demonstration. I recognized some of my friends beneath the masks. In the midst of a tensely formed square of black blockers, there was Morris: bald, unmasked, and relaxed. Upon catching his eye, I waved to him. He looked back at me, eyes bright with enthusiasm, and smiled.

Notes

1   The squatting ban features the following changes in the law: the penalty for being a squatter and for violently resisting is one year and eight months in prison. The penalty for trespassing had changed from five months to one year. Furthermore, the police can evict squatters without a court order and the owner's consent.

2   This phrase in English is the same as the motto in Dutch: *kraken gaat door*, squatting goes on. But in Dutch, this connotes "resistance continues."

3   This activity contrasts sharply with the UK, where up until 2012, squatting residential properties was legal and an estimated 25,000 people live in squats in

London alone. The majority squatted for free housing and only a tiny minority did so to enact an anarchist counter cultural existence. Furthermore, compared to Italy, Spain, and the Netherlands, social centers in the UK are few and far in between and almost immediately evicted by the police. Hence, legal permission, in the UK case, led to squatting for purely "material" reasons. In my experience, visiting squats in London and listening to the personal accounts of friends who have squatted in London, it seems that the majority of squatters do so for material gain. For example, a number of squatters have social housing, but live in squats while they rent out their social housing flats for income. Squats as spaces to use drugs are rampant in the UK, including in "political" squats.

GLOSSARY

Breakers	The people who break open the door during squatting actions
Gezelligheid	A Dutch term that vaguely translates as warm coziness, with connotations of nostalgia and intimacy
Kraakbonzen	A term that translates literally as "squatter bosses"
Kraakspreekuur	*Kraakspreekuren* (pl). Literally translates as squatting information hour. A self-organized group of people, often squatters or ex-squatters, host a weekly drop in service at a social center located in a squat or legalized squat, functioning as a squatters advisory service
Kraker	A squatter
Legalized squat	A formerly squatted building that has become legalized through a formal rental contract or ownership. These buildings tend to provide affordable housing
Social center	A self-organized space run by volunteers that offer free community services mainly aimed at the radical left and the local community
Squat	A space or property in which the residents lack legal permission from owners to reside. Also used as a verb "to squat" a place
Squatter scene	The "scene" is how squatters and people who identify with the radical left refer to the subculture of the radical left
Voku	Short for *volkskeuken*. A restaurant usually run by volunteers held in squatted social centers or legalized squats that serves often affordable food

REFERENCES

Agamben, Giorgio. 1998. *Homo Sacer: Sovereign Power and Bare Life*. Translated by Daniel Heller-Roazen. Stanford, CA: Stanford University Press. http://www.sup.org/books/title/?id=2003.

Alberoni, Francesco. 1984. *Movement and Institution*. New York: Columbia University Press.

Alexander, Jeffrey C. 2004. "Cultural Pragmatics: Social Performance between Ritual and Strategy." *Sociological Theory* 22 (4): 527–73.

Appadurai, Arjun. 1996. *Modernity at Large: Cultural Dimensions of Globalization*. Public Worlds, vol. 1. Minneapolis, MN: University of Minnesota Press.

Avery-Natale, Edward. 2010. "'We're Here, We're Queer, We're Anarchists': The Nature of Identification and Subjectivity Among Black Blocs." *Anarchist Developments in Cultural Studies "Post-Anarchism Today"* 1: 95–116.

Becker, Howard S. 1963. *Outsiders: Studies in the Sociology of Deviance*. New York, NY: The Free Press of Glencoe.

Becker, Howard S. 2008. *Art Worlds*. Berkeley, CA; London: University of California Press.

Behler, Constantin. n.d. "Habitus." *CB's Glossary for Students*. http://faculty.washington.edu/cbehler/glossary/habitus.html.

Benford, Robert D. and David A. Snow. 2000. "Framing Processes and Social Movements: An Overview and Assessment." *Annual Review of Sociology* 26: 611–39.

Bourdieu, Pierre. 1984. *Distinction: A Social Critique of the Judgement of Taste*. Cambridge, Mass.: Harvard University Press.

Bourdieu, Pierre and Randal Johnson. 1993. *The Field of Cultural Production: Essays on Art and Literature*. New York: Columbia University Press.

Caldeira, Teresa Pires do Rio. 2000. *City of Walls: Crime, Segregation, and Citizenship in São Paulo*. Berkeley, CA: University of California Press.

Crane, Nicholas. 2012. 'Are "Other Spaces" Necessary? Associative Power at the Dumpster.' *ACME: An International E-Journal for Critical Geographies* 11 (3): 352–72.

Crossley, Nick. 2003. "From Reproduction to Transformation." *Theory, Culture & Society* 20 (6): 43–68. doi: 10.1177/0263276403206003.

Della Porta, Donatella and Mario Diani. 2006. *Social Movements: An Introduction*. 2nd edn. Malden, MA: Blackwell.

Diani, Mario and Ron Eyerman, eds. 1992. *Studying Collective Action*. Sage Modern Politics Series, vol. 30. London; Newbury Park, CA: SAGE.

Diepen, M. v. and A. d. Bruijn-Muller. 1977. "Kraakakties in Gliphoeve. Sociale Chaos Als Voorwaarde Voor Kapitalistiese Ontwikkeling." *Zone* 2, no. 1e kwartaal: 27–44.

Duivenvoorden, Eric. 2000. *Een Voet Tussen De Deur: Geschiedenis Van De Kraakbeweging (1964–1999)*. Amsterdam [etc.]: De Arbeiderspers.

Eyerman, Ron and Andrew Jamison. 1991. *Social Movements: A Cognitive Approach*. Cambridge: Polity.

Eyerman, Ron and Andrew Jamison. 1998. *Music and Social Movements: Mobilizing Traditions in the Twentieth Century*. Cambridge [etc.]: Cambridge University Press.

Flynn, Nick. 2004. *Another Bullshit Night in Suck City: A Memoir*. 1st edn. New York: W.W. Norton & Co.

Fox, Kathryn Joan. 1987. "Real Punks and Pretenders." *Journal of Contemporary Ethnography* 16 (3): 344–70. doi: 10.1177/0891241687163006.

Freeman, Jo. 1972. "The Tyranny of Structurelessness." *Berkeley Journal of Sociology* 17: 151–65.

Freeman, Jo. 1979. "Resource Mobilization and Strategy: A Model for Analyzing Social Movement Organization Actions." In Mayer N. Zald and John D. McCarthy (eds.) *The Dynamics of Social Movements*, 167–89. Cambridge, MA: Winthrop.

Gamson, William A. 1990. *The Strategy of Social Protest*. 2nd edn. Belmont, CA: Wadsworth.

Gelder, Ken and Sarah Thornton, eds. 1997. *The Subcultures Reader*. London; New York: Routledge.

Goddard, Victoria A. 1996. *Gender, Family, and Work in Naples*. Mediterranean Series. Oxford; Washington, DC: Berg.

Goffman, Erving. 1990. *The Presentation of Self in Everyday Life*. New York: Doubleday.

Gordon, Linda. 2002. "Social Movements, Leadership, and Democracy: Toward More Utopian Mistakes." *Journal of Women's History* 14 (2): 102–17.

Graeber, David. 2009. *Direct Action: An Ethnography*. Edinburgh: AK Press.

Guzman-Concha, Cesar. 2008. "The Squatters Movement in Europe: Sources of Variation and Political Dynamic of the Mobilization." Paper presented at the ISA.

Hamel, Jacques. 1998. "The Positions of Pierre Bourdieu and Alain Touraine Respecting Qualitative Methods." *The British Journal of Sociology* 49 (1): 1–19.

Hannerz, Ulf. 1996. *Transnational Connections: Culture, People, Places*. Comedia. London and New York: Routledge.

Hansen, Thomas Blom. 2001. *Wages of Violence: Naming and Identity in Postcolonial Bombay*. Princeton, NJ: Princeton University Press.

Harvey, David. 1989. *The Condition of Postmodernity: An Enquiry into the Origins of Cultural Change*. Oxford; Cambridge, MA: Blackwell.

Hayden, Dolores. 1996. *The Power of Place: Urban Landscapes as Public History*. Cambridge, MA: The MIT Press.

Hochschild, Arlie Russell. 1979. "Emotion Work, Feeling Rules, and Social Structure." *The American Journal of Sociology* 85 (3): 551–75.

Holmes, Douglas R. 2000. *Integral Europe: Fast-Capitalism, Multiculturalism, Neofascism*. Princeton, NJ: Princeton University Press.

Johnston, Hank and Bert Klandermans, eds. 1995. *Social Movements and Culture*. London: UCL.

Juris, Jeffrey S. 2008. *Networking Futures: The Movements against Corporate Globalization*. Experimental Futures. Durham, NC: Duke University Press.

Laraña, Enrique, Hank Johnston, and Joseph R. Gusfield, eds. 1994. *New Social Movements: From Ideology to Identity*. Philadelphia, PA: Temple University Press.

Maeckelbergh, Marianne. 2009. *The Will of the Many: How the Alterglobalisation Movement is Changing the Face of Democracy*. Anthropology, Culture and Society. New York: Pluto.

Mamadouh, Virginie. 1992. *De Stad in Eigen Hand: Provo's, Kabouters En Krakers Als Stedelijke Sociale Beweging*. Amsterdam: Sua.

Martínez, Miguel. 2007. "The Squatters' Movement: Urban Counter-Culture and Alter-Globalization Dynamics." *South European Society & Politics* 12 (3): 379–98.

McAdam, Doug. 1982. *Political Process and the Development of Black Insurgency 1930–1970*. Chicago: University of Chicago Press.

McAdam, Doug. 1986. "Recruitment to High-Risk Activism: The Case of Freedom Summer." *The American Journal of Sociology* 92 (1): 64–90.

McCarthy, John and Mayer Zald. 1973. *The Trend of Social Movements in America: Professionalization and Resource Mobilization*. Morriston, NJ: General Learning Corporation.

McCarthy, John and Mayer Zald. 1977. "Resource Mobilization and Social Movements: A Partial Theory." *The American Journal of Sociology* 82 (6): 1212–41.

Melucci, Alberto. 1989. *The Nomads of the Present: Social Movements and Individual Needs in Contemporary Society*. Philadelphia: Temple University Press.

Melucci, Alberto. 1996. *Challenging Codes: Collective Action in the Information Age*. Cambridge: Cambridge University Press.

Membretti, Andrea. 2007. "Centro Sociale Leoncavallo." *European Urban and Regional Studies* 14 (3): 252–63. doi: 10.1177/0969776407077742.

Meyer, David S, Nancy Whittier, and Belinda Robnett, eds. 2002. *Social Movements: Identity, Culture, and the State*. Oxford [etc.]: Oxford University Press.

Mitchell, Timothy. 2002. *Rule of Experts: Egypt, Techno-Politics, Modernity*. Berkeley: University of California Press.

Mudu, Pierpaolo. 2004. "Resisting and Challenging Neoliberalism: The Development of Italian Social Centers." *Antipode* 36 (5): 917–41. doi: 10.1111/j.1467-8330.2004.00461.x.

Mudu, Pierpaolo. 2005. "Changing Backdrops in Rome: An Exploration of the Geography of Social Centers." In *Rights to the City*, vol 3: 265–75. IGU – Home of Geography Publication Series. Rome.

Offe, Claus. 1985. "New Social Movements: Challenging the Boundaries of Institutional Politics." *Social Research* 52 (4): 917.

Ong, Aihwa. 1999. *Flexible Citizenship: The Cultural Logics of Transnationality*. Durham, NC: Duke University Press.

Owens, Lynn. 2004. "Kraaking under Pressure: The Decline of the Amsterdam Squatters' Movement." Chapel Hill: University of North Carolina of Chapel Hill.

Owens, Lynn. 2009. *Cracking under Pressure: Narrating the Decline of the Amsterdam Squatters' Movement*. University Park, PA: Pennsylvania State University Press.

Pardo, Italo. 1996. *Managing Existence in Naples: Morality, Action, and Structure*. Cambridge Studies in Social and Cultural Anthropology 104. Cambridge; New York: Cambridge University Press.

Piazza, Gianni. 2007. "Inside the Radical Left of the Global Justice Movement: The Squatted and/or Self-Managed Social Centres in Italy (squatting in Catania)." Paper presented at the ECPR General Conference, University of Pisa.

Piven, Frances Fox and Richard Cloward 1988. *Poor People's Movements: Why They Succeed, How They Fail*. New York: Vintage.

Polletta, Francesca. 2002. *Freedom Is an Endless Meeting: Democracy in American Social Movements*. Chicago: University of Chicago Press.

Portwood-Stacer, Laura. 2010. "Constructing Anarchist Sexuality: Queer Identity, Culture, and Politics in the Anarchist Movement." *Sexualities* 13 (4): 479–93.

Rouhani, Farhan. 2012. "Anarchism, Geography, and Queen Space-Making: Building Bridges over Chasms We Create." *ACME* 11: 373–92.

Rupp, Leila J. and Verta Taylor. 1999. "Forging Feminist Identity in an International Movement: A Collective Identity Approach to Twentieth-Century Feminism." *Signs* 24 (2): 363–86.

Sassen, Saskia. 2001. *The Global City: New York, London, Tokyo*. 2nd edn. Princeton, NJ: Princeton University Press.

Scholl, Christian. 2010. "Two Sides of a Barricade: (dis)order and Summit Protest in Europe." Amsterdam: University of Amsterdam.

Schwalbe, Michael. 1996. *Unlocking the Iron Cage: The Men's Movement, Gender Politics, and American Culture*. New York: Oxford University Press.

Sedgwick, Eve Kosofsky. 1985. *Between Men: English Literature and Male Homosocial Desire*. New York: Columbia University Press.

Seelan, Joost. 1996. *De Stad Was van Ons*. Documentary.

Sennett, Richard. 1977. *The Hidden Injuries of Class*. Cambridge: Cambridge University Press.

Smelser, Neil J. 1962. *Theory of Collective Behavior*. New York: Free Press.

Snow, David A., E. Burke Rochford, Steven K. Worden, and Robert D. Benford. 1986. "Frame Alignment Processes, Micromobilization, and Movement Participation." *American Sociological Review* 51 (4): 464–81.

Tarrow, Sidney G. 1989. *Democracy and Disorder: Protest and Politics in Italy, 1965–1975*: Oxford: Oxford University Press; New York: Clarendon Press.

Taylor, Charles. 1994. *Multiculturalism: Examining the Politics of Recognition*. Princeton, NJ: Princeton University Press.

Taylor, Verta and Leila J. Rupp. 1993. "Women's Culture and Lesbian Feminist Activism: A Reconsideration of Cultural Feminism." *Signs* 19 (1): 32–61.

Tesser, P.T.M. 1995. *Rapportage Minderheden 1995. Concentratie En Segregatie*. Rijswijk/Den Haag: SCP/VUGA.

Thornton, Sarah. 1996. *Club Cultures: Music, Media, and Subcultural Capital*. 1st US edn. Music/culture. Hanover: University Press of New England.

Tilly, Charles. 1978. *From Mobilization to Revolution*. Reading, MA: Addison-Wesley.

Wharton, Amy S. 2009. "The Sociology of Emotional Labor." *Annual Review of Sociology* 35 (1): 147–65. doi: 10.1146/annurev-soc-070308-115944.

Whittier, Nancy. 1995. *Feminist Generations: The Persistence of the Radical Women's Movement*. Women in the Political Economy. Philadelphia: Temple University Press.

Whittier, Nancy. 1997. "Political Generations, Micro-Cohorts, and the Transformation of Social Movements." *American Sociological Review* 62 (5): 760–78.

Zald, Mayer Nathan and John D. McCarthy, eds. 1987. *Social Movements in an Organizational Society: Collected Essays*. New Brunswick, NJ: Transaction.

Zukin, Sharon. 1995. *The Cultures of Cities*. Cambridge, MA: Blackwell.

INDEX

Page numbers in *italics* are figures; with "n" are notes.